MARXISM
AND LIBERALISM

MARXISM AND LIBERALISM

Edited by

Ellen Frankel Paul
Jeffrey Paul
Fred D Miller Jr
John Ahrens

BASIL BLACKWELL
for the
Social Philosophy and Policy Center
Bowling Green State University

© Social Philosophy and Policy 1986
First Published 1986

Basil Blackwell Publisher Limited
108 Cowley Road, Oxford OX4 1JF, England

Library of Congress Cataloging-in-Publication Data

Main entry under title:

Marxism and liberalism.

1. Socialism and liberty—Addresses, essays, lectures.
2. Communism—Addresses, essays, lectures. 3. Liberalism—Addresses, essays, lectures.   4. Marx, Karl, 1818–1883—Addresses, essays, lectures.   I. Paul, Ellen Frankel.   II. Miller, Fred Dycus, 1944–   .   III. Paul, Jeffrey.   IV. Bowling Green State University. Social Philosophy & Policy Center.
HX550.L52M37   1986   320.5′322   85–30676
ISBN 0–631–15165–6 (pbk.)

British Library Cataloguing in Publication Data

Marxism and liberalism.
1. Liberalism   2. Communism   3. Socialism   I. Paul, Ellen Frankel   II. Miller, Fred D. III. Paul, Jeffrey   IV. Bowling Green State University, Social Philosophy and Policy Center
320.5′1   JC571

ISBN 0–631–15165–6

Printed in Great Britain

CONTENTS

INTRODUCTION

The labels *Marxism* and *liberalism* denote two of the dominant ideologies in the world today, ideologies seemingly at war in the realm of ideas and in the real world of politics, as well. But despite the apparent opposition of these two world views and the regimes founded on them, the question of whether or not Marxism and liberalism are compatible continues to attract considerable scholarly attention. Liberal values and institutions – democracy, individual freedom, economic self-determination, peaceful social change – command the loyalty of numerous people from widely different cultural and economic backgrounds. Hence, it is no surprise that many defenders of Marxism argue that Marxist political and social theory is quite compatible with liberal values, or even that Marxist regimes will be the best protectors of these values. It is likewise unsurprising that liberal critics of Marxism argue just the reverse.

This controversy raises issues which are both substantive and methodological. Can Marxist regimes be democratic? What role do concepts like self-ownership and self-realization play in Marxist and liberal social and political theory? Is violence a necessary component of any Marxist revolution properly so-called? Should Marxist theory be judged by the evidence of existing, self-proclaimed Marxist regimes? The contributors to this volume approach these questions from a variety of philosophical perspectives, but with the common goal of elucidating the conceptual connections between Marxism and liberalism. This is an endeavor which should serve to enhance our understanding of both these ideologies and, what is equally important, to enhance our understanding of the national and international turmoil that besets our world.

Marxism and Democracy

A central issue for both critics and defenders of Marx is the extent to which Marxist political and social theory is compatible with the values and institutions of democracy. In a paper entitled "On the Mutual Compatibility of Democracy and Marxian Socialism," Joseph Cropsey pursues three lines of investigation into the issue of whether or not Marxist regimes can also be democratic: the role of choice in each, the "animating spirit" of each, and the intellectual genealogy of each. The first line leads him to the conclusion that the inhabitants of a democracy would not be likely to elect to establish a Marxist regime, since this would require them to give up natural (i.e., self-interested) ends in favor of the "common" good. The second leads him to the conclusion that democracy and Marxian socialism are animated by completely different spirits. And the third indicates that, although the two political regimes have a common percentage, they have evolved in radically different directions. Thus, he concludes, the weight of evidence is very much against the view that democracy and Marxian socialism are mutually compatible.

Alan Gilbert takes a rather different tack in a paper entitled "Democracy and Individuality." Gilbert argues that Marxism and liberalism share a core empirical and moral claim: given that human beings possess certain distinctively human capacities – they are intelligent, empathetic, social animals – justifiable political regimes must facilitate mutual recognition and individual agency. The complex ethical and political conflicts between Marxism and liberalism arise from disagreements over whether or not there is an oppressive ruling class in liberal democratic capitalist societies, and over whether or not existing injustices can be remedied without the radical restructuring of existing social systems. The great weakness of liberalism, Gilbert argues, is that it tends to emphasize the preservation of democratic *procedures* and to be too little concerned with the fact that the masses really do not actively participate in the political process. The strength of Marxian theory, on the other hand, is that it emphasizes the importance of genuine participation in the exercise of political power. Thus, he concludes, Marxism turns out to be a genuine alternative to liberalism as a means to protect and enhance democratic values.

One of the major stumbling blocks for democrats who are, or want to be, sympathetic to Marx has been the "dictatorship of the proletariat." How can a "dictatorship" preserve or enhance democratic values? In "Democracy and Class Dictatorship," Richard Miller argues that the dictatorship of the proletariat should be taken seriously as a democratic ideal and as an important rival to liberal democracy. The clue to why this is so is to be found in Marx's discussions of the dictatorship of the bourgeoisie. The latter, Marx argues, does not depend on any particular set or arrangement of political institutions but, rather, on an institutional bias in favor of the interests of a particular class – the bourgeoisie. Likewise, Miller argues, the dictatorship of the proletariat does not depend on a particular set of political institutions, or even on the presence or absence of coercion. Rather, it requires simply that political institutions be biased in favor of the interests of workers. And it is this bias in favor of the vast majority that renders the dictatorship of the proletariat democratic.

Self-Ownership and Self-Realization

Two concepts that have been central to the controversy surrounding Marxism and liberalism are self-ownership and self-realization. In "Self-Ownership, World-Ownership, and Equality: Part II," G. A. Cohen investigates the conceptual connections between self-ownership and various types of egalitarianism. This should be of central concern to Marxists, he argues, because "the critique of capitalist exploitation and the defense of communist equality require denial of each person's *full* sovereignty over himself," i.e., of self-ownership. But Cohen is no more sanguine about the ability of classical liberalism to preserve the concept of self-ownership. For the *laissez faire* approach to the initial distribution of external resources (i.e., resources which do not, unlike talents and abilities, inhere in a person) that Nozick and others advocate leaves the less talented and the less fortunate in such dire straits that self-ownership is rendered nugatory. And variations on classical liberalism like Steiner's proposal that *laissez faire* be replaced with equal initial distribution preserve self-ownership, but only at the cost of sacrificing any hope for equality of condition. Thus, Cohen believes that there is considerably more to be said about how a socialist constitution could preserve a robust concept of self-ownership without sacrificing equality of condition.

The focus of Jon Elster's "Self-realization in Work and Politics," is the contribution of consumption – construed broadly enough to include aesthetic pleasures and the enjoyment of entertainment – to human happiness and welfare. Elster argues that the good life is characterized much more by self-realization than by consumption. Self-realization is the actualization and externalization (i.e., exercise in the public realm) of the powers and abilities of the individual. Elster rejects the Marxian notion that individuals can reasonably expect (or reasonably be expected) to realize *all* their abilities. But he accepts the view (also found in Marx) that individuals must be allowed to choose freely the activity in which they will seek self-realization. The core of his paper is an extended discussion of whether work and politics can be chanels for self-realization.

Marxism and Totalitarianism

One of the obstacles to answering the question of whether or not Marxism and liberalism are compatible has been the widespread disagreement about whether or not it is appropriate to use existing Marxist regimes as evidence of how Marxist social and political theory will work in practice. Defenders of Marx generally point to some other explanation than Marxist theory for the worst features of these regimes. But Allen Buchanan observes that one of the few things on which modern liberals, classical liberals, and conservatives can agree is that the worst features of totalitarian socialist and communist regimes do stem from the writings of Marx and Engels. His paper, "The Conceptual Roots of Totalitarian Socialism," is an examination of the extent to which this agreement is well-founded. It is a question for empirical social science whether or not Marxist theory *in fact* played a significant causal role in creating the undesirable features of totalitarian regimes. But, Buchanan argues, "it will count heavily against Marxist theory if it can be shown that a system with precisely those deficiencies that are observed in totalitarian socialism is just the sort of system one would reasonably expect to come about through the efforts of persons who relied upon the Marxist conceptual framework for inspiration and guidance." Buchanan identifies three elements of Marxist theory that are linked in this way to totalitarian socialism: Marx's view of revolutionary motivation as flowing solely from simple, rational self-interest; his refusal to provide an explicit theory of democratic, nonmarket social coordination; and his denial that concepts like justice and rights have any important role in the revolutionary process.

David Gordon, in "Marxism, Dictatorship, and the Abolition of Rights," argues that the question of whether or not a Marxist regime is likely to be oppressive must be asked separately about the dictatorship of the proletariat and about the final stage of communism. In response to the first question, Gordon argues that the dictatorship of the proletariat is quite likely to be very oppressive. It will be a matter of no small difficulty to quickly wrest power from the hands of one class, the bourgeoisie, and transfer it to another class, the proletariat. There can be little doubt, Gordon argues, that the proletariat will have to use force against the bourgeoisie and dissident proletarians with little regard for their civil liberties. And Gordon finds confirmation of this view in Marx's own writings on the topic, as well as in the Marxist conception of morality, which weighs the goal of establishing a socialist society more heavily than any costs, including the loss of civil liberties. In response to the second question, Gordon argues that the final stage of communism might also be oppressive, although it need not be. It is difficult to know, since Marx and his followers say very little about what the ideal society will be like (except that it will *not* be capitalist) or how to achieve it. Hence, Gordon concludes, the undesirable features of the dictatorship of the proletariat are of primary importance in determining whether or not Marxist socialism is likely to lead to oppression.

In "Marxian Freedom, Individual Liberty, and the End of Alienation," John Gray also attacks the conventional wisdom that Marxian theory should not be judged by the evidence of existing socialist regimes. In addition to being a paradoxically ahistorical defense of Marxian theory, Gray argues, this conventional view ignores crucial structural characteristics of Marx's theories. According to Gray, Marx construed oppression (unfreedom) as alienation – the sense of being dominated by social forces that one has created but does not control. Alienation can be transcended only by abolishing commodity production and replacing it with production for direct use. And this latter is impossible, Gray argues, because it requires the abolition of the market and with it the information that market pricing produces. And this, in turn, necessitates totalitarian political control to make the planned economies of socialist regimes workable. Hence, Gray concludes, the vision of human freedom embedded in Marxian theory is refuted by the practice of existing socialist regimes.

Marxism and Violence

Virtually all existing self-proclaimed Marxist regimes are tyrannical and show no signs of becoming appreciably less so. Defenders of Marxism generally argue that this is contingent – on historical circumstances, misinterpretations of Marxian doctrine, or something else. But George Friedman argues that the explanation for this fact is to be found in Marx's understanding of violence. Marx believed that revolution was the most desirable, even if not the only effective means to establish a socialist state. And, Friedman argues, revolution and tyranny have at least one characteristic in common: both involve the direct use of violence, i.e., violence which is not mediated by political institutions. Further, Friedman argues, revolutionary violence was not merely instrumentally necessary for Marx. Rather, violence is an indispensable part of the process by which the proletariat becomes aware of itself as a class and as empowered to affect the social environment. It is the experience of violence that teaches the proletariat that it can recreate itself and its social environment. Thus, for Marx violence is a necessary part of the revolutionary process, and not merely a means that is sometimes useful and sometimes not. And, Friedman concludes, it is no surprise that a regime which is borne of violence should depend upon violence for its preservation.

Marx's commitment to (violent) revolution also renders his theories particularly susceptible to the problem of "dirty hands": What are we to do when the only way we can attain some important good is (or seems to be) to commit "wrongful" actions, i.e., actions which violate the requirements of right, or rights, or justice? This problem arises in all spheres of life, but it tends to be especially compelling in politics, where the good attained tends to be general and the wrongs tend to be committed against specific persons. Steven Lukes's central concern in "Marxism and Dirty Hands" is to explore the implications of Marxism for this problem. He argues that Marxism, because it is both ideological and utopian in a distinctive way, is thoroughly unsuited to resolve this problem and, in fact, may have the effect of rendering us insensitive to the importance of the problem. Marxism is ideological in that it ignores the interests of persons in the present and immediate future, insofar as they have no bearing on the goal of "emancipation." Thus, according to Lukes, Marxism is less sensitive even than utilitarianism to the moral requirement that we respect the rights and interests of persons in the present. Further, Lukes argues, Marxism is both utopian and anti-utopian. It is utopian in its insistence that all actions be judged according to the standard of whether or not they contribute to "emancipation." It is anti-utopian in its refusal to specify in any detail at all just what the emancipated world will be like. And this refusal to clarify the standards by which actions are to be judged has rendered it much easier than it might have been to accept even the grossest violations of the requirements of morality.

Much of the tension that characterizes the modern world, tension both within and between nations, stems from the complex theoretical and practical conflicts between Marxism and liberalism. The essays in this volume should enhance our understanding of these ideologies and their roots, underlying values, and consequences.

CONTRIBUTORS

Joseph Cropsey received his undergraduate and graduate degrees from Columbia University. He taught economics at the City College of the College of the City of New York and philosophy at the New School for Social Research before joining the Political Science Department of the University of Chicago. His subject is the history of political philosophy, concentrating on Greek antiquity and the modern period from the sixteenth to the twentieth century. His writings have been on the history of thought and the bearing of thought on politics.

Alan Gilbert teaches at the Graduate School of International Studies of the University of Denver. He received a Ph.D. in Government from Harvard and has done advanced work in philosophy at Cornell. He is the author of *Marx's Politics: Communists and Citizens* and of articles on ethics and social theory in *The American Political Science Review*, *Philosophy and Public Affairs*, *Political Theory*, *The Occasional Review*, and *Nomos*. He is currently completing a book on *Equality and Objectivity*.

Richard Miller teaches in the Department of Philosophy at Cornell University, where he is an Associate Professor. His many writings in ethics, political philosophy and the philosophy of science include, most recently, *Analyzing Marx* (Princeton University Press, 1984) and "Ways of Moral Learning" (*Philosophical Review*, October 1985). He has just completed a book in the philosophy of science, *Fact and Method: Explanation and Confirmation in the Natural and the Social Sciences*.

G. A. Cohen was born in 1941 in Montreal, where, at McGill University, he obtained his B.A., in Philosophy and Politics, in 1961. He then read for the B. Phil. in Philosophy at New College, Oxford, and from 1963 to 1984 he taught in the Philosophy Department of University College London. He became Chichele Professor of Social and Political Theory and Fellow of All Souls, Oxford, in January 1985. He is the author of *Karl Marx's Theory of History: A Defense* (Princeton and Oxford, 1978), and of articles in philosophical and social scientific journals.

Jon Elster is a Professor of Political Science at the University of Chicago and Research Director at the Institute for Social Research, Oslo. Among his publications are: *Leibniz et la Formation de l'Esprit Capitaliste* (1975), *Logic and Society* (1978), *Ulysses and the Sirens* (1979), *Explaining Technical*

Change (1983), *Sour Grapes* (1983), and *Making Sense of Marx* (1985). He is currently working on problems in the intersection of bargaining theory, the theory of collective action, and the theory of distributive justice.

Allen Buchanan received a B.A. from Columbia University in 1970 and a Ph.D. in Philosophy from the University of North Carolina in 1975. He has taught at the University of Minnesota, served as staff Philosopher to the President's Commission for the Study of Ethical Issues in Medicine and Biomedical and Behavioral Research, and is currently Professor of Philosophy at the University of Arizona at Tucson. Buchanan has published numerous articles in social and political philosophy, ethics, medical ethics, and epistemology, and is the author of two books: *Marx and Justice*: *The Radical Critique of Liberalism* (1982) and *Ethics, Efficiency and the Market* (1984). He is currently at work on a book in medical ethics on decisionmaking for incompetent patients.

David Gordon received his Ph.D. from U.C.L.A. He is currently completing a book on individualist political theory. He has written articles on this topic, as well as others, including skepticism, utilitarianism, John Stuart Mill's views on morality-dependent harm, and the generalization argument in ethics. Articles by him have appeared in *Analysis, British Journal of Political Science, Canadian Journal of Philosophy, Ethics, Journal of Value Inquiry, Mind, Political Studies, Politics, Religious Studies*, and other journals.

John Gray, M.A., D. Phil, Oxon., was educated at Exeter College, Oxford, where he read Philosophy, Politics, and Economics. Since 1976 he has been Official Fellow at Jesus College, Oxford. In 1984, he was appointed Distinguished Research Fellow at the Center for Social Philosophy and Policy, and in Spring 1986 he was Visiting Professor in the Department of Government at Harvard. His books include: *Mill on Liberty*: *a Defense* (1983), *Hayek on Liberty* (1984), *Conceptions of Liberty in Political Philosophy* (co-edited with Z. A. Pelczynski, 1984) and *Liberalism* (1985). He is presently at work on a critique of Marxism.

George Friedman received his B.A. from The City College of New York and his Ph.D. from Cornell University's Government Department. He is currently Associate Professor and Chairman of Political Science at Dickinson College, and is the author of *The Political Philosophy of the Frankfurt School*, published by Cornell University Press. He has written several other articles on Marx and Marxism and is completing a book entitled *Marxism and Judaism*.

Steven Lukes teaches politics and sociology at Balliol College, Oxford. He is the author of *Emile Durkheim: His Life and Work*; *Individualism; Power: A Radical View*; *Essays in Social Theory*; and *Marxism and Morality*. With Andrew Scull, he has co-edited a volume of Durkheim's essays on the law; with Martin Hollis, a collection of papers on *Rationality and Relativism*; and with Michael Carrithers and Steven Collins, a collection of papers entitled *The Category of the Person: Anthropology, Philosophy, History*. Most recently he has written the introduction to *The Power of the Powerless*, a translated collection of essays by Vaclav Havel and other Czech writers.

ON THE MUTUAL COMPATIBILITY OF
DEMOCRACY AND MARXIAN SOCIALISM

Joseph Cropsey

Much of the high politics of our time is affected by the hostility and suspicion that pervade relations between the Western democracies and the socialist world. Is it possible that the hostility and suspicion are misplaced, and that the two world systems can find a common ground on which to acknowledge each other as compatible co-denizens between whom there is no difference so potent that the being of one must be a reproach to the being of the other? With a view to this question, I wish to ask whether it is possible for a Marxist society to be democratic or for a democracy to elect Marxism or to elect to remain Marxist. Putting the question in the form, "Is it possible . . ." would enable us to answer it by pointing to even one example of a Marxist democracy, thus to dissolve what seems like a theoretical matter in an empirical medium. This expectation is encouraged by the existence of Marxist regimes that call themselves democratic, but it is, at the same time, frustrated by the obvious unwillingness of the non-Marxist, pre-Marxist democracies to concede to them the propriety of that appellation. In the self-understanding of countries that were democracies before any state was Marxist, democracy is defined by the wide availability of significant choices which cannot be expressed with impunity in Marxist countries or, if they are available at all, then only to a microscopic elite. In the self-understanding of democracies which have at the very least a prescriptive right to be so called, choice or election is decisive for the definition; but can even a well-established self-understanding settle the issue of definition between parties with an interest in contradictory definitions? There is an obvious danger that the question will prove in principle incapable of being answered univocally in a way that is acceptable to both non-Marxist democrats and Marxists who claim to be democrats. This outcome, if it materialized, would furnish evidence of an irreconcilable difference between pre-Marxist/non-Marxist democratic understanding on one hand, and that of Marxism on the other, which would in its own way bear on the original question of their mutual compatibility. It would make clear that each, in its own efforts to embody democracy as it understands democracy, must live by a rule that the other cannot accept. This would leave unresolved, except by appeal to prescriptive right, the legitimacy of each side's claim to the name of democracy; but we may well stipulate the separability of that issue from the one that is of thematic importance to us and proceed directly to the matter of the compatibility of democracy and Marxism by adopting, with the temporary appearance of some arbitrariness, the viewpoint of the side with prescription in its favor, namely, that choice or choosing is of the essence of democracy and freedom is of the essence of choice. That is to say, democracy is a certain condition of choice: where (free) choice is present, democracy is present. This thought points to two somewhat different avenues of further reflection. One is that the theory of democracy is the theory of choice. The other is best put in the form of a question: can democracy be adequately conceived as politics reduced to terms of procedures, rules, or criteria governing the act of choosing, or must it be conceived in terms of the objects of choice, what one might call the substantive ends of the regime, properly to be called democratic. (It is difficult to avoid every resonance of the controversy over which side can rightfully appropriate the name.) How long the two avenues of reflection continue to be distinct from each other remains to be seen.

If democracy is a mode of choice, then the theory of democracy would be the theory of choice and much if not all of our quest for the proper definition of democracy would have to be seen as already completed in the work of the sophisticated writers on the logic of public choice and collective action. Can democracy be adequately understood as the regime whose members' actions are the logic of collective choice converted into practice? It is not necessary for the present purpose to distinguish the economic, strategic, psephistic, and abstractly logical choice-theoretic effluents from the original theory of games because they all participate in a single predominant characteristic: they all pertain to the behavior of agents whose purpose is gain, advantage, or preponderance in relation to one or more similarly motivated actors who presumably have the same equipment for calculation. That the theory of choice has its origin in the theory of games tinctures it not at all with the levity of play but, rather, confers on it all the gravity of the passion for winning.

It might be held that the abstractness of the pure logic of choice renders the theory of collective action marginal to any field of human activity, such as politics, in which the empirical or "pragmatic" is, if not everything, then at least inseparable from everything. For the present purpose, the same point might be made somewhat differently by noting that the pure logic of choice is, *qua* pure, no more democratic than oligarchic, no more peculiar to an American election, for example, than to a maneuver in the Kremlin. This criticism is oblique to my present point, but the objection to choice theory draws attention to a difficulty that we have an obligation to address.

If we think about modern democracy, especially as it is known in the West, we find ourselves contemplating the political setting for the pursuit of private gain, advantage, or preponderance on the part of individuals and groups very much in the spirit of choice-theoretic behavior. But if we ask whether this reveals the essence of democracy itself, we may pause before saying that it does, because it is impossible to ignore the simple definition of democracy as rule by the people or the great multitude, which from ancient times has been supposed to be the poor who will press for their gain and their advantage through their preponderance, but who cannot be thought immune to influences that might deflect them from their egoism. In the interest of not prejudging the question of the mutual compatibility of democracy and Marxism, I should like to leave open the possibility that a people can be influenced significantly by creeds, theories, situations, and doctrines, that they can become practitioners of a divinely-commanded self-mortification, or patriots imbued with a sense of imperial mission, or victims of strategic weakness who surrender to vulnerability and fall thence into hedonism. Who will insist that a people as such must inevitably rule itself according to the dictates of a busy egoism, probable though it may be that they will?

I should like, therefore, to distinguish the *demos* which has come under the influence of some force that is strong enough to turn it away from what I will venture to call the natural ends of the political mass, and the *demos* that in its forthrightness aims at gain and advantage through preponderance. I will venture further to maintain that those goals of self-preference, so familiar through their insistent appeal as to be called natural, are normal to democracy to the point that they seem joined to its essence; that the *demos* can be turned away from its spontaneous inclination only by the application of enormous pressures that arise outside itself and thus imply a divagation from autonomy; that such deviations from the essential tendency of democracy are to be distinguished from those canalizations of self-preference within democratic life such as are indicated in the tenth *Federalist* and that promote the mutual accommodations and concessions that enhance gain. If such a distinction is accepted, then democracy can be understood as directed essentially to certain ends fit to be called natural. Democracy, then, appears as a system of choice or election under the formal principle of autonomy; but it proves to be more than that – a system of election, indeed, but one in which the freedom implicit in election is inseparable in essence from the natural status of the objects of choice. Whether the tension between autonomy and domination by the attractive force of natural desiderata will escape the notice of Marxist or other critics of democracy's self-perception is a question to be kept in mind. For the present, it suffices to observe that undistracted democracy is not essentially a system of means for making choices but, rather, a regimen for superimposing or applying such a system upon or to a substratum of natural ends or the desires for those ends, ends which democracy has no impulse to subvert or replace and which should be considered intrinsic to pristine democracy itself. As Scripture testifies (that it is better to give than to receive is a precept requiring the support of faith in contention with impulse) and as anthropology vainly seeks to deny (with the evidence of the unusual practices of faraway tribes) and as publicized lapses of communists high and low strongly suggest, there is something only too painfully natural about the self-preference that so commonly displays itself as acquisitiveness and that can be confidently regarded as defining the ends that dominate the acts and the machinery of democratic choice.

In proceeding along the two paths indicated at the outset by the reflection that democracy is a certain condition of choice, we have discovered that the two avenues opened thereby – the one indicated by the question whether the theory of choice is not in fact the theory of democracy and the other indicated by the question whether democracy contemplates only the instrumentalities and not the substantive ends of choice – in fact converge on the thought that the means embedded in democracy are peculiarly complementary to the natural ends that those means subserve. This convergence will enable us to progress in our effort to judge the mutual compatibility of democracy and Marxism.

The question of whether or not Marxism and democracy are mutually compatible is vitalized by the empirical fact that the subjects of Marxist governments have hitherto lacked the opportunity freely to express their political judgments, preferences, or choices. It must be understood, however, that what is perceived by liberal democrats as a fact is seen by Marxist advocates as a tendentious interpretation imposed on an undeniable fact that happens to have a meaning contrary to the one attributed to it by liberal democrats. Marxists have no need or desire to deny that they insist as far as possible on one-party government, which is a system that distinguishes a politically favored minority and a passive mass. It is unnecessary to rehearse the arguments of the orthodox and revisionist theoreticians over the role of vanguards, just as it would be irrelevant to impugn the motives of those who justify or lead the one-party elites associated with Marxist government, unnecessary and irrelevant because our attention should be concentrated on the conception of choice, and hence of freedom, on which the visible institutions of Marxist government are erected. For that purpose it is enough to reflect on a few of the best-known tenets of Marxist doctrine, such as those which follow. Society has hitherto been plagued by division; the great One has failed to rise out of the alienation that chokes the happiness of the Many, a multiplicity that is an aspect of the system of property. Multiplicity and alienation are empirically inseparable from the concrete miseries of mankind: massive poverty and loss of freedom among many, and dehumanization of all – a paradigm of slavery. At the bottom of this well of degradation is unreason. Marxism is a doctrine that promises the reign of One over Many

and that sees a salvation in the concomitant triumph of Reason over abominated Passion. But this is a victory that will occur only when the world's
business of production and distribution is no longer left to be conducted
under the signs of greed, hedonism, and combativeness – passions that
generate the outcomes mediately which are accessible to reason immediately
– but rather of reason itself and thus necessarily of philanthropic principles:
reason over passion and One over Many.

The way to this immense consummation is to be led by those who have
been made wise by their wretchedness (abstracting entirely from the paideutic influence of Marxism itself). This is an astonishing proscenium to frame
a drama that lives by rejecting the reason that flows indirectly from passion;
but that difficulty is immaterial to our purpose, which is to find the principle
of choice or election that lies immured in Marxist politics. Led however
restively, by a vanguard however instructed, humanity is to arrive on the
plane of a freedom that goes far beyond emancipation from wage-labor
exploitation and political disfranchisement, and on the plane of a reason that
far transcends the state planning which replaces the balky effectiveness of
market spontaneity. The freedom and reason contemplated by essential
Marxism are revealed as the obverse and reverse of a single coin. They are
so revealed by the meaning of the decisive slogan of Marxism: from each
according to his ability, to each according to his needs. The human community in which that aspiration had materialized would be a One in which
the Many had effectually caused themselves to vanish in a concrete realization of Humanity as such – one for all, all for one. The implicit abandonment by each individual of his pristine self-preference is the deepest sign of
the radical rationalization of life envisioned in Marxism, which in this way
appropriates the moral-political ideal of universality inherited from Rousseau (the general will) and Kant (the categorical imperative). The rule of
reason in this sense could be also the zenith of despotism if it were not
accompanied by, indeed generated by, autonomy. To reason must therefore
be added a freedom conceived so that there is no disparity of radical depth
between freedom and reason. This is accomplished by construing freedom
as that condition of will that has disciplined itself to will freely only what is
worthy of being willed, which is precisely the rational. It is of no concern to
us for the present purpose that the self-discipline of the will is the determined, i.e., unfree result of a purely material condition, namely, the abolition
of the private ownership of the means of production. What matters is that
there is an undoubted ground of choice elaborated in the theory of Marxism
and available for invocation to repel the charge that the subjects of a one-
party regime are simply the victims of oppression.

Here we may abstract from such practical and gravely serious issues as are
implicit in the dogma of a transition period (how long can an unredeemed

promise retain its plausibility let alone its validity?) and concentrate instead on the meaning of the principle of choice that lies within Marxism. To be considered first of all is the fact that the Marxist principle of choice entails the defiance of the claim that the transcendence of self-preference on a massive scale implies or is the subversion of nature and, accordingly, has never been seen. Marxist orthodoxy may not simply demur to the bill of entailment; it must positively insist that widespread transcendence of self-preference is possible, and, hence, that Marxism is invulnerable to the charge of utopianism that is often leveled against it. The social transcendence of self-preference is indeed the subversion, but far more than the subversion it is the outright explosion of nature, of that nature to which has been attributed those human qualities such as egoism which are, as Marxism must affirm, in fact generated in history and replaced in the same medium. We might note in passing how widely this teaching of victory over nature differs from that enshrined in Christianity (with which Marxism is routinely compared) and from that which is prominent in the modern scientific philosophies of "conquest of nature" from Bacon to Hegel. Christianity and science, to use the latter term broadly, understand the effectual reality of unchanging nature and conceive of a victory over it through faith or reason as in no way identical with its demythologization. One is entitled, therefore, to speak of the Marxist conception of choice as being radically anti-natural in the sense that it is hostile to the ideology of nature rather than to the nature whose reality is impugned. I leave for other occasions any judgments of the plausibility or utility of such a conception.

What is one to say about the mutual compatibility of two social systems, both of which claim to embody freedom, but one of which attaches its principle of choice to a well-worn universal, namely, nature, inferred from observation and the other of which derives its principle of choice from the rejection of that universal as outworn and imaginary? That each might adapt itself to the other in ways that, although marginal are yet noteworthy, is not inconceivable. But in order to conceive a democratic Marxism or Marxist democracy in the fullest sense, one must be prepared to tolerate one paradox or another: a democratic mass free to respond to its natural impulses arbitrarily renouncing them and seeking only the good of the whole, or a thoroughly socialized mass conducting its affairs according to the rules of a game whose purpose is to win. (The inappropriateness of game-theoretic analysis of choice to activities in a Marxist society *qua* Marxist seems to follow directly from the expulsion of winning from the ends of a socialist mass more than from the political modes of a society of democratic self-seekers.) It might be argued in favor of the compatibility and, indeed, the veritable synthesis of naturalistic democracy and Marxian socialism that such decisive equilibria as are manifest in the equality of marginal revenues and costs, developed spontaneously in egoist market models, can be simulated and reproduced by the machinery of socialist planning; or one might argue more broadly that the conditions of rivalry and friction can when necessary be introduced in facsimile in a society that exists in order to transcend all effectual disunity. The argument would be weak, however, for even the perfectly effective replication of an outcome of the activity of the democratic animus would signify nothing for the affinity of that animus with the contrary spirit and aspiration of socialism. As much could be said regarding the numerous measures of regulation and redistribution adopted by the democracies, in apparent mimicry of socialism but across the grain of the undiluted egoism of primordial naturalistic democracy.

After all has been said that can be said in a speculative vein, there remains a question that can be answered only empirically. It runs as follows: granting that the principle of democracy is the egoism, even the natural egoism, of the many relatively poor, is it not possible that the preponderant poor may be made to perceive their salvation in the supreme welfare society projected by Marxism? Cannot Marxism promise the most successful satisfaction of the natural desires of individuals by offering the conditions of the hive or the herd? Has modernity in some way brought mankind within sight of a social order in which the *demos* seeks the satisfaction of individual, irrepressible, and natural desires through the instrumentalities of a state in which "nothing and no one can free a person from the compulsory demands of society, its laws that are obligatory for all."[1] There is no way to dispel the empirical possibility of such an outcome; but that eventuality would leave in its wake a question about the society in which the aggressive animus that suffuses individual autonomy and that subserves individual autarky has either become atrophied or, at the very least, is outlawed constitutionally. Is that society not *ipso facto* non-democratic? Nothing that has been learned about human society could justify the conclusion that friction and rivalry belong so singularly to democratic life that democracy is present where and to the extent that they are present; but it is plausible to maintain that where they are absent or banned, democracy – and perhaps politics altogether – has been superseded.

The foregoing points to the second theme under which I propose to consider the mutual compatibility of democracy and Marxian socialism. This theme is identified by the ruling question that arises under it: can we discern with the necessary responsibility and sufficient clarity a primary human temper that animates democratic life, and the comparable one for socialism; and will they if they emerge, be mutually compatible?

The issue of the correspondence between a particular political order and

[1] K. Chernenko, quoted in translation, *New York Times*, September 26, 1984, p. 6.

some human temper, animus, character, or type has engaged the thought of writers known to us since Plato, who connects each regime with the predominant influence of a certain human capacity or passion, or some equilibrium among a number of them. Montesquieu writes of the spirit of laws and is much occupied with "the spirit of monarchy," "the spirit of democracy" and so on, by which he means the deep human drive or motivation that prevails over all others in the specific regime and thus gives its overriding character to the society itself. Kant, at the end of the long footnote on Professor Schiller early in *Religion Within the Limits of Reason Alone*, trenches on a related subject when he reflects on the psychological substratum of goodness in man, though admittedly not man *qua* citizen of a particular regime. When Nietzsche looks beyond good and evil, he discovers in *ressentiment* what he takes to be the deep animus that inspires or pervades all mass politics. And when other writers refer to a democratic and an authoritarian personality, they may have in view certain human propensities or impulsions that are not themselves political, that are primordial in relation to the overt political opinions, choices, and acts, but that have a decisive political influence. I wish to consider in a preliminary way whether or not there are subliminal or, at any rate, affective and, as such, subpolitical correlates of democracy and socialism, with a view to considering the mutual concord or discord of those correlates and, thus, of the concomitant political systems.

From the outset, we must agree to deprive ourselves of the apparent evidence of certain concrete experiences, namely, those of the democratic and Marxist countries, because of the difficulty, insurmountable at least by me, of distinguishing what may be attributed to national character or tradition, what to the peculiarities of British, American, Soviet, Chinese, or Cuban rule, and what to democracy or socialism itself. But part of my concern will be the human traits that are fostered by, as well as the impulses that are drawn upon by, the alternative social systems, and it would be impossible to discuss those plausibly while refusing on principle to observe the available specimens. For example, one might speculate that some cognate of self-assertiveness finds expression in naturalistic democracy, and the social expression of that deep animus is bound to encourage either belligerence or cupidity. But which, in fact, is it? We must leave open the possibility that we shall be unable to dispose of the issue before us – the mutual compatibility of socialism and democracy – without empirical materials that are very elusive.

Setting all such difficulties aside, I will begin my inquiry into what ultimately animates the two regimes with a question: what is democracy? The formal, familiar definition of it as rule by the people is, of course, not incorrect or, not *simply* incorrect, but it is nearly useless for the present purpose. Surprisingly, the respect in which it is close to incorrect proves to be helpful for us now: "the People" in the abstract may be thought to rule but in fact very few people rule, strikingly few seek office, and relatively few manifest a desire to participate in the selection of those who do rule. From this it may be gathered that the decisive human impulse defining democracy is not the passion to rule, but rather, perhaps, the refusal to be ruled by any man or men who claim to rule without the *explicit*, not the merely tacit, consent of "all." This is an indirect expression of at least one formula for equality. The animus within this claim of equality is a species of pride, an ambivalent expression of self-regard: each is as worthy as every other, and no other is more worthy than the first. This pride of jealousy or of invidiousness relies on an opinion of the self and of the other that may be rendered cardinally as well as ordinally: to be as worthy as others who themselves have no such ambition as drives them toward rule and no such merit as raises them above "equality" is to make a proud claim to a modest estate. Lest it be thought that this judgment constitutes an instant disparagement of the dignity of the democratic spirit, it should be pointed out that the generalization of so unassuming a form of pride accomplishes the conjunction of the effectual political impotence of each individual with a sense of his human worth. This notable conjunction could, it is true, be achieved by universal religion, in the absence of each man's political significance, but only where religion might be made to count.

Abstaining from further judgment of the worth of the sense of worth that accompanies the democratic claim of equality, it is easy to see the element of spirited self-assertion that infuses democracy, and to see also the convergence between the self-assertiveness so uncovered and what was previously argued to be the self-asserting end of naturalistic democracy viewed as a medium of choice. It is equally easy to see the similarity, if not identity between the animus of equality and that of marketplace competition, which evinces in behavior a simultaneous self-assertion and other-denial, or "outdoing," as Socrates might have said.[2]

What, in the same vein, is Marxist or modern communism? It is a project for the human condition that, to speak negatively at first, cannot be defined in terms of relation between men and ruling or being ruled because it aspires to the transcendence of rule properly so-called in the classless and, therefore, stateless society. Positively put, communism is a project for uncoerced life. Since the elimination of coercion in the political sense is a concomitant or by-product of the abolition of subordination in the sphere of production, a sphere considered primordial in Marxian socialism, the removal of exogenous constraint or coercion may be considered all-inclusive as encom-

[2] Plato, *Republic*, 349 B–C.

passing the transcendence of politics and economics alike. The formula "From each according to his ability, to each according to his needs" is in its own way an announcement of the transcendence of economics, and may serve as such until a conception of economics becomes available that is free of the implication of scarcity, actual or felt.

The removal of coercion, specifically of state and economic coercion, presupposes the highest degree of conscious sociality among the denizens if the Marxist project is to materialize according to plan. It is imaginable that the socialization of the ownership of the means of production would operate as a mere condition modifying the behaviour of the denizens and causing them to respond to needs and desires in a manner that would have the outward appearance of cooperative good will but was in fact automatic. This outcome would frustrate the intention of Marxian socialism, which is precisely to humanize the members of society, to free them and above all to make them live as human beings do who are conscious that there is no conflict between themselves and any significant "other" in their environment to impose on them and to which they must feel strange. It would be misleading to say that no self would define itself by reference to anything other than itself, but it would not be misleading to say that to the extent that every conscious and self-conscious self must distinguish and thus define itself with reference to others, the socialist self would do so in the consciousness that no other, however distinguishable, is hostile. The condition of the socialist man might be freedom, understood as freedom from coercion and thus, to speak loosely, freedom to live; but the animus or spirit is not freedom but, rather, some state of the soul correlative with that peculiar and peculiarly based freedom. One can only speculate, for every aspect of what we are discussing is in the realm of the projected: there are no empirical materials that would not offer dubious data. One may speculate that the human being living in the absolutely hospitable medium, relieved of every significant frustration or strangeness, would exhibit a vigor of high activity, a spiritedness of productivity in all directions (by hypothesis, compatible with social living). One may equally plausibly speculate that activity presupposes resistance or a monitory other, even if only in the form of a recognized contrivance such as the production quota which must acquire the meaning of a scrutinizing authority and under whose discipline the affected human beings would become intimidated, routinized, or conscientious, depending on the effects of other causes.

It may be a serious defect of the socialist vision that the human product which it projects as its goal simply cannot with any confidence be connected with the causes that are supposed to produce it. The failure of that connection greatly weakens the possibility of comparing empirically the animus of democracy and that of socialism, but it leaves intact the comparison on the plane of aspiration. On that level, it is safe to say that, in envisioning the unalienated man, the man who is at home among humanity, socialism envisions the man whose environment is parental and fraternal (with no sophistications of sibling rivalry relevant) or, in other words, a man whose *sense* of his own dignity, as distinguished from any claimed objective basis for it, is caring or a species of love. The environment from which alienation has been removed is dominated not by justice – to each according to what he deserves – but by caring. I propose, therefore, this second ground on which to reflect on the mutual compatibility of democracy and Marxian socialism: naturalistic democracy tacitly presupposes and without conscious intent may even project the human being in whom the self-preserving and self-serving aggressiveness evoked by Machiavelli and Hobbes is the irreducible, characteristic animus, while modern communism projects the human being in whom the decisive animus will be a species of affectionate sociality. While I freely acknowledge the great lacunae of information that impair the foregoing, I conclude that democracy and socialism conceive of two different and opposing states of man, indeed, of two different kinds of men, and to that extent or in that sense the two systems are mutually incompatible. I leave out of consideration what must be included in any discussion that could claim to be conclusive: how far can the aggressive animus and the affectionate be added to one another to form, in this peculiarly modern milieu, the aggregate of *thymos* and *eros* sought by Plato for the guardians of the excellent city?

That there is room for both of these dispositions in each human being is beyond doubt, but that more than one of them could be primordial is offensive to logic even if not refutable by experience, leaving the synthesis of democracy and socialism possible only in a weak sense, i.e., as the mixture of the two in various proportions but always with one in the ascendant: witness, for example, the Swedish and Israeli societies. There are indeed terms on which the reconciliation of democracy and socialism can be only too easily posited, but they are terms which will outrage the partisans of each and the projectors of their synthesis. According to the famous account of liberalism, both democratic and socialist, presented by Nietzsche, they are equally mean-spirited excrescences of the Judaeo-Christian morality, sharing as their common denominator neither spirit nor love but, rather, the hate-driven resentment felt by the base for the noble. This line of argument favoring the compatibility of democracy and socialism is to be rejected as irrelevant to the practical situation and of little positive help in answering our immediate question.

Finally, I shall take up the theme of the mutual compatibility of democracy and Marxian socialism in a third mode, that of the history of the thought that finds expression in the two social orders. I shall reason from a composite premise that needs to be made explicit, namely, that liberal democracy and Marxian socialism define the essential political possibilities for the modern world into the foreseeable future, and that these concrete political orders can be understood – I will refrain from saying must be understood – by the light of the concepts that are decisively active in each. Those concepts and the arguments in which they are embedded are an important ingredient of modern political philosophy. Thus, the effectual modern political alternative can be referred to and conceived in the terms of modern political philosophy. From this it follows that the mutual compatibility of democracy and Marxian socialism would be the rational consequence or expression of the mutual compatibility or even the unity of the corresponding strands of modern political philosophy, while the mutual incompatibility of democracy and Marxian socialism would indicate a discord and, hence, a disunity within what is called, perhaps simplistically, "modern political philosophy." By a species of logistic metonymy, replacing each regime by its rational surrogate, I shall sketch an argument in which will be considered the relation to each other of the elements of the effectual modern political alternative through a brief presentation of certain modern political conceptions that I take to be preponderant.

It would not be misleading to declare that such classic moderns as Machiavelli, Hobbes, and Locke discovered in nature no higher duty for mankind than to take care of themselves and no more comprehensive freedom than the unlimited right to do so. A conception of rights or freedom in the service of duty and of duties that rest on the same natural ground as rights produces a formidable moral construction, one that seemed problematic only in a few manageable respects, all growing out of the need to explain the origins of civil society out of natural freedom. By the use of explanations that differed from one another in ways that need not concern us, Hobbes and Locke showed the reasons that and the devices by which men gave their consent to be governed. Inseparable from those explanations was the notion that the primary rights of man are not only natural but also inalienable. They accompany man into civil life, in which freedom means nothing less than the exercise of those inalienable rights to life, liberty, and estate. The Hobbesian proposition that the right to the end implies the right to the means thereto was not rejected by Locke, who, in elaborating the evolution of the right of property, the means to life, traced rightful possession to the mixing of one's labor with that to which no one else had a rightful claim. Appropriation is the algetic projection of oneself onto an object through the act of "mixing one's labor" with it, infusing it and thus indelibly marking it with what is, without further analysis of the self, essential to oneself.

Questions of a larger possible meaning of freedom, specifically of freedom of the will, were of course recognized, but they were disposed of by Hobbes and Locke in a naturalistic way, by identifying will with a mental function under the control of a subject capable of suspending judgment. This particular assimilation to each other of will and mind was naturalistic in the sense that it looked in the opposite direction from, for example, Hegel's similar identification which served the intention of Kant, namely, to emancipate the will and thus the subject from natural necessity. This is worth saying, in the present context because it directs attention to Spinoza's exposure of the naturalized will as highly problematic. It was Spinoza's task to reconcile with each other the dictum of "no *imperium in imperio*," no human enclave of exemption from natural causality, and the existence of a true human freedom, that is, a freedom from mere responsiveness in a mechanical whole. He performed this task in the last part of his *Ethics*, by distinguishing activity from passivity, the act of mind from the response of body, having first erected the structure of the unicity of substance within which he could defend himself against the charge that he arbitrarily deprived nature of simplicity. After Spinoza, the articulation with each other of nature and a will compatible with requirements of freedom had to preoccupy Rousseau, Kant, and Hegel in ways that prepared the work of Marx. It may be added in passing that the scrutiny of natural causation undertaken from the perspective of morality and freedom was joined by the scrutiny of natural causation undertaken by Hume from the perspective of epistemology and metaphysics. The Kantian contribution to the patrimony of Marx should be understood as including what Kant owned that he had received from Hume, namely, a disparagement of the empirical, which Kant and then Marx could reconcile with the exalting of history through teleological reasonings that I cannot now take up.

The preparation for the work of Marx that was contained in the thought of his predecessors may be collapsed, for our purpose, into the Hegelian doctrine of personality and, thus, of autonomy. The fulfilment of the human condition requires the conjunction of freedom and reason that emerges when the human subject asserts his subjectivity while or in cheerfully willing all those outcomes whose rationality is evinced in their perfect harmony with the requirements of society, i.e., of the state. The utterance of the human subject in an external thing that is called his property is a stage along the ascent to the ethical life. The classic modern conception of property as being in support of freedom defined by reference to life has been replaced by a conception of property in support of freedom defined by reference to autonomy of will consummated in perfect rational sociality.

Marx's efforts to emphasize his originality and, especially, to widen the distance between Hegel and himself, are not relevant to our present purpose, which is to judge the mutual compatibility of naturalistic democracy and Marxian socialism. My intention in sketching certain developments in modern dogma has been to suggest that the democracy and socialism in which we are interested are the concrete expressions of a set of conceptions that may for some purposes be regarded as the modern unity, and for other purposes must be regarded as a duality. Modernity has been unified in its formulation of the human problem in terms of the mutual adjustment of nature and freedom. It has been deeply divided through the efforts put forth to elevate the conception of freedom out of the gravitational field of mere preservation. Naturalistic democracy grew out of the senior line and Marxian socialism out of the cadet branch of modern political philosophy. Such a purely formal statement of the case gives the impression that they are divided by a family quarrel; but some family quarrels become known as civil wars, and Marx, for whatever his opinion on the subject is worth, inclined to the view that his system is so radically different from what went before that the issue between them must almost inevitably be resolved in violence.

There is a sense in which Marxism may be perceived as itself a synthesis of contrasting elements. Locke's doctrine of property puts heavy emphasis on the mixing of labor, of something irreducibly one's own, with the unformed or unappropriated, and in so doing gave inspiration to the labor theory of value. Marx could not and did not wish to escape the labor theory of value, but he adapted it decisively: he envisioned labor as being trans- formed from toil, the painful and degrading servitude of wage earners, to the satisfying, because uncoerced *activity* of the productive animal destined under the right conditions to actualize in the concrete external all the latent human power otherwise doomed to suffocation within. The scope of Marx's adaptation of the labor theory of property and value, and the dubiousness of the claim that Marxism is an effectual synthesis, may be gathered from the realization that the primordial labor theory tacitly accepts while Marx rejects as a presupposition that man will forever gain his bread in the sweat of his face, i.e., painfully, just as women will bring forth the product of *their* labor. The extent to which Marx fell in with the spirit of revisionist modernity in projecting a human condition unfettered by nature is a measure of the incompatibility of Marxian socialism with naturalistic democracy.

Testing the mutual compatibility of democracy and Marxian socialism by the three criteria proposed in this paper – choice, animus, and genealogy – has produced a signal that is negative, but not overwhelmingly so. I have argued that a human mass left free to express its inclinations could not be expected to choose a social organization dominated by principles that include the need for overturning the very inclinations that rule in the electing mass. I have tried to show that each of the two systems grows from and is nourished by a primal human thrust, and that the aggressive animus of the one contradicts the specific eroticism of the other, leaving aside speculations on the reducibility of hostility and affection to one another. And, finally, I have sketched the developments in philosophic thought that can be regarded as delineating the being and becoming of the two social systems, and find that Marxism and liberal democracy are the phenomenalizations of theoretical projects whose differences are so great, notwithstanding a common parentage, that the compatibility with each other of the respective social orders can only be doubtful. I believe that the weight of evidence available by the means I have used is against their mutual compatibility. Much persuaded of this, I am nevertheless anxious to avoid proving that the bumblebee cannot fly.

Political Science, University of Chicago

DEMOCRACY AND INDIVIDUALITY*

ALAN GILBERT

For many contemporary liberals, Anglo-American democracy seems unimpeachably the best political form. In contrast, adherence to democratic values seems an area in which most Marxian regimes, and perhaps Marx himself, are strikingly deficient. Further, Marxian theory insists on the existence of oppressive ruling classes in *all* capitalist societies and on the need for class struggle and violent revolution to achieve a more cooperative regime – theses which liberal social theories tend to dismiss peremptorily. From the perspective of modern liberal democratic theory, Marxian arguments seem prima facie outlandish and even morally objectionable.

Yet though Marxian theory challenges liberalism, it also affirms and extends certain ethical claims which are at the heart of liberalism: claims about the goods of mutual recognition of persons and self-respect, or a general human capacity for moral personality and individuality. Marxian theory provides an explanation for conspicuous anomalies in the liberal theory of democracy and aims to transcend them. The first section of this essay will sketch the emergence of liberal and Marxian theories of democracy out of ancient theories, and suggest that the leading differences between these two modern theories are broadly empirical and social-theoretical rather than clashes of underlying moral premises. A comparison of liberal and Marxian conceptions of democracy will also highlight the merits of the greatest liberal political theories (those of Montesquieu, Hegel and Mill) in contrast to contemporary relativist alternatives (those of Weber, Schumpeter, Lipset, and Huntington). The second section will try to strengthen the Marxian theory of social individuality as a theory of the self. Since modern democratic theory is essentially a theory of democratic individuality, this section will also underscore the common moral features of liberalism and Marxism. I will suggest that substantial differentials in status as well as class differentials fundamentally impair human well-being and undercut democracy; social equality will be defended. The third section uses this reformulation of Marx's moral and psychological insights into communism to highlight that regime's political, participatory aspects and to criticize Marx's theory of socialism (the first stage of communism) and later socialist

* I would like to thank Lucy Ware for helpful discussions of the theory of the self, status hierarchy and communism. I have also benefited from conversations with G. A. Cohen, John Dunn, David Levine and Walter Gilbert.

experiments. Socialism makes too many concessions to capitalist class and
status hierarchies, concessions which derive not just from an erroneous
approach to counteracting "economic backwardness," but also from a fundamentally mistaken acceptance of deficient social and psychological theories
of human motivation and the self. In such regimes, "liberal" market reforms
do not further democracy; communist egalitarianism might.

1. *The Value of Democracy*

Today's liberal theory of democracy emphasizes either secondary aspects
of democratic practice, or even procedure, at the expense of democracy's
basic moral justification. Thus, contemporary political scientists commonly
stress regular party competition (one set of leaders in office and one or more
loyal oppositions) as a method for generating leadership and effective constitutional restraint on the exercise of power ("the rule of law"). Such arrangements or procedures are assumed to promote (an unspecified conception of)
fairness regardless of particular outcomes. Their justification depends on
their propensity to ward off the dangers of tyranny, that is, the threat to
underlying liberal values represented by the abuse of political and, perhaps,
social power. But these accounts, often characterized as value-free or
relativistic, do not defend the objectivity of liberal values and sometimes
even fail to make them explicit.

At this point, a basic tension arises in many contemporary liberal accounts.
Coherent modern liberal theories, for instance those of Montesquieu and
Hegel, advanced general claims about the political aspects of the good life:
mutual recognition of persons and the universal human capacity for moral
personality. Such theories maintained that liberal institutions (a balance of
governmental powers, impersonal, universal laws which permit individuals to
pursue their own aims within civil society, and the like) would facilitate the
realization of these goods. These theorists regarded slavery and serfdom as
irredeemably hostile to human well-being. In Hegel's phrase, "slavery was
an outrage on the concept of man." The distinctive liberal view of personality
and freedom emerges out of the empirical rejection of ancient and modern
biological claims about a putative duality of human natures that is relevant to
political life – some born to command and others to obey, masters and
slaves, lords and serfs, capitalists and the poor, dominant status groups and
subordinate ones, colonizers and colonized, men and women. The rule of
law and democratic procedures and practices are, where they are justified,
the institutional embodiments of the mutual recognition of persons. Liberal
defenses of procedure, divisions of governmental power, and party competition depend on this substantive claim; they do not supersede it. Contrary to
contemporary denials of the proposition that well-ordered democratic
regimes embody *any* common good, the *common good* of mutual recognition

underlay the diversity of individuality and particular political practices in the older liberalism. Thus, it is ironic that even in the era of the American civil rights movement of the 1960s, liberal political scientists frequently defended a bizarre definition of democracy, which was focused solely on the role of party competition in generating political leadership. According to this definition, the pre-Civil War slaveholding regime, the monolithic control of the Democratic Party (in partnership with the Ku Klux Klan) in the American South through most of the twentieth century, and current South African arrangements all seem to qualify.[1]

Coherent liberal (and radical) arguments claim that individuality – the deliberative shaping of "a life of one's own" within a given historical context – is an intrinsic human good. Intrinsic goods are, very roughly, relationships or activities which elicit determined, even enthusiastic participation in virtue of displaying and developing characteristic human capacities, and which would be chosen for their own sakes. Michael Oakeshott's view of the goods of individuality and conversation defended by civil association (where the law serves as a medium for the pursuit of individual purposes and determines no particular outcomes) may serve as a liberal illustration. Marx's account of the worker-officials of the Paris Commune, engaging in political activity as an "expression of their own nature," rather then to secure money or prestige, provides a radical one. Modern liberal and radical accounts grow out of and modify Aristotle's views. For Aristotle, intrinsic goods are those that focus on the capacity for deliberation or practical reasonableness (*phronesis*) and include life and physical well-being, friendship, the pursuit of knowledge, community, justice, play, artistic creativity, and the like. Modern conceptions of democracy and individuality recognize a more general capacity for deliberation or moral personality than Aristotle allowed. Yet they also underline the centrality of deliberation – a "life of one's own" can only be chosen through reflection on the goods embodied or latent in one's historical situation, given one's capacities and needs.

Unlike Hegel and Marx, however, today's liberal theorists, even including Oakeshott often fail to see the social preconditions of individuality in the historical abolition of slavery and feudalism. The possibility of pursuing a "life of one's own" requires a basic respect from others for one's individual agency, i.e., equal social recognition of the capacity for personality of each person. Montesquieu's dialectic of Roxanne against Usbek and, more philosophically, Hegel's account of master and slave, graphically illustrate the political, psychological, and material aspects of the struggle for mutual recognition. These liberal theories focus not just on what Marxians identify

[1] Alan Gilbert, "Moral Realism, Individuality and Justice in War," *Political Theory* vol. 15 (Feb. 1986); Seymour M. Lipset, *Political Man* (New York: Doubleday, 1963), p. 64; Joseph Schumpeter, *Capitalism, Socialism and Democracy* (New York: Harper and Row, 1950).

as social class, but on differential status as well – the predatory continuum of social honor and prestige in which the stature of one consists only in the diminution of another. Thus, a liberal *might* include racism, sexism, anti-working class prejudice, and, more generally, ideas of fundamental personal and political *insignificance* as aspects of a hierarchy of status. As Hegel's theory emphasizes, humans manifest their capacity for freedom and individuality historically; liberalism is committed to an affirmation of (a complicated, dialectical) moral progress. In Marxian terms, both liberals and radicals defend an idea of an historically discovered *social individuality* which cuts against inequalities of both class and status. Depending on what is true about obstacles to individuality posed by (exploitative) social structures, a sustained recognition of affiliation and politics – an Aristotelian, Hegelian, or Marxian one – may be a prerequisite for achieving individuality. Minimally, in coherent liberal theories, the mutual recognition of persons involved in the abolition of systematically discriminatory practices, as well as the emergence of democratic forms and the rule of law, is a prerequisite for individuality.

A true theory of social structure, democracy, and individuality would specify the conditions under which such mutual recognition is possible. The fundamental controversy between Marxian and liberal theory turns on these empirical issues. Further, given the role of background information or auxiliary statements in science, the confirmation of theories proceeds by detailed comparison of explanations (and in some cases predictions) offered by competing theories. Darwin's contrast between natural selection and creationism in *Origin of Species* provides an important example. Today in the social sciences, as I have argued elsewhere, sophisticated versions of Marxian and liberal theories are leading contenders for truth. A comparison of Marxian and liberal theories of democracy highlights the connection of the basic liberal theses; it helps to formulate the appropriate questions for research and to justify courses of political action.[2]

The main liberal claim is both an empirical (biological, psychological, and sociological) and a moral one: (1) given a very broad characterization of distinctively human capacities, for instance, that humans are intelligent, empathetic social animals, a justifiable political regime must facilitate mutual recognition and individual agency. It must not systematically deny that these capacities exist in any segment of the population. Note that the moral properties mentioned here, i.e., the capacity for moral personality, are identical with or, to use a bit of contemporary philosophical jargon, super-

---

[2] I contrast theories of democracy and argue for the plausibility of a Marxian view in an accompanying paper to this one, "Democracy and the Recognition of Persons," unpublished. See also my "The Storming of Heaven: *Capital* and Marx's Politics," J. Roland Pennock, ed., *Marxism Today*, Nomos vol. xxvi (New York: New York University Press, 1984), section 5.

vene on other empirical properties (such as the psychological capacity for rationality and empathy). Though moral categories cannot be reduced to nonmoral ones, modern discoveries in moral knowledge (i.e. the claim that humans *generally* have a sufficient capacity for moral personality) are linked to claims in these other areas, illustrating a broad unity of knowledge.

Liberals, in addition, advance the following two controversial empirical claims to defend contemporary liberal democracy as the regime which best embodies these moral goods: (2) despite substantial social inequalities (inequalities in wealth and status), no oppressive ruling class exists which might systematically corrupt the use of state power, and the democratic state thus rises above and may at its best be consistently impartial with regard to people's personal affairs in private (civil) society; (3) as a result of (2), existing injustices, however serious (the unjust United States war in Vietnam, racism, sexism, and the like) can be remedied through largely peaceful and legal efforts under the existing or very similar constitutional procedures and party arrangements. A democratic regime is a comparatively plastic, easily reformed one.

A reasonable liberal view is thus committed to core claims about human nature and the good life. It accompanies these claims with a specific social theory about the nature of modern societies (the absence of an oppressive ruling class) and the possibility of social reforms given procedural and constitutional guarantees and particular democratic practices. It seeks to bar tyranny and (unnecessary, mass) violence even in pursuit of just aims. Only in this context is its emphasis on procedures coherent. This account of liberal theories of democracy excludes as anti-democratic or anti-liberal, contemporary views which justify widespread apathy at the expense of substantive equality and mutual recognition.

In contrast, mistaken emphasis on form (procedure) over content goes hand in hand with a currently fashionable version of metaethical relativism. Even the most sophisticated of today's liberals like John Rawls and Michael Walzer – who are critical of major inequalities and political corruption in capitalist economies, who favor some version of democratic market socialism, and who are tempted by doctrines of moral objectivity – have recently affirmed that modern conceptions of equality and freedom flow merely from the conventions of "our" Anglo-American public life. Rawls, for instance asserts, in a Deweyan relativist vein, that the modern conception of an equally sufficient capacity for moral personality is "our" intuition and has no further basis; yet he also advances the opposing view that such a capacity is an objective moral and psychological fact about humans. The former, relativist contention is, however, self-refuting. It denies metaethically what it affirms practically, namely, that we have a sound basis for recognizing equality and a capacity for individuality, in Rawls's sense, as opposed to, say, the Nazi view that humans are divided into distinct and unequal races.[3] To put the matter pointedly, even if relativism were not self-refuting, the condemnation of Nazism or slaveholding is, given the most minimal account of what we know about a good life for humans, far more evident than any likely argument for metaethical skepticism. No liberal view which fails to acknowledge the general capacity for moral personality or to defend metaethically the objective good of individuality can be coherent.

As I noted above, the comparison of liberal and Marxian theories of democracy in capitalist societies shows that they share underlying moral premise (1); their complex ethical and political disagreements arise from clashes over empirical issues in social theory, i.e., from disagreements about (2) and (3). Marx, following Hegel, affirmed the initial liberal claims about human nature, mutual recognition, and individuality. Marxian social theory adds, however, that just as slavery is inconsistent with modern individuality, so "wage slavery" clashes in numerous ways with mutual recognition and self-respect. Marx and Engels concurred with many workers, peasants, artisans, anarchists like Proudhon, and liberals like Mill in condemning "crying" inequalities of riches and poverty, luxury and starvation. As I have argued elsewhere, broad claims made by Marx and Engels about human nature and human needs, including claims about the goods of mutual recognition and solidarity, are sufficient to support this judgment. The differences between their theory and the theories of other radicals, and many liberals also, center on the best explanation of these inequalities and the consequent efficacy of particular stategies for changing them. In opposing appeals to abstract moral principles (for instance, to a putative "eternal justice") as a basis for social theorizing, Marx and Engels sometimes mistakenly contrasted scientific knowledge to ethical opinion and advanced relativist metaethical theses about justice. Yet they proposed communism – the abolition of classes and the wage system – as a *political* arrangement which would overcome the harmful social, political, and moral consequences of capitalist inequality. In contrast to exploitative societies which wrongly claimed to defend the well-being of each of their members, Marxian communism would, in an Aristotelian sense, embody a common good. It would facilitate the concordant flourishing of many goods – political community, knowledge, individuality, and the like – which had clashed in exploitative "prehistory" (e.g., the emergence of political community and science in ancient Athens at the expense of slavery). In this sense, Engels sometimes rightly emphasized that progress in moral knowledge is possible and comparable to advances in other

---

[3] John Rawls, *A Theory of Justice* (Cambridge, MA: Harvard University Press, 1971), pp. 19–20, 506–508; Hilary Putnam, *Reason, Truth and History* (Cambridge: Cambridge University Press, 1981), ch. 5.

branches of knowledge.[4] Thus, Marxians defend the broad judgments about human good (mutual recognition, capacity for moral personality, individuality) which underlie modern liberalism.

However, Marxians reject liberal theses (2) and (3). They argue, instead, that within a liberal democracy, there exists a ruling class which derives its power from its dominant position in the prevailing mode of production, that its presence is shown especially in situations where oppression leads to overt forms of class conflict, and that only large scale, primarily extralegal, and often violent struggles can win substantial reforms, let alone structural changes to achieve a more cooperative society. Marxians have good reason to be suspicious of easy claims about the value of democracy to the masses. Their social theory locates the source of inequalities of class and status in the mode of production, and focuses on the ways in which nonpolitical inequalities systematically distort formal political equality. Like Hegel, they vividly recall that the democratic regime of ancient Athens restricted participation to Greek males and that "democracy" accompanied slavery, the oppression of women, and foreign expansion. Contemporary capitalist, democratic regimes, a Marxian might note, have long histories of colonialism and neocolonialism, formal or informal restrictions on suffrage, persecution of radicals, and the like. Even where democratic forms exist, Marxian theory sees these regimes as in essence dictatorships of the bourgeoisie. While they formally promise respect for persons, they actually operate in ways that denigrate the self-images of workers (and many others). They subject workers (and others) to a hierarchy of status, racism, sexism, apathy, exploitation, unemployment, repression, and unjust wars. These regimes treat human personality and individuality not as if they are diversely embodied, but as if they are something that you could have more and less of, like commodities or status. Injuries to regard for the self and others, nurtured by inequalities of class and status, make formal democracy, in many important respects, a sham. Thus, Marxian social and moral criticism debunks contemporary liberal definitions of democracy, which imply but present no arguments for the claim that historical slaveholding and/or capitalist democracies are regimes characterized by popular rule.

Further, Marxians maintain that because of the existence of predatory ruling classes, liberal regimes and important social reforms have usually arisen from violent revolution and mass, extralegal struggle. Consider, for

---

[4] Friedrich Engels, *Herr Eugen Dühring's Revolution in Science* (New York: International Publishers, 1966), pp. 105, 117. For an account of Marx's moral realism, see Alan Gilbert, "An ambiguity in Marx's and Engel's Account of Justice and Equality," *The American Political Science Review*, vol. 76 (June 1982) and "Marx's Moral Realism: Eudaimonism and Moral Progress," James Farr and Terence Ball, eds., *After Marx* (Cambridge: Cambridge University Press, 1984).

example, the role of the Civil War in the abolition of slavery in the United States, sit-ins and rebellions in the civil rights movement, councils of the unemployed and militant demonstrations in gaining unemployment insurance and social security, sit-down strikes in forging industrial unions, militant student demonstrations and fragging of officers in the anti-Vietnam War movement, and the like.[5] On the Marxian view, sustained social changes in property relations and power will (usually) require revolution. The Marxian denial of the substantive efficacy of formal procedures rests on these controversial claims in social theory, claims which this essay cannot assess. But even though Marxians question the preeminence which liberals place on the regularity of procedures, nothing in the Marxian critique of capitalism requires or licenses the rejection of such procedures in the first (post-revolution) stage of communism.

A fully articulated, morally objective account of Marxism – one which stresses recognition of persons and the dialectical continuity of Aristotelian, Hegelian, and Marxian political theories of cooperation and freedom – preserves the core of the older, objective liberalism. Such an account, however, highlights the empirical differences between the two theories which engender their complex political and ethical disagreements. Marxian theory seeks to realize the moral promises of democracy, not to deny them. It is thus far friendlier to coherent liberal theories of the worth of democracy than either theory is to contemporary, putatively liberal, relativist views.

In turn, many radical democratic theories, like those of Robert Dahl, Benjamin Barber, Michael Walzer, Charles Lindblom, and George Kateb, are critical of contemporary liberal views which celebrate apathy. To justify current regimes, the social scientists whom the radicals criticize advance a strong version of elitism, one which rests on claims about the "authoritarian personalities" or genetic deficiencies of ordinary people. These claims are usually not assessed against alternative explanations, are profoundly antidemocratic, and thus appear to be no more than a crass justification of what is. In contrast, serious democratic theorists, such as the radicals, recognize the weakness of a minimal citizenship, one which involves the ordinary person only in electoral participation and skews governmental policies toward the interests of the wealthy. These admissions render a central Marxian explanatory claim – that the structure of capitalist society discourages working class political activity in numerous ways – prima facie plausible. As Lindblom puts it: "The large private corporation fits oddly into democratic theory and vision. In fact, it does not fit."[6] Such recognitions justify the Marxian search for alternative, egalitarian social and political arrangements.

---

[5] Frances Fox Piven and Richard Cloward, *Poor People's Movements* (New York: Pantheon, 1977).
[6] Charles Lindblom, *Politics and Markets* (New York: Basic Books, 1977), p. 356.

Given this setting, this essay will focus on the internal tensions for Marx's conception of communism posed by Marxian and liberal conceptions of individuality. It will respond to the concerns of what I will call a sophisticated liberal interlocutor, one who emphasizes the objectivity of mutual recognition and individuality, acknowledges that capitalism poses grave problems for liberal democracy, and sees that reform in a more democratic direction without massive social upheaval is unlikely, and yet worries that any version of Marxian communism presents even worse prospects for democracy. In this context, I cannot respond to other concerns, for instance, the concerns of those who think that the abuses coincident with capitalism are not significantly caused by capitalism. My aim is to introduce a new, distinctively Marxian argument about communism and individuality into the controversy between reasonably sophisticated versions of liberal and Marxian social theories.

2. Status Hierarchy, Self-Respect, and Individuality

Thus, my argument starts from the premise that Marx presented a powerful and still telling critique of capitalist democracy. That critique could justify a more cooperative and free regime *if* one is possible. Further, contrary to what many liberals and even socialists believe, Marxian movements have broadly and successfully involved workers and peasants in attempts to forge a new society.[7] Compared to the limited participation (largely restricted to voting) characteristic of capitalist democracies, vibrant radical movements have been *socially* democratic in a very strong sense: they have facilitated political deliberation and action among ordinary, formerly "apathetic" people. Marxian claims about the importance of participation are linked to a theory that massive social inequalities result in the corruption of formally democratic governmental power and generate *many harmful consequences* for working people. Only participation is likely to prevent these harms. The defense of participation is thus a major component of a democratic view in its own right, but becomes even more central on a Marxian account through overriding additional considerations which I cannot fully explore here. Nonetheless, Marx's and Lenin's contention that such movements can be *qualitatively* democratic in a way that liberal democracies are not emphasizes this point.

Against this claim about participation, advanced by revolutionary Marxians and, in a different way, by Hannah Arendt, a liberal may object that such democracy is unfortunately a limited enthusiasm, admirable but short-lived. We must set far lower objectives, the liberal continues, for

---

[7] John Stuart Mill, *On Liberty, Representative Government, The Subjection of Women* (Oxford: Oxford University Press, 1948), pp. 281–290. Rawls, *op. cit.*, pp. 232–233.

durable institutions in a large, complex society. Yet, a Marxian might respond, revolutionary participation has often endured for considerable periods against the odds. Further, radical Marxian alternatives have important achievements to their credit (peasant political initiatives in the lengthy social transformation of agrarian China, worker participation in the Russian Revolution, the Soviet defeat of the massive Nazi onslaught in World War II, and the mobiliztion of workers in anti-facist and anti-racist movements, to name a few). In addition, these revolutions sought to abolish exploitation and the parasitic state, that is, to create a genuine democratic regime by abolishing privileged officer corps and officialdoms of all sorts. But these aims, though they seek to extend those of older capitalist democratic revolutions, are, as the lapsed republicanism of the latter shows, difficult to achieve. In this respect, Marx's broad claim in *Capital* – that proletarian revolutions would be less lengthy, conflict-ridden and violence-prone than their bourgeois predecessors – overemphasizes the force of economic trends in forging communism and underestimates the political obstacles.[8] Yet the achievements of such movements, even if not sustained, and the continuing oppressiveness of capitalist regimes make a Marxian alternative promising.

Still, the liberal has a powerful rejoinder: over time, the most successful revolutionary Marxian movements have, by sophisticated Marxian criteria, given rise to dictatorial, oppressive regimes. These regimes seem hostile to many Marxian political and moral ideas, while more favorable to economic determinist ones which they view as justifying "modernization." The former emphasize participation, deliberation, and the importance of individuality in the creation of communism, while the latter stress the role of putatively neutral experts (planners) who grasp the "laws" of state development of productive forces. Further, while socialist regimes have sometimes undercut status hierarchy (e.g., the advance of large numbers of communist workers into positions of political leadership, Chinese revolutionary attempts to break down divisions between mental and manual work, internationalist policies directed against unequal treatment of nationalities, and anti-sexist policies), these regimes strongly exhibit such a hierarchy. Even if inequalities of status arose (to a greater extent than capitalist differentials) from reward for individual effort, such divisions reflect a competitiveness which undermines respect for the self and others (the public elevation of some *at the expense* of others) and coincide with hierarchies of power, privilege (shopping in special stores, vacations at elite spas, and the like) and wealth. If a class, for instance one composed largely of leading members of the Communist Party, controls the economic "surplus" and state power, and uses both to its own advantage,

[8] Karl Marx, *Capital* (Moscow: Foreign Languages Publishing House, 1957), vol. 1, p. 764; Alan Gilbert, "Historical Theory and the Structure of Moral Argument in Marx," *Political Theory*, vol. 9 (May 1981), sections 3–5.

then the notion that these exploitative systems resemble capitalist ones more nearly than communist ones becomes a plausible Marxian response. Though differences of form and economic dynamic are very important, this basic contrast explains the partial aptness of the often used term "state capitalism" to refer to such regimes.

From these Marxian claims about the unfolding of socialism, however, a liberal might infer that sustained democracy, though admirable on shared moral grounds, is not possible. Criticism of the class bias of capitalist democracies is sound, this liberal might concede, but the failure of a real political alternative parries the force of Marxian insights in undercutting reformist conclusions. Despite human capacities for some degree of cooperation and freedom, no regime can escape the conflicts which marked ancient Athens; democracy and freedom, this liberal continues, must be fused with very substantial victimization. The potential limits to the undoing of oppression do not encompass the realization of a genuine *common* good. This position denies theses (2) and (3) of liberal social theory. For a committed liberal, it is thus not a very palatable alternative; it defends what is evidently a lesser *evil*. But it is certainly a fair and realistic position, one which concedes many reasonable Marxian criticisms of capitalist democracy, given common moral insights, and then dialectically turns those insights against the practice of contemporary socialist regimes to ask whether Marxian theory can provide a plausible account of communism as the realization of social individuality.[9] In the context of this debate, I will not offer a more developed argument about state capitalism (though some might want to defend current "socialist" regimes). Instead, I want to explore the question of whether a Marxian theory has the resources to envision an alternative path of communist development, one which would strengthen and supplement the initial, revolutionary features of these regimes and justify the basic contrast of communist and capitalist democracy.

Further, since Marx left indications which cohere more or less well with his general theory, but no fully worked out ethical and psychological argument, partisans of Marx's communist "theory of the future" need to provide one. Marx's moral claims focus on a notion of social individuality. This section attempts to develop a radical theory of the self, consistent with Marx's insights, in two directions which undercut individualist notions of status hierarchy. In the next section, I will use this modified Marxian conception to analyze tensions within the dictatorship of the proletariat. There I will argue that to make good on their dialectical critique of liberalism, Marxian regimes would have to eschew capitalist and "socialist"

---

[9] Graeme Duncan, "The Marxist Theory of the State," and Steven Lukes, "Marxism, Morality and Justice," G. H. R. Parkinson, ed., *Marx and Marxisms* (Cambridge: Cambridge University Press, 1982), pp. 138–139, 204.

practices, justified by economic determinist arguments, and become more directly communist. Interestingly enough, this argument relies on and develops the moral and political claims which underlie both modern liberal democracy and Marxism.

Social individuality, for Marx, is neither "altruistic" nor "individualistic," but a deliberative combination of solidarity (this is especially important in societies characterized by class conflict and will probably remain so until the extinction of class and status divisions), and other forms of self-expression and self-fulfillment. Thus, in *The German Ideology*, Marx contended:

> The communists do not put egoism against self-sacrifice or self-sacrifice against egoism, nor do they express this contradiction theoretically either in its sentimental or in its highflown ideological form. . . . The communists do not preach *morality* at all, such as Stirner preaches so extensively. They do not put to people the moral demand to love one another, do not be egoists, etc.: on the contrary they are very well aware that egoism, just as much as self-sacrifice, is in definite circumstances a necessary form of the self-assertion of individuals.[10]

Marx opposed moralism, i.e., an appeal to general moral principles as a special kind of motivation abstracted from and opposed to what Hegel called ethical life. As *The Philosophy of Right* shows, to resist moralism (a Kantian moral point of view) is not to reject ethics. In fact, as I have argued elsewhere, Marx recognized that communism facilitates a kind of social and *moral* progress that is fundamentally different from that of capitalist society, one which fuses intrinsic and instrumental goods in contrast to largely alienated, instrumental advance. He emphasized the heroism of international solidarity (such as that of the English workers who vehemently supported abolitionism in the U.S. Civil War even at the cost of unemployment) and of the Communard storming of heaven. Here deliberation and political self-sacrifice (on behalf of a genuinely common good) were central features of Marx's conception of revolutionary politics. He also stressed the importance of sustained political commitment, for instance, in his memorial dedication of *Capital* to his comrade, and "unforgettable friend, Wilhelm Wolff, Intrepid, Faithful, Noble Protagonist of the Proletariat." At the same time, Marx admired the individuality (a healthy kind of "egoism") involved in scientific and philosophical achievements (those of "mighty thinkers" like Aristotle, Hegel, Darwin, Ricardo) and artistic greatness (Milton, Dante,

---

[10] Karl Marx and Friedrich Engels, *The German Ideology* (New York: International Publishers, 1980), p. 104.

Shakespeare, Sophocles).[11] He probably also had in mind mundane (healthy, nonbelittling of or harmful to others) examples of self-concern and self-assertion. For Marx, a society which nutured social individuality embodied a higher ethical life or form of right than its predecessors.

In a recent essay, however, G. A. Cohen has argued that Marx, unlike Hegel, had no reasonable conception of the self. Instead, he contends that Marx's anthropology (his conception of social individuality) is one-sided in emphasizing the realization of productive talents at the expense of ways of life. Cohen is right that Marx failed to spell out the conception underlying his varied remarks about human well-being and sometimes exaggerated the importance of a possibly superhuman display of multiple capacities; he also rightly contends that Marxian theory requires a developed theory of the self. But he overlooks Marx's admiration for the solidarity involved in political community and internationalism. Solidarity is a political relationship and a self-chosen way of being; it is not the realization of a productive talent. He also misses Marx's celebration of deliberative, revolutionary character and of friendship. Marx's anthropology and ethics thus evoke a more robustly political, well-rounded, and definite conception of individuality, and suggest a more adequate theory of the self than Cohen allows. Marx's argument also points to a deeper insight into moral character and individuality than game-theoretic explications of solidarity as "conditional altruism" envision. For an individual chooses such action not just to further other ends, but to realize an intrinsic good (a kind of human cooperation) and to be a certain kind of person (even the kind of person who could sacrifice herself for great political commitments).

The moral psychology that Marx only hints at plays a large role in affirmations of the stability of egalitarian communism, a form of society which eliminates hierarchies of status and egotistic competition. To refine Marx's notion, one needs a complex political and ethical conception, one not based on altruism, but cognizant of relatedness, citizenship, and virtue; one not based on egotism, but insistent on reflective agency and individual integrity for a whole life. As I have argued elsewhere, Marx took as his starting point for such a view the moral psychology of Aristotle.[12]

[11] Gilbert, *op. cit.* (1981), section 4; see also Alan Gilbert, "Marx on Internationalism and War," *Philosophy and Public Affairs*, vol. 7 (June 1978), for a discussion of the English workers' deliberations about abolitionism. Marx, *Capital*, vol. 1, pp. 11, 14, 20, 59, 132, 341.

[12] G. A. Cohen, "Reconsidering Historical Materialism," Pennock, ed., *op. cit.* (1984). Cohen neglects Marx's Aristotelian conception of *human* nature and mistakenly attributes to him a mechanical materialist, narrowly biological view of human personality as a collection of capacities and talents. Marx rightly retained this Aristotelian conception after his adoption of Darwin's theory for other social animals. Gilbert, "Marx's Moral Realism," Farr, ed., *op. cit.* (1984); Jon Elster, *Ulysses and the Sirens* (Cambridge: Cambridge University Press, 1979), pp. 21, 105–106.

Like Aristotle, and more clearly than Hegel, Marx emphasized the participatory political setting for the flourishing of human personality. But two of
the deepest features of a distinctively modern theory of individuality which
develop or transform Marxian (and previous liberal) insights also have their
roots in Aristotle: first, the notion of integrity of the self; and second, the
idea of an objectivity of need which characterizes genuine individuality.
Aristotle does not use the term "individuality." I take a modern conception
of individuality, however, to generalize the capacity for deliberation about a
good life which Aristotle (nearly) restricts to Greek gentlemen. In addition,
one might think here of Hegel's account of the will as a refinement of
Aristotle's notion of deliberation. In *The Philosophy of Right*, Hegel traces the
dialectical moments of a will capable of negating any particular determination, yet sunken in specific purposes or situations. These features are
transformed in the self-recognition of the will as free – mirrored in the
mutual recognition of a modern society – and the expression of that self-
aware will in fully deliberated, particular choices. In its dialectical emphasis
on the generality and infinity of the will, Hegel's conception differs from
Aristotle's; in its recognition of intrinsic goods (political community, love,
knowledge, and the like), his view resembles that of his great predecessor.[13]
Having sketched the relationship between ancient and liberal theories of
deliberation and individuality, I will now turn to the impact of Aristotle's
conception on modern theories of self and mutual respect.

In *The German Ideology*, Marx stressed an Aristotelian idea of love or
friendship based on mutual concern as opposed to the "mutual exploitation" of utilitarianism. But he never explored the psychology of well-
ordered human relationships more deeply. Here, Aristotle's ethical
argument could illuminate and deepen Marx's. Aristotle's theory of friendship (*philia*) in Book IX of the *Nicomachean Ethics* draws its strength from a
conception of the well-ordered self. The good man (or, as moderns would
rightly emphasize, woman) is a lover of self, in that he is a person who has a
certain integrity and self-sufficiency. Such a self contrasts with alien selves,
defined by power, prestige, or money. For Aristotle, the former, healthy
person has a soul ruled by intelligence and can form genuine friendships.
The latter, however, have souls dominated by the corrupt appetites of
Sardanapallus, exhibit an ostensible but deficient love of self, and participate
in defective forms of friendship. Aristotle then traces out a complex psychological dialectic of ability to love oneself as a necessary concomitant of love
for others. Each friend, on Aristotle's account, has the capacity to achieve
insight into the other's good. Further, that good is one's own good: friend-

[13] G. W. F. Hegel, *Grundlinien der Philosophie des Rechts* (Stuttgart: Philipp Reclam, 1970),
pp. 75–103.

ship and solidarity have similar roots in self-love. For a friend can recognize the personality of others and distinguish their needs, based on his own sense of self. His concern involves genuine recognition. Thus, a person capable of such friendship displays individuality. He is capable of a life of his own and has a certain sense of purpose or self-command. In Aristotle's subtle portrayal, a friend need not merely hide from himself, as the evil person does, in the company of others. Since bad people despise themselves, they recall when alone only "unpleasant memories." Lacking integrity, they need blind approval or money in an unceasing attempt to reassure themselves. Others exist for them merely as means, not as independent persons to whose needs they might attend. Further, such people, driven by appetites yet haunted by reason, are always at war with themselves. Their self-hatred rules out genuine friendship.[14] Thus, for Aristotle, the dialectic of self-love and concern for others is at its most intense in friendship; this kind of "social individuality" is also, however, displayed in weaker forms of affiliation, such as citizenship in a *polis*.

Despite major changes, one can detect the resonances of these Aristotelian insights in the modern psychoanalytic theory of the self offered by Heinz Kohut, Harry Guntrip, and Alice Miller. To indicate these striking dialectical relationships, I will briefly describe this theory. In contrast to Freud's misguided instinctual determinism, Kohut's argument focuses on the *social* formation of the self in the context of its early relationships. He contrasts a notion of integrity of self, illustrated in particular examples of flourishing, with that of a fragmented self; the healthy self often overcomes early failures of nurturance through participation in intrinsic human goods (painting, music, friendship, nurturing). Perhaps deliberately recalling Aristotle, Kohut refers to creative activities of these kinds as diverse illustrations and aspects of a good life. What previous psychoanalysis takes as basic and natural – Oedipal anxiety or aggression – he sees as derivative from deficiently human, empathic mirroring.[15]

On this account, parents train their children in the "appropriate" feelings and encourage them to suppress many of their emotions and needs. Such childrearing seeks to mold or even "live through" the child; it presses the child to take care of the parent and fails to respect the child's individuality. The child's suppression of needs in favor of an imposed image leads to an inability to recognize and work through her own emotions, to be fully her

---

[14] Aristotle, *Nicomachean Ethics*, 1166a1–b29.
[15] Heinz Kohut, *The Restoration of the Self* (New York: International Universities Press, 1977), pp. 119–21, and *How Does Analysis Cure?* (Chicago: University of Chicago, 1984), pp. 26–28, 44; Harry Guntrip, *Psychoanalytic Theory, Therapy, and the Self* (New York: Basic Books, 1973); Alice Miller, *The Drama of the Gifted Child* (New York: Basic Books, 1981); Charles Taylor, "What is Human Agency," Theodore Mischel, ed., *The Self* (Totowa, NJ: Rowman and Littlefield, 1977), pp. 133–135.

own person, and engenders self-hatred or, in Aristotle's terms, psychic "civil war." As a Marxian might add, childrearing in accord with sexist stereotypes helps to fragment the self. This social and family dynamic creates a reservoir of repressed emotions and needs which reappear as a kind of second self to haunt the adult's behaviour. On this theory, respect for others, grounded in the childhood experience of the parent's capacity to draw boundaries and acknowledge the child's emotions, stems from respect for (in Aristotle's terms, love of) self. Analogous dialectics of an integrated self and respect for others apply to friendship and political cooperation.

This psychological theory reinforces the Marxian claim that current stereotypes of the "good" man or woman – for men, achievement in the status-ridden, alienated public world, "mastering" and suppressing one's emotions, and treating family relationships as the province of women; for women, a greater sense of connectedness but also submergence and loss of self in family relationships and an uncertain sense of self in public life – *harm both*. Ethically, as Carol Gilligan has suggested, men are bound over to the "heartless" world of abstract right and (at least partly) artificial, distorted selves; women are (without deliberation) plunged into a quasi-Aristotelian and Hegelian world of connectedness, need, and ethical life. To the extent that they are influenced by such deeply rooted stereotypes, both lack social individuality. These sexist stereotypes often dovetail with other socially created sources of self-deprecation and self-hatred, for instance, the internalization by their victims of anti-working class and racist ideologies.[16] Despite greater contemporary criticism by ordinary people of such nefariously imposed self-images, a Marxian maintains, capitalism continues to further such divisions; communist egalitarianism transforms and defeats them. If it is true, the contemporary theory of the self, coupled with the insights of social theory regarding gender, racist, and anti-working class stereotypes, deepens Marxian and liberal conceptions of personal life, individuality, friendship, and respect for self and others.

Further, one can use this Aristotelien and contemporary theory of integrity of the self to undermine relativist misconceptions of individuality. An Aristotelian theory of human goods already rules out the relativist calculation of "preferences" characteristic of Bentham's utilitarianism, neoclassical economics, and emotivism. For these views contend that we have no real (objective) needs, not even the need to be recognized as a person. They adopt the corrupt notion that humans aim for infinite amounts of power or wealth. But contemporary psychological theory suggests that an individual

---

[16] Carol Gilligan, *In a Different Voice* (Cambridge, MA: Harvard University Press, 1982). Jean Baker Miller, *Toward a New Psychology of Women (Cambridge, MA: Beacon Press, 1966)*. Lillian Breslow Rubin, *Worlds of Pain* (New York: Basic Books, 1976). Richard Sennett, *The Hidden Injuries of Class*.

needs to shape a life of self-chosen purpose and coherence. As David Levine has rightly argued, individuals do not need an infinite supply of resources for such a life. (What would one do with an infinity of ever bigger and better yachts?) A scholar needs certain books, a woodworker certain tools, friends the availability of common activities in which to enjoy and reflect their personalities. Over a lifetime, as Marx suggested, an individual might pursue a variety of activities with differing requirements; given conflicts of need, she would have to choose which ones to regard as central. While these projects would involve considerable, varying resources, however, a notion of the coherence and integrity of self would objectively limit each individual's needs.[17]

On a Marxian version of this conception, politics and friendly regard are part of individuality. Yet in an important sense, such social activities and ways of being concern primarily the individual.[18] They are done for their own sake, for reasons suited to the activity or relationship itself. Participants are not motivated by the *social* hierarchy of prestige and money characteristic of capitalism and other exploitative societies. In an Aristotelian sense, such relationships and activities are natural achievements, and the needs connected with them express individuality. They reveal what is humanly (socially) natural as opposed to what is (also socially) corrupt. Thus, Marx drew an important analogy between the workers-officials of the Commune and Milton writing *Paradise Lost*; the activities of each expressed their natures:

> the whole sham of state-mysteries and state pretentions was done away with by a Commune mostly consisting of simple working men, organizing the defense of Paris ... doing their work publicly, simply, under the most difficult and complicated circumstances, and doing it, as Milton did his *Paradise Lost*, for a few pounds.[19]

Marx contrasted these activities and relationships with those of "unnatural" capitalist politicians or hack writers of political economy texts who

---

[17] David P. Levine, *Needs, Rights and the Market* (unpublished), ch. 1. Elster, in "Exploitation, Freedom and Justice," Pennock, ed., *op. cit.* (1984), pp. 298–299, worries that many individuals might have preferences for resource-expensive goods; their demands might conflict with communist equality. Either Aristotle's or Levine's theory of objective human goods undercuts the notion that such needs would be a frequent, let alone overwhelming component of individuality.

[18] Levine's theory, even more than Cohen's initial presentation of Marxian communism as the abolition of social roles in *Karl Marx's Theory of History: A Defense* (Princeton, NJ: Princeton University Press, 1978), pp. 129–133, overemphasizes the abolition of (harmful) "social" divisions. It fails to stress sufficiently the care and energy involved in healthy social connectedness.

[19] Gilbert, "Marx's Moral Realism," Farr, ed., *op. cit.* (1984); Marx and Engels, *Writings on the Paris Commune*, trans. Hal Draper (New York: Monthly Review, 1971), p. 153; Marx, *Theories of Surplus Value* (New York: International Publishers, 1952), p. 186.

labor only for pay or status. To head off any potential misunderstanding, I should again emphasize that the kind of mutual recognition and connectedness characteristic of politics, though analogous to that of friendship, is markedly less intense. But a theory of the self which emphasizes that each individual shapes a life of integrity by choosing among varied, intrinsic goods deepens Marx's conception of natural activities and relationships. Such a theory stresses that although we can easily identify extreme examples of evil and insufficiency of self (murder, rape, drug addiction), diverse enactments of self have no common measure. In that sense, modern liberal and Marxian theories embrace individuality.

As we have seen, both views have a distinctively social component. Against the historical backdrop of slavery and serfdom, liberalism is based on a recognition of the equal worth of persons or, more exactly, of their equally sufficient capacity for agency, and liberalism embodies these goods in formal democracy and impersonal laws. Yet capitalism produces constant inequalities of worth, hierarchies of status. Private enterprise (like utilitarianism) tries to encompass the diverse enactments of individuality or personality in a single currency. It induces constant striving for relative social position and undermines equality. Private enterprise is thus inconsistent with the basic moral insight into the mutual recognition of persons and social individuality characteristic of coherent modern liberalism, and not just of contemporary radicalism.

Levine's argument attaches objective needs to self-enactment and, hence, grounds a right to work or a right to income not just on "preferences," but in the recognition of individuality; yet he articulates no definite Aristotelian conception of a broad list of human goods or values in which individuals might participate. Though the Aristotelian view is, in this respect, more sophisticated and would strengthen Levine's account, even Levine's economic theory, which makes *almost* all human goods relative to individual choices, emphasizes the recognition of a single central good, that of individuality or of an equally sufficient capacity for moral personality (the capacity to be a self). His argument shows that an objective defense of mutual recognition and individuality is at the core of every coherent (non-self-refuting) modern political theory.

The criticism of private enterprise for abridging these goods also applies to modern socialism. Except in contrast to feudalism, the reward structure of private enterprise bears remarkably little relation to the alleged individual "merit" or hard work which is its putative moral justification. But socialism is sometimes deemed to reward desert, to generate the meritocratic status hierarchy promised but not realized by liberalism. Thus, socialist justice realizes the previously utopian currency of capitalism; social status, economic inequality, and differential estimates of persons are based on merit. Yet that currency remains distorted. In fact, it appears to flow from and reinforce a deficient self – one that will work only for fear of starvation or to gain a place in a hierarchy at the expense of others – rather than a healthy self which acts out of a particular conception of a life of integrity and an awareness of the appropriate reasons for activities. Under socialism, the specific virtues often claimed for capitalism (for instance, ingenuity or initiative) are also (often) elicited in the service of defective selves. The unhealthy sense of self, cultivated by private enterprise and market socialism, contradicts the sense of individual well-being and self-respect needed to deliberate on great political issues and, hence, to encourage the political participation which sustains a genuine democracy. A status- and wealth-bound theory of justice coheres neatly with an elitist sanctioning of apathy and is thus strikingly anti-democratic.

Given an appropriate theory of individuality and need, as Levine contends, liberal arguments which stress the importance of self-respect and mutual recognition, like those of Rawls and Dworkin, would require the elimination of (capitalist and socialist) hierarchies of status and wealth. Instead, the best method for distributing resources, short of full communist distribution according to need, would be the allocation of equal individual incomes. These incomes would include a *social* minimum necessary for decent medical care, education, housing, and transportation, for this sphere has important standard features and is comparatively easily susceptible to planning (but even here, citizens might want to encourage individual decisions about provision of these goods). Beyond this sphere, however, given equal incomes, individual would have enough discretionary funds to realise their other main needs without the inegalitarian distortions and "self"-seeking at the expense of others characteristic of capitalist (and Soviet and Chinese) status hierarchies.[20] A partial market, driven by individually generated demand, would remain for the distribution of those goods not already dispensed according to social need; one might call the goods available on this market *individuality-related goods*. That market, however, would neither govern the sale of labor-power nor lead to differential wages and a status hierarchy.

This view parries Hayek's interesting criticism of socialist planning. In a modern economy with shifting needs, Hayek has suggested, only a market can respond adequately to the judgments of individuals. Planners cannot know beforehand the outcome of complex individual deliberations and will generally get them wrong.[21] This version of communism acknowledges the

---

[20] Levine, *op. cit.*, conclusion; Elster, in Pennock, *op. cit.*, 298–299. I leave aside the forging and repair of basic means of production for social wealth which, in a planned economy, are also not governed mainly by a market.

[21] F. A. Hayek, "The Use of Knowledge in Society," *American Economic Review*, vol. 35 (Sept. 1945).

grain of truth in Hayek's argument, but insists that planning based on democratic discussion can overcome the harms of unemployment and degradation, which are impelled by an absence of resources characteristic of capitalism, and secure other important collective goods.

On this view, the definition of work would be expanded. For example, such incomes would be extended to those involved in the nurturing of children. In addition, at least sufficient incomes would be provided to support children. Every person would thus have a claim to a share of social wealth. In an important sense, the first stage of communism would move to abolish wages or, at least, reduce their dominion. (Citizens might require, for example, that nondisabled adults work in order to obtain a share.) In such a society, an egalitarian economic and social order, since it would sustain a healthier sense of self, would dialectically reinforce thoroughgoing political democracy, and vice versa. The communist actuality of self and mutual respect would supersede hierarchies of status.

A liberal critic might object that this communism would still restrict individual choice of occupation. Granting the rest of the argument, such a person might say, that restriction points to an important conflict of goods, one pitting egalitarianism against individuality. Given the seriousness of this conflict, certain types of liberalized capitalism or market socialism could better realize Marxian moral aims than this version of communism. A Marxian might respond, however, that this stage of communism would still further individuality much more than capitalism, yet also achieve egalitarianism. Within this economy, individuals would be able to choose jobs according to their interest in the work itself, rather than for pay. Further, they would not be driven to seek undesirable forms of work by lack of resources. These and other changes – if Marxian social theory is right, the overturning of racist and sexist discrimination, and the like – would further self-expression in work.[22]

Yet given the level of social need, some desirable jobs would be competitively restricted, by relevant criteria. Other, comparatively undesirable ones would be shared or perhaps even externally rewarded in ways which would not lead to status differentiation. For instance, routine work could either be shared (housework, street cleaning by neighborhood associations) or differentially remunerated (perhaps by a shortened work day). Yet some aspects of such necessary labor also further individuality: the order and decoration in housework, for example, is often aesthetically important; participation itself is integral to the sharing of lives, self-reliance, and responsibility. Given the decline of status and gender stigmatization, individuals would appreciate these aspects more keenly.

The impact of such remaining limitations on individuality might also

[22] On conflicts of goods, see Alan Gilbert, *op. cit.*, Ball and Farr, eds. (1984).

diminish with the subsequent flourishing of communist productivity and the general shortening of the work day. Nonetheless, the critic might still invoke Marx's qualms about necessary labor: the self-realization characteristic of artisans who control their own production process – and routine endangers the interest in even that work – is rare in industrial circumstances. So are jobs which nurture self-enactment and self-disclosure. Even in communism, many would realize their individuality more directly outside of work than within it.

A theory of the self focused on leisure and politics reinterprets Marx's claim in *Critique of the Gotha Program* that nonnecessary "work becomes life's prime want": activities and relationships which realize individuality become "life's prime want."[23] Necessary work within a communist economy is one aspect of *personal differentiation* and individuality, but neither the only, nor even the central aspect. Further, accompanied by a political emphasis on mutual recognition, a notion of the integrity of self stresses that the sphere of necessary work should not be an arena for inegalitarian pay and *status differentiation*.

We can now separate different features of Hayek's epistemological defense of the market. A theory of the self recommends individual deliberations about ways of life. The choice of books, musical instruments, recreation equipment and leisure activities, kinds of education, items for a home, and the like cannot be left to the homogenizing guesses of planners: hence, the need for an individuality-related market. Given a preceding distribution of income – an egalitarian one – this market will, epistemologically speaking, secure the relevant information. But a comparable Hayekian epistemological argument in favor of an inegalitarian labor market fails because of the need to curtail status hierarchy and further individuality. A neoclassical economic argument, with its impoverished conception of self as a mere bundle of homogenized preferences, cannot draw this distinction. Thus, a coherent theory of the self clarifies Hayek's epistemological argument by distinguishing individuality from individualist misconceptions.

This discussion of individuality, labor markets, and status differentials also highlights a distinctively communist feature of Marx's reservations about modern theories of justice. Many conceptions of distributive justice, including ones based on socially necessary labor time, propose a distorted uniform standard to measure merit and allocate resources. Such conceptions give rise to status hierarchies which violate individuality and any genuine sense of a common good. In contrast, a dialectical Marxian conception of justice envisions the abolition of classes (and statuses) as the social precondi-

---

[23] Karl Marx and Friedrich Engels, *Selected Works* (Moscow: Foreign Languages Publishing House, 1962), vol. 2, p. 24.

tion for individuality. The communist political association, which makes such abolition possible, embodies the Marxian sense of a common good. This conception of justice assesses need and "merit" based on diverse choices about and manifestations of individuality. Thus, only a theory of the self which stresses a range of intrinsic goods and the integrity of individual choices of *disparate* ways of life is appropriate on this account. As Charles Taylor has suggested, particular contrasts mark realizations of disparate goods – one may be a defender of truth or a merchant of words, an insightful friend or an obtuse sycophant, politically motivated or a mercenary. This point applies centrally to the concept of a person or an individual. Contrary to quantitive (zero-sum) principles of status hierarchy, one cannot, in relation to others, be more or less a person, more or less an individual, though in qualitative terms one can become a murderer, a tyrant, or a moral monster who forfeits that equality. Individuality can, in a different though very important sense, go more or less deeply – an artist or a person can realize a style or self more fully, become more or less an individual. The notion of social individuality incorporates these two aspects or perspectives which are fused in the concept of a person. The Marxian conception criticizes previous uniform, rights-oriented, or utilitarian conceptions of "justice" (non-Aristotelian ones), and might seem, given the abolition of previous (corrupt) social determinations, not to be a theory of justice at all. This subtle communist indictment of prevalent theories of justice perhaps contributes to Marx's mistaken metaethical deemphasis on ethics and justice in his overall historical theory.[24]

A standard liberal and economic determinist Marxian objection to this egalitarian argument focuses on the need for material incentives as the spur to productivity. Given human deficiencies and the need to accumulate, this objection insists, communism cannot outproduce its socialist and capitalist competitors. This peculiar contention makes productivity appear to be the sole criterion of human well-being. In response, Elster and Cohen have recently suggested that only arduous (i.e., other than self-imposed) work under circumstances of scarcity requires material incentives.[25] These cir-

---

[24] In "Marx on Morality and Justice," Parkinson, ed., *op. cit.*, Lukes rightly sees communist "justice" as beyond rules concerning distribution, but misses the dialectical retention of fundamental rules preserving life and the mutual recognition of persons. These extensions of previous social and political achievements partly explain what Lenin referred to as the long familiar "elementary social rules" which would be more easily observed in communism; Lenin, *Selected Works*, 2:373. Contrary to Lukes, the ends of communism and the standards justifying revolutionary action in "prehistory" are not rigidly separated. On a dialectical view, how could definite aims concerning the human good license their utter violation in "prehistory?" Lukes's explanation of the putatively "beyond morality" character of Marxian theory of the good – its beneficent transcendence of the conflicts of scarcity coupled with an alleged moral agnosticism toward such conflicts – thus mirrors the self-refuting aspects of relativist Marxian metaethics which he otherwise astutely criticizes.

[25] Cohen, in Pennock, ed., *op. cit.*, p. 246.

cumstances hinder the expression of human nature. The development of productivity and civilization increasingly engender a healthy sense of self-confidence and release the (humanly) natural creativity and skill which Marx identified with communism. In a great, dialectical, epochal change, the foregoing accounts suggest, self-generated choices ultimately supplant scarcity and money as instigators of productivity. Unlike the situation in alienated "prehistory," individual deliberations (and historical advance) now integrate intrinsic and instrumental goods.

Elster's and Cohen's important thesis, however, understates the role of connectedness and relationships (politics, friendship, nurturing) in communist creativity, the decisive social elements in the realization of individuality. In his 1958 "Critique of Soviet Economy," Mao pointedly distinguished the mistaken Soviet emphasis on material incentives (wage differentials and individual bonuses) as the driving force of socialism from a Marxian view of political insight as an intrinsic good, inspiring action and production for its own sake, and serving as the main instigator of revolutionary development. As Mao wrote:

> Page 486 [of the Soviet text] says, 'In the socialist stage labor has not yet become the primary necessity in the lives of all members of society, and therefore material incentives to labor have the greatest significance.' Here 'all members' is too general. Lenin was a member of the society. Had *his* labor not become a 'primary necessity' of his life?[26]

The instance of Lenin here stands for the Communards and, as we shall see, millions of subsequent communists. A Marxian theory of the integrated self, objective need, and political community, based on Aristotle, Kohut, Levine, and diverse political achievements (e.g., the polis, modern nonslave holding societies, the Commune, and subsequent revolutionary movements and regimes) provides a stronger, more coherent psychological and economic account of how the fundamental historical changes, emphasized both in Elster and Cohen and in more political versions of Marxism, might occur.

Revolutionaries have sometimes inappropriately referred to this political element in individuality as a "moral incentive." The notion of moral "incentives" is in fact an alienated, economic determinist one, as if the way to understand all human relationships and activities were in the common currency of "economic development" or "modernization." On this curious view, the income and status hierarchy enshrined by Teng Hsiao-p'ing or the contemporary Soviet regime, and mass revolutionary efforts to forge an egalitarian cooperative society are treated as mere "instruments" in "socialist" industrialization. The well-being and integrity of individuals in work and

[26] Mao Tsetung, *A Critique of Soviet Economics* (New York: Monthly Review, 1977), p. 83.

politics is at best merely incidental – an alien accompaniment – to some larger social purpose. In contrast, on a Marxian conception such integrity is a vital and commonly acknowledged component of social and political cooperation. That conception emphasizes mutual recognition. At stake in these conflicting views of socialism and communism we thus have two sharply opposed theories of social life and individuality.

Levine sees his argument about the self and mutual recognition as a modification of the claims of classical political economy, including Marx's, about an objectively defined level of subsistence. Levine elaborates a flexible notion of objective need, suited to capitalism's promises about individuality and the wealth of civilization, rather than a clearly inadequate, merely physical standard. His theory, as we shall see, also challenges the role of the "law of value," and consequent wage and status differentials in Marx's notion of socialism (the first stage of communism). In the context of an Aristotelian and Marxian conception of social *individuality* and the self, however, Levine's view of the objective needs of individuals articulates and reinforces a central aspect of the Marxian theory of communism.

3. *Revolutionary Democracy, Income Equality, and the Decline of the Market*

The term "dictatorship" plays a large (and, from a Marxian point of view, partially obscuring) role in the controversy between Marxians and liberals over the revolutionary state. Liberal arguments often extend an appropriate ancient moral contrast between regimes into a rigid dichotomy between democratic "societies" and dictatorial ones. Neoclassical and pluralist theories make the fundamental coerciveness of modern democracy (its character as a regime which *rules* somebody) almost invisible, though as I have argued elsewhere, such theories cannot adequately account for apathy and glaring social inequalities.[27] Marxians, of course, despise tyranny just as much as liberals do. But they more easily extend this critique from the Prussian monarch or Napoleon to the factory foreman with the watch whose rule is also a petty, exploitative "despotism." Thus, they view democratic regimes dialectically (as a democracy for slaveholders, a dictatorship for slaves; a democracy for capitalists, a dictatorship for immigrants, workers, and most of the middle classes; a democracy for workers and their allies, a dictatorship for capitalists). In this context, any analysis of the Marxian view of the dictatorship of the proletariat should affirm its democratic aspect. Marx envisioned a regime in which the centralization, concentration, and separation of the exploitative, "parasitic" state apparatus and its accompanying ideological aura (control of weapons but also status divisions) dissolved into an armed, politically active populace of equals. For both Marx and

[27] Alan Gilbert, "Democracy and the Recognition of Persons," unpublished.

Lenin, the political vigor of the Paris Commune – contrasted with the deathly quiet of dictatorial domination under capitalism – provided the inspiration for their theory of the dictatorship of the proletariat. Yet that theory was very rough – barely sketched in Marx.

Marx's basic conception of the first stage of communism involved the dominance of revolutionary devices (political democracy, egalitarian pay for officials, distribution of significant social resources according to need, and vigorous political advocacy of the future of the movement: the abolition of classes and the wage system). But he also made concessions to capitalist practices and motivations which potentially conflicted with those revolutionary aspects. His conception was captured in the famous dialectical image of communist life emerging stained by the "bloody birthmarks" of capitalism. Studying the Paris Commune, Marx adopted a complex and struggle-oriented, if not very precise, view of the likely course of communism:

> The Commune does not do away with the class struggle ... but it affords the rational medium in which that class struggle can run through its different phases in the most rational and humane way. It could start violent reactions and as violent revolutions ... the catastrophes it might still have to undergo would be sporadic slaveholders' insurrections, which, while for a moment interrupting the work of peaceful progress, would only accelerate the movement by putting the sword into the hand of the Social Revolution. ... The [workers] know that this work of regeneration [the lengthy transition to communism] will be again and again relented and impeded by the resistance of vested interests and class egotisms.[28]

In asking why the revolutionary democratic aspects of socialist regimes have ultimately dissolved into dictatorship, those sympathetic to Marxism need to specify different noncommunist features of socialist practice and their dialectical interplay with revolutionary politics and the state. Since Marx could not base his theory on large-scale communist experience, revolutionary features of twentieth century communism are relevant to this inquiry. A plausible Marxian argument must combine deeper theoretical insights into communism with at least some evidence for their practicality.

In this context, revolutionary socialist regimes have employed three kinds of concessions, all of which require evaluation: (1) some arising from noncapitalist or insufficiently capitalist economic backwardness; (2) others arising as ordinary market incentives, universally characteristic of socialism; and (3) still others emerging from wars forced on communist revolutions by external capitalist powers. These regimes have legitimized the

[28] Draper, *op. cit.*, pp. 154–155.

first type of concession by a strong emphasis on the low level of productivity which existed in the initial revolutionary settings (such justifications insist on *special* features of the Russian and Chinese revolutions). We might call them *Economic Determinism-Justified Concessions to Backwardness*. (Roughly, an economic determinist version of Marxism insists that the development of productive forces shapes successive social forms, and that the level of productive development *narrowly* circumscribes possibilities for a genuinely cooperative politics.) The second type has been legitimized by economic determinist and liberal arguments about scarcity, fear- or pay-based motivation, and desert-based justice which apply to *socialist* regimes in general. On these accounts, even following a socialist or communist revolution, a new regime must rely heavily on monetary rewards to elicit economic participation. We might call these policies *Individual Desert-Based Market Concessions*. They have sometimes been taken to further liberal decentralization against the dictatorial features of highly centralized, planned regimes. They are, thus, invoked as desirable mechanisms by theorists who attempt to unite Western democracy with market socialism.[29]

Both the fierce repression of social uprisings and international ruling-class intervention against successful ones e.g., the Sparatacus revolt, the German peasant war, European intervention against the French Revolution, the June insurrection, the Paris Commune, foreign intervention in the Russian Civil War and the Nazi invasion, the twenty-year Chinese military struggle, the fascist responses in France, Austria, Italy, Spain, Germany, and Chile, the U.S. interventions in Vietnam and against the Sandinistas in Nicaragua, etc., have justifiably oriented serious radical movements toward violence and war. To defend themselves against counterrevolution, radical regimes have sometimes adopted highly centralized forms of military organization, recruited officers from the old standing army, and so forth. We might call these *Crisis- or War-based Concessions*. Contentions about (the threat of) such interventions have also licensed the first two kinds of concessions. Unfortunately, if liberal theses that capitalist democracies are comparatively plastic, easily reformed, decent regimes are mistaken, as they

---

[29] These concessions lead to the perpetuation of what Roemer has called status exploitation in socialism. He attempts to justify some of this inequality with a game–theoretic argument as "necessary socialist exploitation." Since, on his account, there are no *direct* beneficiaries of "exploitation," the latter characterization is puzzling. More importantly, Roemer ignores the impact of such differentials on the fundamental issue of who controls the state and the possibility of broader systemic harms to workers arising out of socialist inequalities. He thus criticizes the law of value to clear away misconceptions which hinder the development of current socialist regimes. See the useful discussion in Roemer, *A General Theory of Exploitation and Class* (Cambridge, MA: Harvard University Press, 1982), pp. 248–249; and "Should Marxists Be Interested in Exploitation?," *Philosophy and Public Affairs*, vol. 14 (Winter 1985), p. 64. This argument questions the putative necessity of socialist "exploitation" and challenges the law of value, based on an explicit conception of communism as social individuality.

well may be, the need for revolutionary regimes to prepare for war, though not to make the other two types of concessions, will continue. War-based concessions in particular exerted an enormous, mainly anti-democratic influence on the Bolsheviks. For instance, the attack by numerous foreign-sponsored armies and assassinations and attempted assassinations of leaders (Volodarsky, Uritsky, Lenin) led the Bolshevik regime to reverse its original ban on capital punishment, to abandon its attempt to work with other parties, and to erode formal democratic practices. Further, the need to defend itself legitimized recruitment of former tsarist officers and officials. It also reinforced arguments for economic determinism-based concessions to backwardness: installation of former capitalists to manage plants; recruitment of professionals of bourgeois background to organize university and cultural life; etc. Finally, this argument sustained *individual desert-based concessions*, the use of material incentives and wage differentials among noncommunists and finally, in the mid-1930s to prepare to combat Nazism, a decisively anti-Communelike concession: the introduction of wage differentials in the Bolshevik party itself. These and other economic, social, and political concessions all sustained an older capitalist-like state structure and economic regime and eroded revolutionary democracy. These aspects of Soviet history might be taken to suggest that standard liberal democratic and market modifications of the "parasite state" features of contemporary Soviet rule are at least a "lesser evil" alternative.

Yet, dialectically, within these ferocious conflicts, given the justice of their cause, revolutionary regimes had important successes, such as initiating popular *levées-en-masse* and nurturing worker and peasants participation in political leadership. These policies contributed to the radical elan of these regimes, their democratic and voluntary aspects. Such features surfaced in the Russian Revolution and flourished in China. Thus, the new Soviet regime relied heavily on revolutionary workers in winning the Civil War and in subsequent industrial construction. The Bolsheviks had become a predominantly working class party by 1914; they overwhelmingly recruited workers through the mid-1920s; and they insisted on a maximum wage for party members (roughly that of a skilled worker). Later, they utilized egalitarian distributive policies in the massive effort to defeat Nazism in World War II.[30]

Going further than the Soviets in a revolutionary democratic direction, the Chinese communists mobilized a multimillion member peasant revolutionary army. They emphasized an egalitarian supply system (distribution of

---

[30] Jonathan Adelman, "The Formative Influence of the Civil Wars," *Armed Forces and Society*, vol. 5 (November 1978); Gilbert, *Marx's Politics Communists and Citizens* (New Brunswick, NJ: Rutgers University Press, 1981), ch. 10–11.

scarce goods according to need) and the abolition of signs of rank. Further, they applied these policies in the large regions of China which they had liberated before 1949. Though they appealed to nationalism and tolerated the "national bourgeoisie," their original military and social organization among peasants exhibited neither the backwardness-concessions of the Soviet economic and political structure nor the market ones (they neither recruited former Kuomintang officers nor relied on wage incentives). The success of this political effort was dramatic. In his *Critique of Soviet Economics*, written during the Great Leap Forward, Mao utilized the political heroism of past Chinese (and even bourgeois) revolutionary experience to criticize the Soviet overemphasis on material incentives:

> Our party has waged war for over twenty years without letup. For a long time we made a nonmarket supply system work. Of course at that time the entire society of the base areas was not practising the system. But those who made the system work in the civil war period reached a high of several hundred thousand, and at the lowest still numbered in the tens of thousands. *In the War of Resistance Against Japan the number shot up again from over a million to several millions. Right up to the first stage of Liberation our people lived an egalitarian life, working hard and fighting bravely, without the least dependence on material incentives, only the inspiration of revolutionary spirit.* At the end of the second period of the civil war we suffered a defeat, although we had nothing but victories before and after. This course of events had nothing at all to do with whether we had material incentives or not. It had to do with whether or not our political line and our military line were correct. These historical experiences have the greatest significance for solving our problems of socialist construction.[31]

Historic successors, however, often critically modify rather than transform earlier patterns that they admire. In 1949, the Chinese Communists adopted many components of the Soviet model. These features included backwardness-concessions (e.g., recruitment of former capitalist managers, reliance on educators of privileged background) and extensive market-based concessions (e.g., wage differentials to encourage noncommunists to cooperate with the new regime and even differentials *within* the communist party). Thus, Mao's 1958 critique both articulated the role of egalitarianism in a lengthy struggle involving millions of people and yet sought to blunt the contemporary political radicalism of many cadre and peasants ("the ultracommunist wind"). But Chinese revolutionary experience revealed the democratic possi-

[31] Mao, *op. cit.*, p. 85.

bilities of revolution – it provided striking counterexamples to the *Economic Determinist Backwardness Concessions* exhibited in Soviet military organization, economic determinism-justified free market policy, the lack of reliance on and even oppression of peasants, and the *Individual Desert-based Market Concessions* which were especially evident in the Soviet Communist Party. But Soviet and post-liberation Chinese practice pitted one important sector of society – spurred by pay and status differentials – against another: revolutionary workers, and peasants motivated by the need to associate and forge communism. Pre-mid 1930s Bolshevik egalitarianism, as well as the pre-liberation Chinese supply system and Chinese opposition to the brute status associated with military rank had strengthened the revolutionary, democratic side of this dialectic. Abandonment of the principles of the Commune and facilitation of status divisions, one might think, decisively reinforced the reactionary side. In general, policies elevating members of the former elite to positions of power, lack of trust in the workers and peasants, primary reliance on market incentives, and failure to insure conflict-laden discussion and deliberation about the future of the movement can all foster the emergence of dictatorship.

In explaining the consolidation of ordinary "socialist" dictatorships, a liberal emphasizes the narrow political practices of the regime; a Marxian attempts to tie such practices into a broader theory of the (re)emergence of an exploitative, oppressive class structure. It is far easier to sustain a dictatorial regime than a genuine Marxian revolutionary democracy. Former exploiters and would-be new ones have advantages in expertise, experience, and often in organizational skills, particularly insofar as the state exists as a centralized entity isolated from society. They draw strength from the weight of nonradical traditions and psychology, for instance, those underpinning the prevalence of material incentives, divisions of nationality, sexism, etc. Given the novelty of communist politics, a qualitative shift in the political character of a state to the right – away from a basically revolutionary to an exploitative state apparatus – *can* occur mainly through a kind of corruption, signaled by the emergence of substantial status differentials, without fierce, overt class war.[32] The outburst of the cultural revolution in China and its suppression, or left-wing Polish worker revolts, however, indicate the depth of social conflict; the crushing of the Chinese "ultraleft" provides an important counterexample to the claim that revolutionary socialist regimes peacefully *evolve* into exploitative ones.

Particular political experiences of war and mass radical involvement, often reflecting different strategies, decisively affect these outcomes. The exhaus-

---

[32] Paul Sweezy and Charles Bettelheim, *On the Transition to Socialism* (New York: Monthly Review, 1971), p. 74.

tion among ordinary people which stemmed from the enormous effort required to ward off the unparalleled physical and psychological brutality of the Nazi onslaught, coupled with the prevalence of a pro-status outlook and a hierarchical political approach, contributed to the evolution of a reactionary Soviet leadership. (That combination of factors offset the considerable exhilaration of the victory over Nazism.) In contrast, the greater dissemination of communist ideas among ordinary people and a greater respect for peasant radicalism during the lengthy civil war and World War II helped to instigate a left-wing countermovement in China against the emergence of a socialist status hierarchy, illustrated by some important features of the Great Leap Forward and the Cultural Revolution.

From a liberal perspective, market concessions in socialist societies create polyarchy (workers' self-management seems at least more participatory than Soviet "one man management"). Yet given the market advantages enjoyed by certain well-positioned firms, uneven success, and differential wages, even a predominantly self-managing system could breed substantial inequalities, exacerbate status differentials, and bend the state apparatus to serve a privileged group. Further, as the Yugoslav case illustrates, such a system neither arouses political participation nor does it threaten the existing dictatorship. Though lacking even the appearance of democratic self-management, the Soviet regime has extensively utilized "material incentives" since the mid-1930s. A 1937 Soviet philosophy textbook described the sense of a common good that this system elicited:

> This mutual penetration [of opposites] is manifested in the form of piecework, the insistence [on] differential wages . . . the bonus system, diplomas . . . and other forms of encouragement designed to enlist all the powers of the individual in the service of society.[33]

Here, the visible hand of planners arranges the market, but the effect on income and status differentials, motivation, and political outlook, is broadly similar to the Yugoslav model. Once the Bolsheviks relied so substantially on material incentives, more radical appeals became hard to sustain. As Mao suggested,

> [the 1950s Soviet textbook of political economy] makes it seem as if the masses' creative activity has to be inspired by material interest. At every opportunity the text discusses individual material interest as if it were an attractive means for luring people into pleasant prospects. This is a reflection of the spiritual state of a good number of economic workers and leading personnel and of the failure to

[33] M. Shirokov, ed., *Textbook of Marxist Philosophy* (Moscow: Leningrad Institute of Philosophy, 1937), p. 167.

emphasize political-ideological work. Under such circumstances there is no alternative to relying on material incentives. "From each according to his ability, to each according to his labor." The first half of the slogan means that the very greatest effort must be expended in production. Why separate the two halves of the slogan and always speak onesidedly of material incentive? This kind of propaganda for material interest will make capitalism unbeatable![34]

Liberal views on the coincidence of market incentives and democracy arose against the background of the coerciveness and denial of personality that feudalism embodied; that contrast is the source of Hayek's and today's Chinese market socialists' peculiar emphasis on collective forms of production as regressive "roads to serfdom." Against feudalism, even unhealthy motivations nonetheless served the emergence of individuality; a less politically dominated economy, characterized by self-seeking, was superior in human terms, not just in productivity, to a serf-holding one. In fact, as Montesquieu rightly suggested, a greater emphasis on individual personality and initiative augmented productivity and helped sustain the rule of law. But in a communist context, so Marxians maintain, that contrast is no longer valid. Even "merit-based" market concessions, when they play a significant role, aid old and new status-derived, exploitative interests by undercutting an egalitarian social and political structure. This change can occur whether there is central planning (utilizing material incentives) or a mix of market and planning "mechanisms." Both liberal and economic determinist theories rest on an inadequate (alienated) view of human psychology which the modern theory of the self counteracts. Thus, a Marxian might insist that the whole liberal concern with plan or market, centralization or decentralization, focuses our attention on the wrong questions. Rather, the fundamental issues are: what is the extent of participation and discussion; to what extent do differentials based on status persist along with their corresponding and fundamentally inegalitarian ideologies; and which social class (or strata) controls state power? The reliance on market practices, recommended by liberals, does not mitigate and may often have the paradoxical effect of strengthening (exploitative) dictatorships. Given the triumph of reactionary regimes in Russia and China, Marxians need to develop a theory of how the tensions between political community and the market, the politics of social individuality and status-based ideologies of "individualism," integrated and defective senses of self, may be overcome and decline averted.

Against this argument, however, a liberal critic might insist that modern politics and industrial organization are heavily bureaucratic. Even if mass organizations (for example, soviets or village associations) flourish for some

---

[34] Mao, *op.cit.*, p. 79

period during a revolution, the victory of a one party regime will eventually lead to their atrophy. A sophisticated liberal might even grant that a centralized revolutionary organization, bringing radical proposals into the political arena, instigating discussion and action among the most oppressed, and respecting the views of others (aside from exploiters and armed counterrevolutionaries), can be a democratic force during a revolution and in the initial postrevolutionary stage. Yet, he might add, too many forces in communist society appear to lead to sharp status differentiation and the corruption of the party. Ultimately, the liberal maintains, the party will hinder, not facilitate mass democracy. Even where serious radical challenge is possible (the "ultraleft" in the cultural revolution), it is still relatively easy to turn a centralized state apparatus and party into a reactionary dictatorship and to use it against the masses. Thus, a decent version of party competition, allowing some, perhaps politically tepid, loyal opposition, but coupled with a tradition of free, even if nonthreatening, speech, is the best one can hope for. Once again, this liberal defense is qualified by numerous concessions to Marxism. It also does not foresee or does not deal creatively with major political conflicts and changes.[35]

Yet this liberal might turn Marxian justifications of particular policies based on revolutionary history against a broader Marxian argument. The liberal might even grant the initial seriousness of Bolshevik attempts to work with other parties. Given the pressures of war and civil war, however, the left Socialist Revolutionaries, infuriated by the Treaty of Brest-Litovsk, launched a campaign of assassination against Bolshevik leaders and ultimately joined the counterrevolution. The outlawing of such parties, the liberal would note, just shows how limited the possibility of electoral competition for leadership under revolutionary circumstances is. Thus, the liberal would think that it is better to prize even very limited traditions of democratic competition, where they exist.

Even where a Marxian response acknowledges their importance, however, it would probably emphasize neither interparty competition nor even competition for leadership within a communist party – an important topic in its own right. (As the foregoing liberal objection indicates, why would such changes alone sustain transformation in an antihierarchial, antisocially dictatorial direction?) Instead, the Marxian might look to a possibility indicated by Chinese revolutionary experience. There the Communist Party proposed a systematic strategy: (1) learn from the experience of the masses (their response to oppression, such as the peasant revolts in Hunan, and later efforts to redistribute property as a means of abolishing poverty); (2) elabor-

---

[35] A. J. Polan, *Lenin and the End of Politics* (Berkeley, CA: University of California Press, 1984), pp. 125–128, 61–68.

ate central policies and broad justifications for furthering the revolution (a policy of relying on peasant-based armed struggle, and the formation of mutual aid teams and cooperatives to generate sufficient wealth to ensure life-sustaining shares); (3) return these ideas to the masses in each locale for discussion and implementation (in nonparty village associations as well as party organizations); (4) investigate the results and criticize previous policy (learn from extra-party criticism, and self-criticism); formulate a new (modified) policy and again take it to the masses. Later policy reiterates the second cycle, starting with evaluation of revolutionary activity and self-criticism (substituting step 4 for initial steps 1 and 2). As Mao put it:

> In all the practical work of our Party, all correct leadership is necessarily "from the masses, to the masses." This means: take the ideas of the masses (scattered and unsystematic ideas) and concentrate them (through study turn them into concentrated and systematic ideas), then go to the masses and propagate and explain these ideas until *the masses embrace them as their own, hold fast to them, and translate them into action*, and test the correctness of these ideas in such action. Then once again concentrate ideas from the masses and once again go to the masses so that the ideas are persevered in and carried through. And so on, over and over again in an endless spiral, with the ideas becoming more correct, more vital and richer each time.[36]

As William Hinton's *Fanshen* vividly demonstrates, these policies enabled peasants to emancipate themselves from rule by the landlords, create democratic associations which permitted discussion and deliberation on basic forms of social organization and leadership, criticize village leaders and communists (not coextensive groups), and initiate cooperative production. Such achievements were much more than an outburst of revolutionary enthusiasm; these processes were sustained for a considerable period. Further, they reveal an important merit in radical centralization which is not simply conditioned by the presence of a highly centralized, brutal enemy. Mao's *On Practice* rightly suggests that the formulation, implementation, and criticism of a general line can have aspects of a (social) scientific experiment: how does one move, given previous experience and a broad Marxian theory, from a cooperative political community combined with residual aspects of status ideology to communism? But serious political experimentation, much more sharply than other branches of inquiry, requires democracy and participation: individuals must "embrace these ideas as their own, hold fast to them," act on them, assess the consequences, and help develop them

[36] Mao, *Selected Works* (Peking: Foreign Languages Press, 1965), vol. 3, p. 119.

further. Only the self-understanding and self-respect of participants, not the rule of experts, can generate and sustain Marxian communism.[37] In this context, mass governmental organizations need a durable vigor and integrity.

Other features of initial Chinese communist political practice cut against the emergence of a status hierarchy. That regime sought to undermine status inequalities by combining leadership with periods of manual labor, soldiering with contributions to civilian production, coordination in battle with political discussion. That movement tried to facilitate *mass* criticism, not just intraparty criticism, of the practices and lifestyles of leaders. Regular investigation of the working and living conditions of ordinary people to nurture responsiveness would, it was hoped, sustain a radical, nonbureaucratized leadership. Revolutionary newspapers featured stories exemplifying broad criticisms of officialdom. For example, when an official, a former employee of a Shanghai boiler factory, returned for a month's work, his fellow workers put up a poster criticizing him and, after several days, reminded him: "If we put up a wall poster, it was not because we had anything against you or because there weren't enough workers. But you used to be a worker like us and now that you're on top, we only see you at official assembly meetings! We don't want you to forget the workers here." "When someone becomes a cadre it should not be for honors or so that he will never have to go back to work. If you don't use a hammer anymore, you will change."[38] As subsequent Chinese experience has revealed, these egalitarian policies toward leaders will not offset the impact of large-scale pay and status differentials. Broad criticisms of status hierarchy are also no substitute for tracing out relevant inadequacies of policy and style of leadership. In addition, outside of the Cultural Revolution, criticism from below often affected local rather than national leaders. Nonetheless, strengthening those Chinese innovations which attacked status hierarchy and created opportunities for popular criticism of policies and leaders seems a likely way of facilitating revolutionary democracy.

Furthermore, the Chinese strategy incorporated Marx's notion of articulating the "future" of the movement, continuing class conflict leading to the "abolition of the wage system," within the (socialist) "present." In contrast to the Soviet emphasis on the predominance of material incentives, Mao's *Critique of Soviet Economics* interpreted appeals to *material* interests in a broader light. First, he distinguished a collective material interest – the solidarity of the working class which produces material benefits for all – from "material" interest in the sense of the competitive interest of some at the expense of others. The Soviet view focused exclusively on the latter. Second,

---

[37] William Hinton, *Fanshen* (New York: Vintage, 1966).
[38] Jean Chesneaux, *China* (New York: Pantheon, 1979), pp. 221, 169.

he gave this common interest an Aristotelian or Marxian interpretation as an intrinsic good, valuable as an end in itself, not just as an instrument to other ends. These ideas were connected to Mao's later advocacy of a Paris Commune type of state as an ideal (Mao, of course, opposed the Shanghai Commune at the height of the Cultural Revolution):

> hard, bitter struggle, expanded . . . production, the future pros-pects of communism – these are what have to be emphasized, not material interest. The goal to lead people toward is not 'one spouse, one country home, one automobile, one piano, one television.'

Critics of revolution within the Communist Party had advanced a plodding, anti-political conception: "a ten thousand league journey begins where you are standing." Emphasizing the integrity and energy of political thinking, Mao vividly responded:

> but if you look only at the feet without giving thought to the future, then the question is: what is left of revolutionary excitement and ardor? What energy is left for travelling.[39]

This dialectical Marxian stress on the future of the movement suggests a qualitative point about communist discussion and criticism. As in the Paris Commune, to some extent in the Great Leap Forward, and most explicitly, in the Cultural Revolution, popular deliberations must concern the organiz-ation and interplay of revolutionary political and social power: the connec-tion between mutual recognition in politics, status differentials, the potential for reactionary dictatorship and the stages of communism; the international situation, war, dependency, and what constitutes internationalism; and the like. Thus, Soviet factory discussions which are restricted to suggestions for implementing particular planning objectives do not by themselves qualify as genuinely democratic.[40] To be democratic, these or other assemblies would have to encompass debate and criticism concerning the general political purposes and dynamic of a communist regime, as well as the implementation of an economic plan. An atmosphere of respect and mutual recognition between leaders and citizens would have to be an integral, one might almost say tangible, aspect of communism.

Mao's emphases on mass participation, on deliberation and criticism, and on eroding divisions between manual and mental work recapitulate and render more exact Marx's admiration for the politics of the Commune and his dialectical strategy for the future of the movement, culminating in the abolition of class and status. Mao and many activists in the cultural revolu-tion sometimes mistakenly interpreted a distinction between a radical and a

[39] Mao, *Critique*, p. 112.
[40] Polan, *op. cit.*, pp. 93–94.

conservative view as a contrast between serving the people and serving oneself, selfless altruism and predatory egotism. That contrast neglects the central distinction between the politics of mutual recognition of persons and genuine individuality, and the "individualist" advancement of some at the expense of others. In the latter, "individuals" are always dominated by the spell of external social forces and relations (of money and competitive prestige), and uninvolved or restless in ordinary activities and relationships. Such "self-seeking" individuals are, so to speak, never themselves. But the Chinese communist emphasis on the social and political aspects of an integrated self and its role in revolutionary participation points in a very different, more humane direction.

Thus, the left-wing aspects of Chinese experience provide some grounds for a democratic defense of communism. In the light of my previous argument on status, the Maoist view of practice and reliance on the masses needs a stronger psychological and political theory of the self, and a sharper moral emphasis on (social) individuality than Mao's own formulations allow. An appropriate conception of practice must be nonutilitarian, insisting on the unification through deliberation of intrinsic and instrumental goods. Even with such a theory, one less marred by an economic determinist lack of confidence in the rationality of oppressed classes (notably peasants, but also workers), than even the most radical arguments and policies of the Communist International, a fundamental contradiction between scientific insight and participation, centralism and democracy would remain. In this context, democratic discussion and involvement require something closer to the atmosphere and organization of the Commune, or perhaps of aspects of the Chinese Cultural Revolution, than the habitual practice of even comparatively left-wing Communist regimes (e.g., Mao's).[41]

In fact, revolutionary democratic aspects of Chinese experience produced a left-wing critique of inegalitarian practices. For example, peasants in the Great Leap Forward challenged pay differentials in the party and postliberation abolition of the egalitarian supply system. Even more strikingly, a demonstration of a million workers in Shanghai, in February 1967, agitated for a governmental structure modelled on the Paris Commune. Here an Aristotelian "extreme democracy" emerged dialectically to challenge the inadequacies of socialism. Mao and the Chinese Communist leadership ultimately suppressed these radical forces.[42] Ironically, Mao's clearest argument on the role of politics occurs in a work which primarily emphasizes the

---

[41] One needs to distinguish revolutionary aspects of the cultural revolution from xenophobic ones.

[42] Maurice Meisner, *Mao's China* (New York: MacMillan, 1977), pp. 327, 321–322; Charles Bettelheim, "The Great Leap Backward" in Bettelheim and Neil Burton, *China Since Mao* (New York: Monthly Review Press, 1978), pp. 100–107.

role of the "law of value" against the left. Following Marx's and Mao's insistence on learning from revolutionary practice, however, one might draw critical conclusions from these experiences about the law of value, status hierarchy, and the undercutting of revolutionary democracy. Such inferences cut sharply against some of Marx's arguments and Mao's own stand in the Cultural Revolution.

Thus, in *Critique of the Gotha Program*, Marx explicitly maintained that socialist justice – the principle of equal pay for equal work according to a suitable (labor-time) standard – would realize the promise of bourgeois justice (overcome the contradiction between this form and its previous exploitative content) and yet engender considerable social inequalities. In Marx's first stage of communism:

> Content and form are changed, because under the altered circumstances no one can give anything except his [or her] labor and because, on the other hand, nothing can pass to the ownership of individuals except individual means of consumption. But as far as the distribution of the latter among the individual producers is concerned, the same principle prevails as in the exchange of commodity-equivalents: a given amount of labor in one form is exchanged for an equal amount of labor in another form.
>
> Hence, *equal right* here is still in principle – *bourgeois right*, although principle and practice are no longer at loggerheads.[43]

For Marx, the labor-time standard was dialectically "stigmatized by a bourgeois limitation." This uniform measure produces unequal results for unequal labor. It would benefit the single person compared to one who must support a family. To make Marx's claim more pointed, one might note that given previous forms of special oppression – racism, sexism, enforced lack of skill – unchecked by special compensatory, internationalist policies, the law of value would perpetuate differences in income and status between men and women, citizens of a comparatively advantaged nationality and those of other nationalities, skilled and unskilled workers and so forth. Thus, under socialism, even if Horatio Algers become more frequent, Horatio Algers remain a comparative rarity. Marx considered such an elevation of the standard of individual desert over that of social need to be a "defect." If we take into account racism, sexism, and the corruption of democratic politics, Marx's worry becomes considerably more troubling. As the last section suggested, a general argument about social individuality based on the theory of the self and a critique of status hierarchy makes the source of Marx's concern clearer.

[43] Marx, *Selected Works in One Volume* (New York: International Publishers, 1974), p. 324.

Given revolutionary experience and a better theory of the self, a contemporary Marxian might want to take this argument further than Marx did, arguing for a communist system of social distribution of necessary goods and otherwise equal incomes. Note again that this proposal does not wholly abolish the market – there remains an area in which individual choices strongly affect particular lines of production. What it does abolish, however, is market-based differential incomes and status inequalities. It thus leaves a sphere for the healthy development of individuality, described in the previous section, but does not undercut and probably strengthens political equality and whatever approximation of a Paris Commune type of state can exist in the modern world. (Our world differs from that of the Commune, e.g., simply arming the citizenry does not exhaust our inventory of weaponry.) An explicit defense of social individuality needs to accompany this egalitarian policy. In that context, however, egalitarianism seems far more likely to facilitate genuine participation and deliberation than market socialism.

Highly centralized versions of the dictatorship of the proletariat have received their putative justification from intense social conflicts, nurtured by war and the economic concessions of socialist regimes. Prima facie, removing economic concessions and nurturing individuality should undercut the authoritarian elements in communism. Those elements of democratic centralism pertaining to social experiment can be better captured – in fact, can *only* be captured – without authoritarianism. Despite the threat of war, these changes should facilitate internal democracy, enabling discussion and a much greater rivalry of strategies than any radical regime has so far permitted. That rivalry must at least apply to mass organizations, but these changes might also provide a framework for interparty or intraparty competition. Systematic advocacy of racism and sexism, or the explicit revival of capitalism would still, under most circumstances, be curtailed. But a communist regime might encourage a far greater range of democratic practices than existing liberal regimes with their systemically encouraged apathy of the poor and disadvantaged (to mention only one of many interrelated, harmful consequences of an exploitative social structure, if Marxian social theory is right). Nonetheless, political life has peculiarities which cannot be avoided simply by economic and social measures, even those affecting the status of rulers. Given political experience, any easy Marxian response to a sophisticated liberal critic of anti-democratic practices among communist regimes is misguided; this section has only sketched some directions in which a reasoned Marxian reply might be sought.

Nonetheless, a Marxian defense of a dictatorship of the proletariat, with greatly increased participation and equality of status and income, provides a difficult but not implausible response to this liberal challenge. For the capitalist alternatives have often featured fascism, colonialism, neocolonialism, and, even in leading capitalist democracies, predatory wars and extreme forms of oppression. For instance, in the 1920s and 1930s, liberal regimes introduced racially inspired limitations on immigration, bans on ethnic intermarriage, and differential policies in education which were later alleged to be distinctive of fascism (the 1924 U.S. immigration law sought to maintain a "pure Nordic stock," and thirty states had miscegenation laws). Given the decisive Soviet role in World War II, one might speculate about an intriguing counterfactual: what would the political regimes in Europe and the United States look like now if Russia had lost in the winter of 1941? Today's Western democracies play a large role in sustaining repressive regimes in less developed countries, and as Samuel Huntington's influential argument on the emergence of elite authoritarianism as a response to "distempered" democracy illustrates, even the current limited democratic institutions are under significant threat at home.[44] The common liberal contention that capitalism, liberal democracy, and nonbelligerent policies are aligned under "normal" conditions of class conflict needs a deeper defense than it has so far received. So do claims about the possibility of fundamental, egalitarian social change through electoral competition. The foregoing, very controversial arguments for a modified revolutionary democracy are thus linked to a broad web of comparatively well-supported Marxian historical and explanatory claims which are in stark contrast to liberal ones.

Marx's theory of full-blown communism emphasizes contribution to the community and realizing oneself in particular activities, not the competition of isolated "selves" motivated and ruled by money. Thus, Marxian communism differs fundamentally *in both social theory and ethics* from the theory and practice of market socialism and from conceptions of an individual desert-based distributive justice. A Marxian theory of democracy stresses the political activity and deliberation of ordinary people, not primarily procedural or formal features. Yet this complex view of communism still shares with liberalism core modern moral and political insights into mutual recognition and individuality. It stands or falls on radical claims about the forms of durable human cooperation.

As I have argued elsewhere, the distinctively political and moral features (features concerned with human well-being) of Marx's theory play a fundamental role in the general dialectic of Marxian political strategy and historical explanation. Given the broad change from prehistory to fully human history, they do so especially in the achievement and preservation of com-

---

[44] Stephan L. Chorover, *From Genesis to Genocide* (Cambridge, MA: MIT Press, 1975), Chapters 3–5; Samuel P. Huntington, "The Democratic Distemper," Samuel P. Huntington, Michel Crozier, and Joji Watanuki, eds., *The Crisis of Democracy* (New York: New York University Press, 1975).

munism.[45] Now, a left-wing socialist regime could avoid the use of wage differentials, especially in the party and government, and emphasize what Mao called the collective interest; it could also launch more thoroughgoing campaigns to undercut differentials between women and men and between nationalities based on the preceding regimes; it could cultivate lively political association even more strongly than did the Chinese Communists. Persisting in such policies, such a regime might far surpass the egalitarianism and democracy of previous socialist practice.

Yet even such a left-wing socialism probably would encompass a now covert, now open war between revolutionary elements and those which breed a strongly inegalitarian, one might say, procapitalist, mentality. After all, differentials in the party merely extend normal, extraparty market practices. If such differentials are so essential for noncommunists, why should communists "suffer?" An economic determinist emphasis has made cooperation wildly contingent on the level of productivity. But if human insight, accumulated knowledge, political experience, and mutual respect are going to play a larger role, why shouldn't cooperation flourish, as a Rawlsian might suggest, in quite moderate economic circumstances? An egalitarian policy of distribution according to need (equal incomes) might undercut the features of socialism which engender status differentials. For communism, if Marxian theory is right, does away not merely with the crude exploitation of capitalism and state capitalism, but with racism, neocolonialism, fascism and war. These would obviously be enormous, compelling accomplishments. A communist society, also and just as importantly, is a society of common commitment to individuality and self-respect. It is an egalitarian, anti-status society. A fully worked out Marxian theory would have to elaborate the relationship between the abolition of status hierarchy and remaining concessions; between broad political discussion and criticism focused on the future of the movement, and formal procedures; between equal incomes and projected full distribution according to need, and so forth. This essay has only posed a fundamental, very difficult problem for both Marxian and liberal political theory. The recognition of persons, foreshadowed by democracy, is still more promise than actuality.

Political Science, University of Denver

---

[45] Gilbert, "Historical Theory," 1981.

DEMOCRACY AND CLASS DICTATORSHIP

RICHARD W. MILLER

Clearly, Marx thought he was promoting democratic values. In the *Manifesto*, the immediate goal of socialism is summed up as "to win the battle of democracy."[1] Marx sees the reduction of individuality as one of the greatest injuries done by a system in which most people buy and sell their labor power on terms over which they have little control.[2] As they supervised translations and re-issues of the *Manifesto*, Marx and Engels singled out just one point as a major topic on which their view in 1848 had been superseded. The forms of government needed to be changed to give people more control over the state, a change in structure pioneered by the Paris Commune.[3]

And yet Marx's phrase for the workers' state in which the battle for democracy has been won is "the dictatorship of the proletariat." This has always seemed an obstacle, probably the highest, for democrats who want to be sympathetic to Marx. One way to remove the obstacle is to take the phrase as florid talk of something banal or uncoercive. Some think Marx only had in mind the very temporary need for a provisional government, relatively bold and nonprocedural in its uses of coercion, as such governments always are. Or perhaps the dictatorship of the proletariat is nothing more than a state governed by concern with workers' well-being, which was neglected before.

While Marx does not say much directly about the dictatorship of the proletariat, what he does say makes this particular reconciling project hopeless. In a letter of 1852, he singles out the need for a dictatorship of the proletariat as one of his three distinctive insights in social theory.[4] The need for a provisional government is hardly such a novel or central thought. And the dictatorship of the proletariat has a lot to do with coercion of a biased and, sometimes, dramatic sort. Writing in 1881, he describes an essential function of the workers' state as "intimidating the mass of the bourgeoisie."[5] Another sign that the dictatorship of the proletariat is not a temporary device is Marx's conception of what follows it, namely, a society without a state, "an

[1] Karl Marx and Frederick Engels, *Selected Works in One Volume* (New York: International Publishers, 1968), p.52.
[2] See, for example, Marx, *Grundrisse* (New York: Vintage Books, 1973), p.488, and Marx, *Economic and Philosophical Manuscripts of 1844* in his *Early Writings* (New York: McGraw-Hill, 1963), pp.122ff.
[3] Marx, *Selected Works* pp.32ff.
[4] Marx and Engels, *Selected Correspondence* (Moscow: Progress Publishers, 1975), p.64.
[5] *ibid.*, p.318.

association, in which the free development of each is the condition for the free development of all."[6] In the *Critique of the Gotha Program*, Marx emphasizes the profound psychological transformations that will have to prepare the way for stateless, communist society, transformations that follow the founding of socialism and a workers' state. As the political side of this long process, the new class dictatorship is hardly a stopgap. At any rate, it is a stopgap only from the most cosmic perspective.

I want to explore a very different way of reconciling class dictatorship and democracy, one that depends on taking seriously Marx's dramatic ways of talking about the workers' state. When its nature and rationale are understood, Marx's dictatorship of the proletariat turns out to be genuinely different from liberal democratic paradigms, yet his proposal that this is the right way to realize democratic values is at least as plausible as liberal democratic ideas. Of course, what is plausible can be wrong. But the minimal claim that democrats should take the dictatorship of the proletariat more seriously has a practical outcome. Neglect of the rationale for the dictatorship of the proletariat has distorted the basic terms in which we assess United States foreign policy and the course of world affairs.

THE DICTATORSHIP OF THE BOURGEOISIE

Marx's few but important words about the dictatorship of the proletariat are best approached indirectly, by first investigating his views of politics before it and after it. Why did Marx think that the state under capitalism was in general a dictatorship of the bourgeoisie, so that "the modern representative state," not just obviously repressive arrangements, embodied "the exclusive political sway" of that class?[7] And, having distinguished state-power as such from a mere coordinating apparatus, why didn't he think that the destruction of capitalism should be followed immediately by the destruction of the state?

Marx's general descriptions of the capitalist state are splendid metaphors, in some ways quite misleading, like all splendid metaphors. The state is "a committee for managing the common affairs of the whole bourgeoisie."[8] This suggests an ongoing conspiracy, in which political figures routinely consult with businesspeople to get their orders of the week. Aside from being a silly view of politics, this literal reading does not fit what Marx says about particular political events. For example, the Louis Napoleon dictatorship, in his view, is both an arrangement in which the French state reached its

[6] *Manifesto, Selected Works*, p.53.
[7] *ibid.*, p.37.
[8] *ibid.*, p.37.

highest development thus far, and one in which the bourgeoisie, "freed from political cares," tended to the business of business.[9]

Also, Marx says the capitalist state is "an engine of social despotism," "the national war-engine of capital versus labor."[10] This suggests that the state only responds to workers' demands coercively, at least when capitalists would prefer that no such demands were made. This fits the talk of class dictatorship nicely, but hardly accords with Marx's real respect for certain reforms under capitalism, such as the Ten Hours Bill and the Factory Acts.

What is needed is a conception of bourgeois dictatorship that warrants the metaphors but does justice to Marx's grasp of the facts of political life. As with the dictatorship of the proletariat, one should avoid, if possible, reducing the more florid talk to innocuous truisms, for example, that money is a source of political influence. The metaphors would not be warranted, then, even as metaphors. And novel options for political theory might be lost.

As I argued more extensively in *Analyzing Marx*, a plausible but non-trivializing version of the idea of bourgeois dictatorship might be set out in three parts.[11] First, Marx is claiming that basic developments in government policy under capitalism are in the interests of one class, the bourgeoisie. So government acts as if it were an executive committee for managing the common affairs of the bourgeoisie. Here, it is crucial to recognize that an institution exclusively serving the interests of one group will often satisfy demands of another group, even if it is clearly in the interests of the dominant group that those demands did not exist. All that is required is that stability be an interest of the dominant group, that the institution play a role in fulfilling this interest, and that acquiescence on the part of the opposed group helps create stability. To say that Reagan, Shultz, and Weinberger attend to Soviet demands, sometimes satisfy them, and, as a result, do things that would not be in the interest of United States world-power were it not for the existence of the Soviet demands, is obviously not the same as saying that these gentlemen are double agents, serving both United States and Soviet interests. Thus, the difference between the two ways of attending to interests is dramatic, in practice. And the fact that government is concerned with stability and acquiescence is one of the few platitudes that political theorists of all persuasions share. So it follows from the view that the state is a bourgeois dictatorship that concessions will be made. This is not just a means by which Marxists explain away recalcitrant data. What is distinctive of Marx's view is the expectation that major concessions to workers' interests will require vigorous demands and threats to stability. Of course, since

---

[9] *The Civil War in France, Selected Works*, p.290.
[10] *ibid.*, pp.289, 290.
[11] See R. Miller, *Analyzing Marx: Morality, Power and History* (Princeton: Princeton University Press, 1984), Chapter 3.

stability is not the only bourgeois interest and acquiescence is not the only means to it, there will also be an expectation of frequent repressive responses like Wilson's Red Scare, Roosevelt's jailing of three national leaderships of the Communist Party, and Truman's purge of the federal civil service, and of destabilizing acts when bourgeois interests demand them, for example, the prosecution of unpopular wars.

This regular connection between government action and bourgeois interests is no accident, on Marx's view. In any given period of time, definite mechanisms maintain it. The particular mechanisms that he describes are diverse and strikingly nonconspiratorial. For example, in *The German Ideology* he speaks of the bourgeoisie as having "purchased" the state, by means of the national debt.[12] If the most important businesspeople are appalled by government policy, they will, without any need for explicit coordination, throw a government into fiscal chaos, by refusing to float government loans. This truism suggests another, daunting to any political activist who is not self-consciously revolutionary. Antibourgeois political action lowers the "animal spirits" of investors and firms (in Keynes's elegant phrase), resulting in unemployment and industrial stagnation. In the sphere of ideology, politics will, of course, be shaped by outright bourgeois ownership of major media and substantial influence on others – "the press, the pulpit and the comic papers, . . . all the means at the disposal of the ruling class," as Marx sums up the nineteenth-century repertoire.[13] Major elected leaders and officials enjoy high salaries, and lead lives dominated by the subculture of the bourgeoisie.[14] In these and other ways, Marx thinks that the objective framework for political activity can systematically bias government action toward the bourgeoisie, even in a parliamentary regime based on universal suffrage.

Marx's conception of the mechanisms of bourgeois rule underwent one important change, significant in itself and for his conception of workers' rule. In the *Manifesto*, parliamentary democracy is presented as the ultimate form of bourgeois rule.[15] But subsequent developments, above all the rise to power of Louis Napoleon, convinced him that the political structures of mature bourgeois rule are extremely diverse, change as the social context makes old structures inadequate, and sometimes include pervasive nonparliamentary repression. In his French political histories, he emphasizes the extreme flexibility with which the bourgeoisie has supported now one political arrangement, now another, as their interests have changed, moving from democratic representation and a people's militia to the first Napoleon's

---

[12] Marx and Engels, *The German Ideology* (New York: International Publishers, 1977), pp.79ff.
[13] *Selected Correspondence*, p.222.
[14] See *The Civil War in France, Selected Works*, p.291.
[15] *Manifesto, Selected Works*, p.37.

dictatorship to the restored Bourbon dynasty to constitutional monarchy to a democratic republic to the dictatorship of Louis Napoleon. The common thread is not some distinctive institution, but the social interest served by all these political arrangements.[16]

Many, perhaps most, liberal-democratic activists in the United States think that Marx is largely right in claiming that present-day bourgeois democracies are biased toward the interests of big business, and have this bias because of persistent and deep-rooted social mechanisms. The disagreement between Marx and these activists (the third aspect of Marx's theory of bourgeois rule) concerns what it would take to break the connection between government policy and bourgeois interests. According to Marx, a revolution is required. More precisely, a movement that changes the basic role of government will have to develop and use the capacity for large-scale, disciplined, and violent political action. Thus, while Marx sometimes said that a socialist government might be elected in Britain, "he never forgot to add," Engels reports "that he hardly expected the English ruling classes to submit, without a 'pro-slavery rebellion', to this peaceful and legal revolution."[17] And, of course, an ultimately successful socialist party would have organized workers for armed struggle in this civil war. If Engels neglects to say that His or Her Majesty's Armed Forces would not be the bulwark against counterrevolution, this is surely because it goes without saying.

Engels's hedge is the whole upshot of the occasional references to peaceful transformation that have led Lichtheim, Avineri, and many others to portray Marx as maturing into a nonrevolutionary.[18] This secondary literature is a pity, because the older Marx's emphasis on change in bourgeois political forms gives his revolutionary strategy a rationale it had lacked. Since many people are killed in revolutions, and revolutions often fail, why not take the gradualist course of voting for the lesser of two evils in a parliamentary democracy? It took Louis Napoleon to make the answer clear: a bourgeoisie losing by the old parliamentary rules of the game will break those rules, even deserting its old representatives for upstarts who advocate more direct and efficient repression. (Evidently, the chance of an elected, genuinely socialist regime was for Marx a transient and local piece of luck, the proslavery rebellion to one side.)

Marx's conception of the dictatorship of the bourgeoisie sheds considerable light on the dictatorship of the proletariat, sometimes by way of contrasts, sometimes by way of similarities. Even when it is a parliamentary democracy, a capitalist state is undemocratic because most people have so

---

[16] See *The Eighteenth Brumaire of Louis Bonaparte, Selected Works*, pp.169–77; *The Civil War in France, ibid.*, pp.289ff.
[17] Marx, *Capital*, I (Moscow: Progress Publishers, n.d.), p.17.
[18] See *Analyzing Marx*, pp.114–36.

little effective influence over the terms of their lives. And this is not because the state does not intervene enough in economic life – even though laissez-faire regimes can be a mask for real economic subordination. Rather, the social system confines the ultimately decisive means of political influence to the bourgeois minority. If the dictatorship of the proletariat "wins the battle for democracy," it must be because it skews influential mechanisms toward the great majority, instead. By way of similarity, the bourgeois state embodies different structures from context to context, more coercive as class struggle is more intense. A common social function is the common thread. This institutional diversity seems to be part of the logic of class dictatorship in general. So the failure to identify the dictatorship of the proletariat with one set of institutions is not just a token of Marx's general reluctance to write "recipes for the kitchens of the future." A working class committed to a single political recipe would lose.

STATELESSNESS

Marx sharply distinguishes the coordinating groups that modern material needs require from state power as such. State power, as against mere coordination, is in itself a denial of freedom, incompatible with a free association in which the full development of each is the condition for the free development of all. While Marx never completes such contrasts with an explicit definition of the state, his basic idea is clear enough. A state is an organized minority group of "people of authority," people who often and successfully demand to be obeyed because of their social role, who collectively dominate the use of force in the society, and who monopolize permission to use force.[19]

Marx thinks that the state, no matter which class's it is, is an evil. He praises the Paris Commune for beginning to dismantle the state as such, and denounces the state as a "parasite feeding upon, and clogging the free movement of society."[20] His last important work, *The Critique of the Gotha Program*, ends with mockery of those socialists who think that needs for freedom can be completely satisfied while there is a state.[21]

Especially in *The Civil War in France*, Marx emphasizes the separateness of the state from the rest of society, a separation that becomes more burdensome as government becomes more centralized in response to modern social needs. Though Marx himself was blind to Rousseau's genius, his worry is distinctly Rousseauiste. People who govern have special power and a special

[19] See *Manifesto, Selected Works*, p. 53; *The Civil War in France, Selected Works*, p.289.
[20] *ibid.*, pp.291, 293.
[21] *Critique of the Gotha Program, Selected Works*, pp.330ff.

social life. It is too much to expect them to subordinate their corporate will to the general will indefinitely. Less pessimistic than Rousseau, Marx thought that socialism could set in motion changes in outlook and economy that would make the state unnecessary. But why wait? Why replace the dictatorship of the bourgeoisie with another species of leviathan? The rationale for a dictatorship becomes clearer after one asks why Marx wanted any state at all.

Socialist society arises out of capitalist society and is "stamped with the birthmarks of the old society from whose womb it emerges."[22] This is the beginning of Marx's argument for retaining some individual economic incentives at first, even though they are bound to separate some workers from others. Presumably, the same kind of rationale exists for retaining the state. And such reasons are not hard to find. Capitalists, even ex-capitalists, have networks of acquaintance and tactical skills exceeding the average worker's. They can rely on the legacy of centuries of bourgeois ideology – individualist, racist, nationalist, and elitist. As long as individual incentives persist, the consequent differences will weaken socialism through resentment and disdain. So, without any organized coercive apparatus, the bourgeoisie will make a comeback.

So far, the argument emphasizes dangers from former members of the bourgeoisie. If this is the whole story, then the dictatorship of the proletariat has something of the transience of a provisional government. But Marx's discussions of other birthmarks afflicting socialism suggest other, analogous dangers. The continued use of individual material incentives recognizes the tendency of many workers to base self-esteem on being better off than others, and the repugnance that skilled workers and professionals would feel if they were treated on an equal footing with the unskilled. The concessions recognizes these tendencies, and tends to perpetuate them. Hence, opposition to the more egalitarian aspects of socialism is to be expected among strategically placed people, ex-capitalists to one side. Also, the rationale for Marx's opposition to the state suggests that the state itself is bound to give rise to well-situated groups inclined to become a new ruling class. Relatively rambunctious students of a teacher sympathetic to Marx sometimes point out that even a mere coordinating apparatus might have the will and capacity to become a new bourgeoisie. Until outlooks have changed in the direction of basing self-esteem on helping the community, this is certainly true. One solution might be to have no state in the interim, hoping that the stateless climate will breed a thoroughly classless psychology. Veterans of any popular political movement have seen or experienced the result. Without a structure of authority, responsibility, and influence by the rank and file, coordinators become very self-centered controllers. In the anti-Vietnam-War movement, groups in which quasi-governmental structures were seen as par-

[22] *ibid.*, p.323.

liamentary, Marxist, or Stalinist b***s*** were eventually run by a clique of half-a-dozen people meeting in a restaurant booth. At the national level, Marx's alternative is a state structure with new means of popular influence. However, the new means are bound to be imperfect. Within this structure, efforts to rule society in the interests of an elite are bound to have some support.

Especially in Stalin's regime, the idea that widespread class struggle persists under socialism was a basis for antidemocratic repression. So it is important to see that the underlying idea is plausible in point of fact, as well as in abstract theory. Without resolving questions of which societies have been genuinely socialist, it is sometimes relatively clear that a society is moving toward socialism or away from it. Russia after 1917 and Nicaragua after the overthrow of Somoza moved to the left (though, explicitly, not to socialism in the latter case.) In both of these cases, and in numerous others, it takes no paranoia to see that a deposed elite refused to give up without a fight. For the last twenty-five years, the Soviet Union has been moving away from socialism, in the direction of greater inequality, more privileges for the managerial and bureaucratic elites, and more reliance on the essential tool of the capitalist labor market, the threat "If you don't like it here, get a job elsewhere." Adult mortality rates have shown a dramatic increase, unprecedented in an industrialized nation, while Western reporters are periodically shocked when worse-off Russians express nostalgia for the good old days of Stalin. The movement to the right seems to have had upwardly mobile members of the party and government apparatus as its base of support. A somewhat similar movement to the right in China seems to have rural entrepreneurs and the dominant lineages of villages as its social base. Looking much farther backwards, that class struggle persists after a successful revolution seems a lesson of bourgeois history. If disgruntled grand aristocrats had only themselves to rely on, the eras of Cromwell and of Robespierre would hardly have been followed by many decades of restoration and counterrevolution.

THE DICTATORSHIP OF THE PROLETARIAT

Marx's conception of politics before and after the dictatorship of the proletariat has turned out to have important implications for the workers' state. Marx's argument for the new class dictatorship is implicit in the rationale for any post-revolutionary state: a biased apparatus of coercion is needed to consolidate the social transformation of the new society. The criticism of bourgeois rule suggests why the new state is a victory for democracy: because it is part of an arrangement of political resources that connects government action with the interests of the vast majority. Since a broadening of political influence is involved, there will be changes in specifically political institutions. But no one pattern of institutions need correspond to the dictatorship of the proletariat, any more than one corresponded to the dictatorship of the bourgeoisie.

Still, we want to hear a great deal more. In particular, Marxists ought to have realistic proposals about how political influence could be dispersed while a complex, modern economy is coordinated, and about how government can deal effectively with class struggle without itself becoming a ruling class. A simile from engineering may make clearer the sort of realism one might reasonably demand. Since birds can fly, it has always seemed possible, in principle, that humans can, aided by machines. But the attempt was not worth risking wealth and limbs until a great deal of aerodynamic and mechanical work suggested particular means as well worth trying.

The praise of the Paris Commune in *The Civil War in France* is Marx's post-Leonardo, pre-Wright brothers sketch of how the dictatorship of the proletariat might work. In particular, he describes a number of innovations that gave the majority power that they lack in capitalist democracies. Under the Commune, the standing army was replaced by a people's militia. All officials, including police, were elected and subject to immediate recall. No official of the Commune was allowed to make more than the average skilled worker.[23] (A similar restruction was a condition for membership in the Soviet Communist Party through the early 1930s. When it was abolished, to attract professionals into the party, this was widely seen as a move to the right, by observers as different as the United States Ambassador and Anna Louise Strong.[24])

Since Marx, descriptions of post-revolutionary societies have sketched other institutions that could be innovations in democracy. I have hedged this claim abundantly because all descriptions of these societies are highly partisan, pro or con. It is all the more frustrating, then, that there are few detailed and concrete accounts of events within these institutions, for example, of what was said in a Soviet factory committee circa 1930 or of a typical meeting of a Cuban block committee today. I will only offer these further examples as plausible means to make a dictatorship of the proletariat more democratic. (I should confess a source of prejudice, however, concerning the actual existence of democratic innovations that have not been conclusively documented. As an over-aged member of SDS, I saw groups

[23] *The Civil War in France, Selected Works*, pp.291ff.

[24] The Webbs report the original income regulations, and admit the first departure in a poignant footnote, in Sidney and Beatrice Webb, *Soviet Communism: A New Civilization?* (New York: Scribner, 1936), p.349. For further discussion of the "Great Retreat" of the early thirties, see Jerry Hough and Merle Fainsod, *How the Soviet Union is Governed* (Cambridge, Mass.: Harvard University Press, 1980), pp.161–65.

rise to the challenge of combining democracy with effective action. I have seen no record of these events, since. On one memorable occasion, a combined meeting and sit-in at McGovern headquarters at the 1972 Democratic convention, events unfolded before network cameras, whose monitors showed that the networks were choosing to broadcast pictures of delegates with funny hats.)

The Communards had no time to address themselves to the most glaring deficiency in capitalist democracy: the absence of democracy in the workplace. Indeed, large factories tend to resemble prisons in physical layout as well as in interpersonal structure. Descriptions of Soviet experience up through the early 1930s include interesting innovations such as the following. Party members at a factory were subject to periodic review by the workers, and could be put on probation or expelled for arrogant, callous – in short, for bossy behavior. Workers had resources, time, and permission to post "wall newspapers" in which they could express both organizational suggestions and antimanagerial complaints. Many decisions were made by a "triangle" of managers, a workers' committee, and a party committee, the latter usually dominated by manual workers.[25]

Another kind of innovation, which is especially striking in descriptions of Cuba after Batista's overthrow, is the delegation of much police and administrative responsibility to local neighborhood associations. After all, for most city dwellers in industrial capitalist societies, the tyranny of the local "bad cop" is what repression basically amounts to, while helplessness in the face of the landlord or the social service bureaucracy is the most routine form of powerlessness.[26]

Of course, all of these devices can be manipulated or made irrelevant. Still, they suggest ways in which the structure of political resources could be rearranged so as to bias government action in favor of the interests of the vast majority. So long as they are not advertised as a panacea, the concrete description of such institutions is also important in two other ways. First, each clearly could represent a gain in democracy, even though all are obviously compatible with biases in coercion and participation that make the workers' state a class dictatorship. So they are means of reconciling class

---

[25] Though the Webbs have a frustrating tendency to rely on official sources, they present a newspaper report of the review of Party members at a factory which is detailed and plausible, as far as it goes. See *Soviet Communism*, I, pp.381–387. They describe other aspects of workers' participation in the early thirties, with brief eyewitness accounts, on pp.172–193. There is a thoughtful and plausible discussion of institutions of workers' participation before the Great Retreat in Gregory Bienstock, *et al.*, *Management in Russian Industry and Agriculture* (London: Oxford University Press, 1944), Chapter III. Anna Louise Strong's relatively early memoir, *I Change Worlds* (London: Routledge, 1935) contains some nuanced observations of the psychological climate of this period among rank and file Soviet activists.

[26] For a concise description of Cuban block associations by a skeptical but reasonably open-minded reporter, see Fred Ward, *Inside Cuba Today* (New York: Crown, 1978), pp.69–75.

dictatorship with democratic values. Second, none of these institutions requires going to a meeting every evening. In mainstream political theory, arguments from the laziness of the many seem to have replaced arguments from the intelligence of the few as the main justification for rule by elites. A life in politics is not to everyone's taste, and so (we are told) it is just as well if only a few have real political power even when everyone has the vote.[27] Yet when one thinks of genuine democracy as a problem of social engineering on which the Communards did pioneering work, one thinks of distinctively democratic institutions that simply do not require a perverse love of committees.

The gap in Marx's discussions of the dictatorship of the proletariat is the absence of any similarly detailed sketch of how freedom might be restricted. The very phrase "dictatorship of the proletariat" implies organized coercion of a class-biased sort. And the rationale for having any state at all is a case for such coercion, in the abstract. Marx does approve of the Commune's most famous act of violence: taking hostage the Archbishop of Paris and ultimately shooting him.[28] But this approval caused quite enough of a stir without the supplement of thought-experiments as to how the Commune might have been coercive if it has survived. After all, people on the Continent were exiled, imprisoned, and blacklisted for supporting the Commune throughout the rest of Marx's life. His comment in 1881 that a dictatorship of the proletariat would have met the Commune's need to "intimidate the mass of the bourgeoisie"[29] shows that he took the need for coercion seriously. But it hardly describes specific means of coercion compatible with his distrust of government as such.

Here is a piecemeal list of coercive measures a workers' state might choose and which could collectively merit the metaphor "dictatorship of the proletariat" without, in themselves, making government into tyranny.

(1) The advocacy of certain especially vile and dangerous ideologies might be outlawed. In the 1940s, the New Jersey state legislature nearly passed a "racial libel" law making it a criminal libel to advocate the inferiority of a racial, religious, or ethnic group. Would New Jersey have taken a step toward tyranny if this law had passed and had been sustained? Not obviously so.

(2) Leading politicians of the old major parties and officers in the old armed forces above a certain rank might be barred from holding office.

[27] See, for example, Gabriel Almond and Sidney Verba, *The Civic Culture* (Boston: Little, Brown, 1965), pp.337–41, and Robert Dahl, *Who Governs?* (New Haven: Yale University Press, 1961), pp.305ff.

[28] *Civil War in France, Selected Works*, pp.308ff.

[29] *Selected Correspondence*, p.318.

(3) Manual workers might be preferentially promoted to leading political and governmental positions, with similar biases in training and educational opportunities.

(4) In the early phases of socialism, prosecutions for counter-revolutionary conspiracy might be less safeguarded by due process than other prosecutions, and punishments might be especially severe, in order to set an intimidating example. During the Civil War, Lincoln had Confederate sympathizers in the border states imprisoned, and suspended *habeas corpus*. The Supreme Court collaborated with him by refusing to hear these cases until the war was over and the cases were moot. Did Lincoln and the Court injure democratic values?

In general, a good way to imagine what a dictatorship of the proletariat might be like, in its repressive aspects, is to imagine what it would have taken for Reconstruction to succeed in the South.

The Reconstruction era was a time of unparalleled interracial cooperation, especially between former slaves and white tenant farmers. When W.E.B. Dubois adopted a simple expedient of historical integrity, and studied the minutes of Reconstruction legislatures, he began to uncover a rich history of thoughtful, radical deliberations concerning changes in property ownership, forms of cooperative work, and social services. In some states, such as South Carolina, tenant farmers' unions and biracial political coalitions brought society to the verge of genuine transformation.

As the antebellum elite complained, these movements were protected by the bayonets of an occupying army. Former Confederate officers – in effect, the old plantation-owning elite – were barred by law from political activity. This could be portrayed as a punitive violation of elementary democracy – as it was most famously in Griffith's *Birth of a Nation*. On the surface, the accusations of undemocratic coercion look valid. The old elite had not only been disarmed but much of their wealth had been taken away or destroyed. And the deposed elite were a minority. Yet they were forcibly excluded from political life.

In fact, the old elite had an enormous reservoir of power in their extensive regional network of acquaintanceship, their business, political, and military skills, the difficulties in coordinating economic life on a new pattern, and the persistence of anti-black ideas even in people who supported the new order for a time. Movements for change were disrupted by the Ku Klux Klan and by economic sabotage. When an interracial alliance won the governorship of South Carolina, leading members of the old elite organized racist mobs to destroy the printing presses and meeting houses of that alliance and to maim or hang leading figures in Reconstruction. When the occupying army was withdrawn, under the Hays-Tilden Compromise, the repression and degradation of the plantation-owning elite was replaced by a long night of their repression and degradation of almost all blacks and many whites. The legacy of this era seems the main threat to democratic values in the United States today.

What would it have taken to consolidate the gains of Reconstruction? For Marxists, the question presupposes an impossibility. The alliance of the industrial bourgeoisie of the North with the agricultural bourgeoisie in the South once the former's national supremacy was established was as inevitable as the reconciliation of elites in late seventeenth-century England and mid-nineteenth-century France. Still, the thought experiment is revealing, in that it shows how a structure of biased coercion might enhance democratic values, on the whole. If the advocacy of racist ideas had been banned, that would have been a help. If former slaves and poor whites had been preferentially promoted to positions of economic leadership, and preferentially given training, that would have helped, too. The more radical officials of the Freedmen's Bureau had begun such measures, and their defeat is usually seen as the first great setback for Reconstruction. Finally, it would have been a help, to put it mildly, if the old elite could have been prevented from organizing armed violence of the kind that overpowered the Fusion government in South Carolina. It is hard to see how this could have been done without the stern pursuit of suspected Klan members and the like, including convictions without full due process and the hanging of especially eminent and influential organizers to set an example. Even more than actual Reconstruction, this would have been no regime of equal rights for all. Yet it might have enhanced liberty for the great majority.

OBJECTIONS

When people seek to reduce subordination, enhance participation, and otherwise promote democratic values, Marx's dictatorship of the proletariat is, I would propose, the most important rival to liberal democracy with its emphasis on equal and impartial laws governing suffrage and advocacy. Both rival outlooks rest on broad and flexible theories of social and political power. So it would be foolish to attempt a quick rebuttal of all objections that might be raised to one or the other political outlook. I will only discuss a few objections to Marx's approach that are extremely common but, I think, off target.

Often, proposals for a certain bias in coercion are countered by a slippery-slope argument that they will, most probably, lead to totalitarianism. A ban on the advocacy of racist views is expected to produce a regime of thought control, in which all substantial disagreements with leading government policies are repressed. This expectation could be true, in principle. In fact, the slippery slope does not seem to exist. In Britain, the Official Secrets Act, broad and severe libel statutes, and such archaisms as the crime of insulting the monarch are all very real infringements on what we in the United States consider to be our First Amendment rights, to say nothing of our philosophical ideals of free speech. France has a law against falsifying history, and this law has served as the basis for prosecutions. Britain and France are not police states.

A second, intimately related worry concerns Soviet history. The repression epitomized by the Great Purge of the mid-1930s is sometimes said to show that restrictions on equal participation are bound to destroy democratic values, at least when proudly proclaimed and supported by a Marxist rationale. But repression and legal restriction were not, in fact, connected in this way. The Soviet Constitution which was enacted under Stalin's leadership includes guarantees of equal rights not very different from those in the United States and quite as liberal as those in Britain or France. The charges on the basis of which people were imprisoned, set to forced labor, or killed were almost always the serious political crimes of any nation – spying, sabotage, assassination, and treason.

There was a dramatic change in Soviet political arrangements around the time of the Great Purge, a shift away from the dictatorship of the proletariat in its distinctively democratic aspect. The restriction on Party members' income was lifted. Professionalism in the armed forces came to be celebrated, with the restoration of traditional ranks and their paraphernalia. Patriotism was made the main motive for combat. Managers' prerogatives in the workplace were increased. Was the regimentation of the 1930s simply a reflection of an all-powerful leader's paranoia? Or was it the inevitable consequence of other aspects of Marxism? I would suggest that neither explanation is right. In his writings and in his encounters with hostile and shrewd observers – Churchill, for example – Stalin did not convey the impression of a disordered mind.[30] He did have arguments to offer against democratic and egalitarian arrangements. And these arguments do rely on one familiar strand in Marxist theorizing, technological determinism. What is essential (the basic argument runs) is to make the technological basis of production in Russia modern, industrial, centralized, and efficient. Social consciousness is bound to adapt to these arrangements, and to do so in the direction of a communist society. If, in the meantime, democracy is suppressed, careerism is encouraged, and socialist appeals are replaced by patriotic ones, this is a realistic means of laying the foundations for full

---

[30] See, for example, Churchill's description of his Moscow visit of 1942 in *The Second World War* (Boston: Houghton Mifflin, 1950), Chapters 4 and 5.

socialism and democracy, in a society presently afflicted with internal divisions and powerful, hostile neighbors.[31] There is, then, a rationale for Stalin's politics in ideas that thoughtful Marxists have sincerely held. But was Marx a technological determinist? In *Analyzing Marx*, I argued at length that he was not. Here, I will simply point to the generally acknowledged basis for doubting that he was. Not a single important historical explanation in Marx fits a technological determinist pattern. I hope I need not add (though I will) that technological determinism is simply a framework in which Stalin could make his case more easily. Marxist technological determinists can certainly be anti-Stalinist, moved by obvious humane concerns. Still, if there were a tension between a fundamental part of Marxist theory and highly democratic political programs, the idea that social change is adaptation to technological needs would, I think, be its source.

One further objection cuts much deeper. Socialism is supposed to be in the interest of the great majority. Indeed, a socialist economy such as Marx describes could not function unless most people were aware of this interest. How else could efficient production go on when the goad of unemployment is removed? Thus, there should be an enormous weight of numbers on the side of a socialist regime. And yet (the objection goes) violations of liberal democratic guarantees are inconsistent with this assumption of broad support. The dictatorship of the proletariat implies a distrust of the proletariat that is bound to degenerate into widespread repression.

Part of the Marxist answer is an appeal to the residual resources of capitalism under socialism that I have already described. However, this objection forces Marxists to describe more clearly the special vulnerability of socialism to such challenges, despite the broad interests socialism supports.

A plausible response begins with the fact that support for a new social arrangement is not an all or nothing matter. Some will hate the goals of the new regime. Others will be so extremely committed to them that they would see decades of disruption and hardship in their own lives as life-enhancing challenges, if the goals are still pursued. However, a great many others (including, I would guess, myself) would support those goals, but with less and less commitment if those goals do not produce concrete benefits in their own lives, on account of disruption, inefficiency or violent opposition to the new regime. The new ideas sound good in theory to many who wonder if they can work in practice, and who take the current gains and losses as an experimental test that can go either way. Yet others have a split outlook, in which prosocialist ideas are dominant for the time being, but could become subordinate. Perhaps they are committed to working-class solidarity, but also

[31] See, for example, Stalin's *Report to the Seventeenth Congress of the C.P.S.U.* (1934), especially pp. 276–84 and *Dialectical and Historical Materialism* (1938), pp. 320–22, in *The Essential Stalin* (New York: Anchor Books, 1972).

deeply suspicious of workers of another race. This will be especially common if, as has always happened for the past century, social change is crucially helped by a special crisis, in particular, a disastrous war. Finally, many people in what used to be the upper middle class will have especially important skills, and mixed feelings about socialism. They will acquiesce in the new arrangements if they prosper, but their tolerance for disorder and hardship is, typically, low.

This diverse array of kinds of support is characteristic of any new social arrangement. There was a similar diversity of responses to that relatively tiny shift, the independence of Britain's North American colonies. The ambiguities of support ought to be characteristic not just of the establishment of socialism, but of consequent shifts to a more cooperative society, say, the abolition of wage differentials or the change from collective farms to communes. These ambiguities are quite consistent with a desire, on the part of the vast majority, that the new arrangements succeed. Yet the ambiguities of support make a new social arrangement especially vulnerable to failure. It is true that the vast majority of people cannot be trusted to be iron-willed cadre who will tolerate decades of failed harvests, idled factories, and risky military duty. Too many will be like most of my friends and me. A long-established society, depending on ingrained habits, can lurch from disaster to disaster for much longer. And the crucial disasters for a new society are of a size that the residues of capitalism can create. The grain of truth in the charge of distrust is this: the dictatorship of the proletariat is not based on that Kantian form of respect in which people are treated as if their lives were wholly governed by their most ultimate and general principles. Still, outside of special philosophical circles, few people think it an insult if they are thought to have a more limited and material side.

DICTATORSHIP, DEMOCRACY, AND CONFUSION

I hope to have shown that Marx's dictatorship of the proletariat is worth taking seriously as a democratic ideal. That it is not, in the United States, is a source of much distortion in political thinking. In particular, it creates an unreal and, in some ways, racist framework for thinking about the so-called Third World. Since World War II, a great many countries have ceased to have the characteristic institutions of parliamentary democracy. And nostalgia for these institutions, in those countries, is often confined to a tiny elite. Whatever their distrust, even hatred for the present regime, relatively few people in Ghana, Pakistan, or Nigerai seem to mourn the passing of Anglo-American institutions. If democratic values are identified with those institutions, the upshot is that most nonwhite people simply do not care about democratic values. Perhaps their national cultures are not mature enough for democratic values, as Gabriel Almond and Sidney Verba suggest. Or perhaps, as Jeane Kirkpatrick implies, democracy is only on the agenda after severe social antagonisms are overcome.[32] In one way or another, like Her Majesty's Indian subjects according to J.S. Mill, most are not ready for democracy.

The logic of the dictatorship of the proletariat suggests a very different assessment. Post-colonial regimes that displayed the full array of Anglo-American institutions were nonetheless dictatorships of the former imperial bourgeoisie and of local elites. Their restoration is not an issue for many people because of, not despite the fact that they care about democratic values. Similarly, what one would like to know about the Sandinistas is not the details of the latest elections, but the real work of neighborhood associations and the class composition of the bureaucracy. And one's enthusiasm about the passing of the military regimes in Argentina, Uruguay, and Brazil ought to be muted by the knowledge that those regimes had already established their point about the limits of parliamentary democracy: if broadly based social movements have a chance of succeeding under parliamentary rules, the rules will be changed.

Since the case for Marx's version of democracy is not esoteric, why isn't it taken more seriously? Mainly, no doubt, because of very direct limitations on the spectrum of respectable political ideas. Good words for the dictatorship of the proletariat sound pro-Soviet or worse (i.e., Stalinist). The pressure is especially strong because it is the democratic side of capitalism, not the economic side, which retains a capacity to inspire great numbers of people. In the United States, even though not many people regard themselves as socialists, not many hate the very idea of a collective economy or cherish the very idea of production by private firms.

Though ideological pressures and a real concern for what went wrong in Russia are more important causes, a certain style of thought about political power also plays a role in making it hard to take seriously the idea that a class dictatorship could be a worthy democratic ideal. We are used to dividing democratic values into two categories, Isaiah Berlin's positive and negative liberties or Benjamin Constant's freedom of the ancients and freedom of the moderns. On both sides of each divide, we take up the standpoint of someone who may be acting alone, pursuing goals in competition with others. The negative liberties proscribe interference with the individual's activities, when these activities are of certain general kinds. The positive liberties give the individual resources to pursue goals successfully. Of

---

[32] See Gabriel Almond and Sidney Verba, *The Civic Culture* (Boston: Little, Brown, 1965), esp. Chapters 1 and 13; and Jeane Kirkpatrick, "Dictatorships and Double Standards," *Commentary*, vol. 68 (November 1979), pp.34–45.

course, if no one wants to interfere, then negative liberty is redundant. And if the individual is only succeeding because of an arrangement of roles and resources in society at large, positive liberty is not directly involved. Though liberal democrats can certainly be socialists, a market analogy may make their competitive assumption clearer. Income is supposed to give me a positive liberty that laissez-faire protections would not provide. I have a resource to get what I want. But the actual structure of consumer preference is not a positive liberty, for me, though it may have considerable impact on my powers. *When we think of positive liberties we think of resources that an individual can, broadly speaking, own.* The existence of Saint Patrick's Day does not add to my positive liberty, as extra income would, although I owe to supermarket tactics around that day my ability to buy my favorite Irish marmalade at an affordable price.

Obviously, the dictatorship of the proletariat produces losses in negative liberties, that is, infringes general guarantees of non-interference by the state. Political theorists sympathetic to Marx are apt to claim overriding gains in positive liberty, i.e., in capacities to influence government in one's interest. No doubt, there would be some gains of this sort, say, if wall newspapers were a basic form of political communication, or police powers were delegated to block associations. But especially at the level of national policy, the gains are less dramatic. More precisely, devices that Marx takes, and plausibly so, to enhance democracy do not fit the category of positive liberty as it is usually conceived. Breaking the connection between political power and economic privilege is a gain in democracy. But my personal ability to influence policy would not be substantially enhanced if political leaders made no more than $25,000 a year. What could be changed thereby is the tendency of government to take some interests seriously, rather than others. Similarly, abolishing the standing army would not enhance a worker's ability to get her way in the face of opposition. But it might enhance the ability of people like her to get their way through the survival of a regime attending to their interests.

Positive and negative liberties are important. And the democratic values that do not fall in either category are still, in a real sense, individualist. If measures like those taken by the Paris Commune make society more democratic, this is because of changes in the lives of individuals, not just effects on abstract historical trends. But in thinking about democracy, as in other matters, we are apt to reason as if only gains in an individualistic *competitive* framework mattered. The resources that concern us are apt to be means of influence possessed by individuals, by which individuals can triumph over the powers and desires of others. In fact, most people may be missing democratic resources that no one can own.

Philosophy, Cornell University

SELF-OWNERSHIP, WORLD OWNERSHIP, AND EQUALITY: PART II

G.A. Cohen

I. INTRODUCTION

1. The present paper is a continuation of my "Self-Ownership, World Ownership, and Equality,"[1] which began with a description of the political philosophy of Robert Nozick. I contended in that essay that the foundational claim of Nozick's philosophy is the thesis of self-ownership, which says that each person is the morally rightful owner of his own person and powers, and, consequently, that each is free[2] (morally speaking) to use those powers as he wishes, provided that he does not deploy them aggressively against others. To be sure, he may not harm others, and he may, if necessary, be forced not to harm them, but he should never be forced to help them, as people are in fact forced to help others, according to Nozick, by redistributive taxation. (Nozick recognizes that an unhelping person may qualify as unpleasant or even, under certain conditions, as immoral. The self-ownership thesis says that people should be free to live their lives as they choose, but it does not say that how they choose to live them is beyond criticism.)

Now Nozick believes not only that people own themselves but also that they can become, with equally strong moral right, sovereign owners of the potentially indefinitely unequal amounts of worldly resources which they can gather to themselves as a result of proper exercises of their own and/or

---

* For improving comments on a previous version of this paper, I thank Ronald Dworkin, David Gordon, Alice Knight, Derek Parfit, John Roemer, Hilel Steiner, Steven Walt, and Erik Wright.

[1] That earlier paper appears in a volume of lectures delivered at the Leonard Symposium held at the University of Nevada at Reno in October, 1983, to be published by Cornell University Press, and edited by Frank Lucash. I shall henceforth refer to this article as "Self-Ownership: I." Most of "Self-Ownership: I" also appears in *New Left Review*, No. 150, March/April, 1985, under the title "Nozick on Appropriation."

[2] In so designating what is foundational and what is derivative in Nozick, I am denying that he thinks that freedom comes first and that, in order to be free, people should be self-owning. For he gives us no independent purchase on freedom which would enable us to tie freedom and self-ownership that way around. His real view is that the scope and nature of the freedom we should enjoy is a function of our self-ownership. That is why he does not regard the apparent unfreedom of the proletarian – see section 6 below – as a counterexample to his view that freedom prevails in capitalist society. For the proletarian forced daily to sell his labor power is nevertheless a self-owner, indeed must be one in order to sell it, and is, therefore, nevertheless free, in the relevant sense.

others' self-owned personal powers. When, moreover, private property in natural resources has been rightly generated, then its morally privileged origin insulates it against expropriation or limitation.

Now, a union of self-ownership and unequal distribution of worldly resources readily leads to indefinitely great inequality of private property in external goods of all kinds and, hence, to inequality of condition, on any view of what equality of condition is, be it equality of income, or of utility, or of well-being (if that is different from utility), or of need satisfaction (if that is different from each of those), or of something else yet again. It follows that inequality of condition is, when properly generated, morally protected, and that the attempt to promote equality of condition at the expense of private property is an unacceptable violation of peoples' rights. When people enjoy the freedom to which they are entitled, inequality is unavoidable.

Two kinds of response to Nozick were contrasted in "Self-Ownership: I." In the first, a premise that equality of condition is morally mandatory is used to deny his starting point, the thesis of self-ownership. But this first response (so I claimed) suffers from the defect that the idea of self-ownership has an initial appeal which so swiftly derived a rejection of it will not undermine. In work which goes beyond the present paper, I hope to undermine it in the more painstaking way I think is necessary. But here I investigate a second possible response to Nozick, which was described, but not explored, in "Self-Ownership: I." In this different response, equality of condition is not put as a premise, and the principle of self-ownership is not rejected, on that or any other basis. Instead, one strives to reconcile self-ownership with equality (or not too much inequality) of condition, by combining self-ownership with an egalitarian approach to worldly resources. The strategy is to concede to right-wing liberalism its more attractive thesis, which is its assertion of each person's rights over his own being and powers, while attacking its less plausible one, which is its view of the original moral relationship between people and things, the moral relationship, that is, between people and things which have not as yet been acted on by people.

In "Self-Ownership: I," I questioned Nozick's blithe assumption that such "virgin" things may be regarded as quite unowned and therefore (virtually) up for grabs; one scarcely need share that assumption *even* if one accepts that people are full owners of themselves. Now, the most radical alternative to the view that things are, in their native state, quite unowned, is to regard them as jointly or collectively owned by all persons. Part II of this paper studies an attempt to combine such a conception of the original moral relationship between people and things with the principle of self-ownership.

But, before embarking on that study, I should explain why the present paper appears in a volume devoted to the theme of Marxism and liberalism. The relationship of the paper's theme to liberalism will already be plain enough. Its relationship to Marxism will be more apparent in the light of a distinction between left-wing and right-wing liberalism, which I shall now proceed to draw.

Consider three types of entity over which a person might claim sovereignty or (what is here equivalent to it) exclusive private property: the resources of the external world; his own person and powers; and other people. Liberalism, to idealize one of its traditional senses, may be defined as the thesis that each person has full private property in himself (and, consequently, no private property in anyone else). He may do what he likes with himself provided that he does not harm others. Right-wing liberalism, of which Nozick is an exponent, adds, as we have seen, that self-owning persons can acquire equally strong moral rights in unequal amounts of external resources. Left-wing liberalism is, by contrast, egalitarian with respect to raw external resources: Henry George, Leon Walras, Herbert Spencer (at least in his earlier phase), and Hillel Steiner illustrate this position. Rawls and Dworkin are commonly accounted liberals, but here they must be called something else, such as social democrats, for they are not liberals in the traditional sense just defined, since they deny self-ownership in one important way. They say that, because it is a matter of brute luck that people have the talents they do, their talents do not, morally speaking, belong to them, but are, properly regarded, resources over which society as a whole may legitimately dispose.

Now, Marxists have failed to distinguish themselves from left-wing liberals with regard to two large issues. They have dealt with these issues as though it were unnecessary for them to reject liberalism as I have just defined it, but I think they cannot, in the end, avoid rejecting it, and one of the purposes of the present paper is to force upon them a recognition that they must do so.

The first issue is the critique of capitalist injustice. In the official Marxian version of that critique, the exploitation of workers by capitalists derives from the fact that workers lack access to physical productive resources and must therefore sell their labor power to capitalists, who enjoy a class monopoly in those resources. Hence, for Marxists, the injustice of capitalism is (ostensibly) a matter of unfairness with respect to rights in external things, and its exposure requires no denial of the liberal thesis of self-ownership. Unlike social democrats, who forthrightly conceive state intervention on behalf of the less well off as securing justified constrained helping, and who must therefore reject the thesis of self-ownership, Marxists affect to regard the badly off as not unlucky, but misused, forcibly dispossessed of the means of life and therefore harmed, and, under that construal of their plight, the demand for its redress needs no foundation stronger than left-wing liberalism.

The second issue is the nature of the ideal society. In the Marxist conception of it, external resources are communally owned, as in the leftest of left liberalisms, and the individual is effectively sovereign over himself (even if not as a matter of constitutional right), since the free development of each is, in the famous phrase, the condition of the free development of all. A premise of superabundance makes it unnecessary to press the talent of some into the service of the prosperity of others for the sake of equality of condition.

I argue in "Self-Ownership I"[3] that both the critique of capitalist exploitation and the defense of communist equality require denial of each person's full sovereignty over himself. Being egalitarians, Marxists must, in the end, abandon their flirtation with self-ownership: a combination of self-ownership and equality of external resources will not supply what Marxists demand. Since this paper discusses the consequences of various such combinations, it has a direct bearing on matters of central concern to Marxists.

II. REWARDS TO ABILITY AND INABILITY UNDER JOINT OWNERSHIP

2. We inquire here into the upshot of uniting self-ownership with joint ownership of the external world, with a view to shedding some light on the distributive effect of self-ownership in a world whose parts are not open to unilateral privatization.

For the sake of starkness, though at the possible expense of generality, imagine a society of two people, who are called Able and Infirm, after their respective natural endowments. Each owns himself and both jointly own everything else. With suitable external resources, Able can produce life-sustaining and life-enhancing goods, but Infirm has no productive power at all. We suppose that each is rational, self-interested, and mutually disinterested (devoid, that is, of spite, benevolence, and all other motivations into which the welfare of others enters essentially), and we ask what scheme of production and distribution they will agree on. We thereby investigate the reward which self-owned ability would command in one kind of world without private property.

Now, what Able and Infirm get depend not only on their own powers and decisions but also on what the world is like, materially speaking. Five mutually exclusive and jointly exhaustive possible material situations, not all of which are interesting, may readily be distinguished:

    i. Able cannot produce per day what is needed for one person for a day, so Able and Infirm both die.

[3] See Part I of "Self-Ownership: I."

ii. Able can produce enough or more than enough for one person, but not enough for two. Infirm lets Able produce what he can, since only spite or envy would lead him not to. Able lives and Infirm dies.

iii. Able can produce just enough to sustain both himself and Infirm. So Infirm forbids him to produce unless he produces that much. Able consequently does, and both live at subsistence.

iv. If Able produces at all, then the amount he produces is determined independently of his choice, and it exceeds what is needed to sustain both Able and Infirm. They therefore bargain over the distribution of a fixed surplus. The price of failure to agree (the "break point") is no production, and, therefore, death for both.

v. Again, Able can produce a surplus, but now, more realistically, he can vary its size, so that Able and Infirm will bargain not only, as in iv, over who gets how much, but also over how much will be produced.

The interesting cases are iv and v, in which bargains will be struck.[4] It is a controversial question, in the relevant philosophical and technical literature, what one should expect the outcome of such bargaining to be. But it seems clear that the inputs to the bargaining process will be what are called the utility functions of Able and Infirm, including the disutility of labor for Able and the disutility of infirmity for Infirm. What will matter, in other and less technical words, is their preferences, what they like and dislike, and how much. And the crucial point is that Able's talent will not, just as such, affect how much he gets. If the exercise of his talent is irksome to him, then he will indeed get additional compensation, but only because he is irked, not because it is his labor which irks him. In short, he gets nothing extra just because it is he, and not Infirm, who does the producing. Infirm controls one necessary condition of production (relaxing his veto over use of the land), and Able controls two, but that gives Able no bargaining advantage. If a good costs $101, and you have one hundred of the dollars and I only one of them, then, if we are each rational and self-interested, you will not get a greater share of the good if we buy it jointly, just because you supply so much more of what is required to obtain it.

Here, then, joint world ownership prevents self-ownership from generating an inequality to which egalitarians would object, and while the Able and Infirm story is an extremely special one in several respects, the particular point that talent as such yields no extra reward even under self-ownership where there is also joint ownership of external resources is, one would think, generalizable. (I do not say that no inequality repugnant to egalitarians can arise in the Able/Infirm situation, but only that either there will be no such

---

[4] I am supposing that it is not open to Able to wait until Infirm dies in order to become the sole owner of everything: assume that he would himself die no later than Infirm does in the absence of production.

inequality, or its source will not be Able's ownership of his own powers, but the influence of the parties' utility functions on the outcome of the bargaining process.)

3. In section 4 I shall describe a seemingly fatal objection to the argument of section 2, and one from which, as I try to show in section 6, we can learn a great deal. But here, somewhat digressively, I develop a relatively minor objection to the argument, and one which, I am embarrassed to say, I lack the competence to assess with assurance.

The objection questions the claim that self-ownership has no unequalizing effect in a jointly owned world. The following model may be used to develop the objection. Consider two sets of farmers. Members of the first set own all the land jointly. Members of the second set each own some land privately, in varying amounts, but in no case enough to live off, and all jointly own a further tract of land. Talent and fertility are such that the material position for each set of farmers is a multi-person version of either iv or v of section 2. If I am right in section 2, then the upshots of bargaining under the two distributions should be identical whenever the material possibilities are the same.

The objection is that a farmer in the second set could threaten to destroy (part of) his private plot, whereas no one can threaten to destroy anything which is held jointly. If such threats would be credible, then it seems that privately well-endowed farmers could assert leverage over privately less well-endowed farmers. And if they could do so, then so could Able in the case, not excluded above, in which he has it in his power to let (part of) his talent decay. What I do not know how to assess, because of my uncertain grasp of bargaining theory, is whether such a Schellingian[5] threat would be credible and therefore effective *under the assumption that everyone is rational*. If it would be, then those with greater power to produce could get more in a jointly owned world for reasons which go beyond the consideration that their labor might be irksome to them.

But this objection to the argument of section 2 is, as I said, relatively minor, even if it is sound. One reason why it is minor is that it achieves purchase only in the rather peculiar case in which Able can indeed diminish his own productive power. But a more important reason for considering the objection secondary is that no right-winger would want to defeat the Able/Infirm argument on so adventitious a basis. He would want, instead, to overcome it by pressing the more fundamental objection to which I now turn.

4. Whatever should be said about the objection of section 3, there remains a deeper and seemingly fatal objection to the lesson drawn in section 2 from the Able/Infirm story. That lesson is that, without denying self-

---

[5] See Thomas Schelling, *Strategy of Conflict* (New York: Oxford University Press, 1960).

ownership, and without affirming equality of condition as an underived principle, one may move towards a form of equality of conditon by insisting on joint ownership of the external world. And the seemingly fatal objection is that to affirm joint ownership of the world is, as the story of Able and Infirm might be thought to show, inconsistent with preservation of self-ownership. For how can I be said to own myself if I may do nothing without the agreement of others? Do not Able and Infirm jointly own not only the world but also, at least in effect, each other? Does not joint world ownership entitle a person to prohibit another's wholly harmless use of an external resource, such as taking some water from a superabundant stream,[6] and is it not, therefore, inconsistent with the most minimal self-ownership (and independently indefensible to boot)? It looks as though the suggested form of external resource equality, namely, joint world ownership, cancels the self-ownership with which we had hoped to combine it.

There are two possible replies to the objection that self-ownership lacks substance when it is combined with joint ownership of the world. The first, which is neither interesting not promising, and which is explored in section 5, is to argue that joint world ownership does not, in fact, deprive self-ownership of all substance, since, to put the point crudely, economics isn't everything. The second reply, which I regard as both correct and very important, and which is mounted in section 6, is to accept that joint world ownership renders self-ownership merely formal, while showing, however, that present polemical purposes do not require it to be anything more than that.

5. The first reply says that people have vital interests in matters other than production and the distribution of its fruits, matters on which joint world ownership might have no, or only a reduced, bearing. It would then be false that joint world ownership would, consequently, render individual self-ownership nugatory.

But this reply seems to be incompatible with the fact that all human action requires space, which is jointly owned if the world is.[7] (Even the mental activity of an immobile agent requires the space he occupies.) Or, if that is thought farfetched, then consider, instead, that all human action requires nourishment, which requires food, which comes from the external world. It seems to follow that a universal veto on what anyone may do with the external world affects every department of life, and not just the domain of

---

[6] This is John Locke's example; see his *Second Treatise of Government*, paragraph 33, and "Self-Ownership: I," for a discussion of it.

[7] On the importance of space as a resource, see my *Karl Marx's Theory of History*, Oxford and Princeton, 1978, pp.50–52. For strong claims about the relationship between freedom and rights over space, see Hillel Steiner, "Individual Liberty", *Proceedings of the Aristotelian Society*, 1974–5, pp.44ff.

production. It looks, indeed, as though joint world ownership fully determines the outcome, whatever may be laid down officially about who owns whose powers.[8] Assume, for example, that everyone jointly owns everyone's powers. Will they not then negotiate with each other exactly as they would if each officially owned himself, as long as the external world is jointly owned by all?

There is, perhaps, one "action" which could be performed without the permission of others in a jointly owned world as long as there is self-ownership, and possibly not without it, namely, letting oneself die: in the absence of self-ownership one has noncontractual obligations which might preclude letting oneself die without their permission. (I speak of letting oneself die rather than of (other forms of) suicide, since active suicide might require external resources, and letting oneself die is achieved by refraining from using any.) But even this suggestion may be incorrect, since the world's joint owners might be thought to have the right to forbid one to die on the ground that one's dead body might pollute some of the world's resources.

6. But now let us recall our polemical task, which is to address Robert Nozick's contention that honoring people's self-ownership requires extending to them a freedom to live their own lives which is incompatible with the equality of condition prized by socialists. The recently suggested response to that contention was that self-ownership is, contrary to what Nozick says, compatible with equality of condition, since the inequality which Nozick defends depends on adjoining to self-ownership an inegalitarian principle of external resource distribution, which need not be accepted. When, instead, self-ownership is combined with joint ownership of the world, its tendency to generate inequality is removed.

The objection to that response (see section 4) was that the resource distribution under joint world ownership renders the self-ownership with which it is officialy combined merely formal. *But that objection would, for immediate polemical purposes, be laid to rest, if it could be shown that the self-ownership defended by Nozick is itself merely formal,* for he could not then maintain that what he defends generates inequality of condition.

To be sure, Nozick would like us to think, what he evidently himself thinks, that the self-ownership he favors is more than merely formal. In Chapter III of *Anarchy, State and Utopia* he pleads that each person should be

---

[8] If, that is, the joint world ownership is itself substantive rather than merely official. For consider a regime in which a person P owns both himself and everyone else, with all other resources being in joint ownership. Then either that joint ownership remains real (because P's ownership of everyone is truly consistent with their exercise of rights over things), in which case the statement in the text applies; or the joint world ownership is itself unreal. I provisionally conclude, pending further possible counterexamples, that joint world ownership either fully determines the outcome, rendering other provisions merely official, or is itself merely official.

free to live his own life, a *desideratum* which is supposed to be secured by the rights constituting Nozickian self-ownership.[9] But Nozick also thinks that the circumstances of the most abject proletarian – call him "Z"[10] – who must either sell his labor power to a capitalist or die, is consistent with nonviolation of the relevant rights.[11] And if that is so, then Nozick could not object that Able's self-ownership is merely formal, since, whether or not it is indeed merely formal, it is not less substantive than Z's.

If Able and Z lack substantive self-ownership, then that is because neither can do anything without the agreement of Infirm and the capitalist, respectively. But they are, nevertheless, different from chattel slaves. For while each can do nothing without another's agreement, it is also true that there is nothing which either need do without his own agreement: neither Infirm nor the capitalist has rights of sheer command which are not grounded in a prior contract to obey. By contrast, the slave's master may unilaterally determine what the slave must do.

The resulting dilemma for Nozick is severe. Either capitalism does not preserve true self-ownership, since Z's self-ownership is not robust enough to qualify as such; or, if it does so qualify, then true self-ownership allows the enforcement of equality of condition, since Able's self-ownership is at least as robust as Z's, and no inequality follows from self-ownership in the Able/Infirm world.

Notice, moreover, that both Able and Infirm are in one respect far better placed than Z is. For each of Able and Infirm must strike an agreement with the other in order to survive, and, since both are rational, it follows that the

---

[9] See *Anarchy, State and Utopia* (New York: Basic Books, 1974) pp.28–35 (on side constraints) and pp. 42–45, 48–51 (on leading one's own life).

[10] After Nozick, *op. cit.*, pp.262–4, for a critique of which see my "Robert Nozick and Wilt Chamberlain," J. Arthur and W. Shaw, eds., *Justice and Economic Distribution* (Englewood Cliffs, 1978), pp.257–60; "Freedom, Justice, and Capitalism," *New Left Review*, No. 126 (March–April 1981), pp.8–11; "Illusions About Private Property and Freedom", John Mepham and David Ruben, eds., *Issues in Marxist Philosophy*, (Hassocks, Sussex: Harvester Press, 1981) pp.226–239.

[11] Z is abject because he owns no private property, and he will therefore contract, on adverse terms, with someone who does own some, if he can find a propertied person willing to contract with him. His predicament might be thought dire, but Nozick does not think that he has a just grievance. For a propertyless person has a grievance, in Nozick's view, only if his propertylessness renders him worse off than he would have been had the world remained in Lockean common ownership, without private property, and Nozick believes that proletarians are unlikely to be, in that way, worse off. He would say, of those propertyless persons who do manage to sell their labor power, that they will get at least as much and probably more in exchange for it than they could have hoped to get by applying it in a Lockean state of nature; and, of those propertyless persons whose labor power is not worth buying, that, although they might therefore, in Nozick's non-welfare state, die, they would have died in the state of nature anyway.

See Part II of "Self-Ownership: I" for an extended critique of Nozick's way of testing whether propertyless persons have a just grievance.

survival of each is assured. By contrast, no capitalist need strike an agreement with Z in order to survive,[12] and Z's very survival is, therefore, not guaranteed.

To put the main point differently: Nozick says that a propensity to inequality is unavoidable when people are allowed to live their own lives. Yet he must hold that, despite the constraints on his life choices, and despite his adverse power position vis-à-vis others, Z leads his own life. But it then follows that Nozick is wrong that, when people lead their own lives, equality of condition cannot be guaranteed, since Able and Infirm lead their own lives at least as much as Z does, and the constitution under which they live guarantees a certain equality of condition.

At the beginning of this paper, I said that it was a strength in Nozick's position that the thesis of self-ownership was inherently appealing. But what exactly, we should now ask, possesses appeal for us; what sort of self-ownership do we feel moved to insist that people should enjoy? Is it (i) merely formal self-ownership, that bare bourgeois freedom which distinguishes the most abject proletarian from a slave, or is it (ii) a more substantive self-ownership which we can associate with the idea of controlling one's life? If (i) is the right answer, then we win both the polemic against Nozick and the larger struggle to reconcile socialist equality with the liberty which (almost) everyone favors. But I think most of us believe that people should have more sovereignty over themselves than either Able or the proletarian enjoy. This does not, of course, rescue Nozick. On the contrary: whereas it seemed that right-wing liberalism had the virtue of affirming self-ownership, it now turns out that it refuses to affirm self-ownership of an attractive kind. But it is also true, for similar reasons, that socialists should not favor joint world ownership. If they want to equalize rights over external resources, they must find another way of doing so.

The natural next step is to ask what kind and degree of control over external things each person must have to enjoy the self-ownership most of us believe in, and then to ask whether self-ownership united with such control is compatible with socialist equality. These questions compose a real challenge to contemporary left-wing political philosophy, even after Nozick has been set aside. The freedom of which he speaks, which turns out to be a very confined freedom, can be reconciled with equality, but it remains to be shown that socialist equality can be reconciled with a freedom more worthy of the name.

I do not here pursue the project described in the foregoing paragraph. But I would like to mention what I feel certain would be one of its results. It is

[12] Some would question this contrast between the capitalist and the worker. I defend it in section XIII of "The Structure of Proletarian Unfreedom," *Philosophy and Public Affairs*, vol. 12 (Winter 1983), pp.20–23.

that a defensible socialist constitution must contain a bill of individual rights, which specifies things which the community cannot do to, or demand of, any individual. To those who say that socialism is, or could lead to, tyranny, socialists often reply that, on the contrary, socialism is complete democracy, that it brings within the ambit of democratic decision issues about production and consumption which capitalism excludes from the public agenda. That reply, I now think, is markedly unsatisfactory. For socialist democratic decisions require either a unanimous or a majority vote. If they require unanimity, then a rightless socialist constitution negates substantive self-ownership, as the Able/Infirm story shows. And majority vote without a bill of rights also legitimates unacceptable tyranny over the individual.

Much more must be said about specifically socialist constitutions, but here I leave that task for another occasion. We now move, instead, to Part III, in which I study a constitution which institutes a form of equality of resources which unquestionably preserves self-ownership, without, however, protecting equality of condition.

III. THE STEINER CONSTITUTION

7. Let us now take stock. In "Self-Ownership: I" I urged that two theses had an initial intuitive appeal: first, that each person has the right to dispose of himself as he pleases, provided that he does not harm any one else, and second, that the resources of the commonly inhabited external world should be treated in an egalitarian fashion. This suggested the project of identifying an economic constitution which was faithful to the stated intuitions and which might yield something like a socialist equality of condition. To clear the way for that project "Self-Ownership: I" subjected Nozick's theory of appropriation, which rejects the second intuitive thesis, to a scrutiny from which it emerged multiply scathed.

I have just considered a more egalitarian view of the original moral relationship of persons to things, one in which no one can operate with them without the consent of all, namely, joint ownership. It seems, however, that joint ownership of the world is inconsistent with substantive personal rights of a kind we all cherish (though not with the right-wing construal of those rights). If so, I have up to now failed to describe a constitution which is true to both self-ownership and worldly egalitarian intuitions.

A different economic constitution, which does seem to preserve both intuitions, combines self-ownership with private ownership of initially equal parts of the world's resources. Unlike joint ownership, which forbids a Nozickian formation of unequal private property by placing all resources under collective control, the new proposal, which I shall call the Steiner constitution,[13] institutes private property from the start, but it forbids the inegalitarian Nozickian scramble by privatizing resources in an initially equal division. The Steiner constitution is not Ronald Dworkin's constitution, which Dworkin calls "Equality of Resources," since Steiner equalizes external resources only, whereas Dworkin also favors an equalizing compensation for inequality of personal talent.[14] In fact, and as we shall see in section 9, Dworkin contends, in my view unsuccessfully, that a constitution of the Steiner type is incapable of consistent justification.

At first blush, joint ownership and equal division look to be equally egalitarian ways of treating external resources, but, whether or not they really are both egalitarian and equally so, their outcomes are utterly different. Consider, again, Infirm and Able. Suppose that Steiner is in force, so that each owns an equal amount of land. Suppose, further, that Able could work both plots of land and thereby produce more than enough to sustain both himself and Infirm, and that Able can also produce at least enough to sustain himself by working his own land only. Then Able's precontractual "breakpoint" would be much higher than Infirm's: Infirm's would be death, but Able's would be whatever standard of living he could achieve by working his own land only. If, then, Able contracts to support Infirm in return for some of the product of working Infirm's land, he is likely to supply Infirm with his subsistence only, since he has Infirm over a barrel. And if the product Able could keep for himself after tilling Infirm's land is not, in his view, worth the additional labor he must spend to get it, then Able will let Infirm die.[15] So in this case, and, no doubt, generally, joint ownership is kinder than equal division to the less able. Note, further, that Infirm would fare even worse under Lockean common ownership. Common ownership would allow Able to till as much land as he wished without giving Infirm anything, and, unlike the Steiner constitution, would endow Infirm with nothing to offer Able in return for Able's support.

Notice that, under many circumstances, equal division will generate capitalism. If people's talents and/or luck are sufficiently unequal, relatively high fliers might so transform their original shares that they could profitably hire others to work on them at wages superior to what those others could

---

[13] I so name it because it is Hillel Steiner's solution to the problem of justice in distribution when the issue of successive generations, which I do not address here, is set aside. See Hillel Steiner, "The Natural Right to the Means of Production," *Philosophical Quarterly*, vol. 27 (1977), pp.48–49.

[14] I do not know whether Dworkin thinks that the equalizing compensation ought, if possible, to be total. These pages of "Equality of Resources,"*Philosophy and Public Affairs*, vol. 10, no. 4 (Fall 1981) suggest more than one anwer to that question: pp.299, 301, 327, 337.

[15] I suppose, once again (see footnote 4), that Able may not wait until Infirm dies in order to pick up his share. Suppose that Infirm forestalls that by designating his land as his burial plot.

glean from working their own resources. Low fliers would then have reason to sell their shares to their more fortunate brethren and become their wage laborers.[16] By contrast, joint ownership turns into capitalism only if every joint owner agrees that it should, or agrees to an equal (or other) division out of which capitalism develops. And capitalist societies which develop out of an initially equal division will tend to display more inequality (or display the same inequality sooner) than those capitalist arrangements with joint ownership in their prehistory, even if both sorts will also tend to display less inequality than those growing out of Nozickian appropriation.

Unlike joint ownership, equal division does not guarantee subsistence for Infirm, even when that is materially possible, and it therefore contradicts a basic welfare state principle. Equal division under self-ownership must therefore be unacceptable to anyone who believes in even a minimally demanding principle of equality of condition, and *perhaps* it could therefore be argued that equal division does not, in fact, respect the egalitarian intuition about external resources.[17] But, however that may be, self-ownership together with equal division will not yield the equality of condition prized by socialists. And since joint ownership, which might yield that equality, rules out the substantive personal rights definitive of self-ownership, a constitution of the sort I described in section I, combining self-ownership with equality of worldly resources and securing equality of condition, has not been discovered here.

8. A comparative examination of the convertibility into one another of equal division (ED) and joint ownership (JO) constitutions supports the view that, *if* self-ownership is to be maintained, then ED is the preferable form of external resource equality. What follows is not intended as a case for ED over JO *tout court*, though some of it might also be so viewed, but only for ED

---

[16] There is less tendency to such an upshot when the greater talent of more productive people cannot be developed, and/or exercised to differentially productive effect, except as a result of a division of labor in which less productive people are essential participants. But socialists and left-wing liberals are inclined to exaggerate the extent to which that is likely to be so.

   For a set of statements urging some such dependence of the more on the less productive, see William Galston, *Justice and the Human Good* (Chicago: University of Chicago Press, 1980), pp.207, 211–12; and two authors he quotes: David Miller, *Social Justice* (Oxford: Clarendon Press, 1976), pp.105–06; and Leonard Hobhouse, *The Elements of Social Justice* (London: George Allen and Unwin Ltd., 1922), pp.140–41. Part of the claim is nicely put by Bishop Latour in Willa Cather's *Death Comes for the Archibishop* (New York: Alfred A. Knopf, 1927). He says to his friend, the excellent cook, Father Joseph Vaillant: "I am not deprecating your individual talent, Joseph . . . but, when one thinks of it, a soup like this is not the work of one man. It is the result of a constantly refined tradition. There are nearly one thousand years of history in this soup" (p.39). For a persuasive attempt to block inferences which socialists might wish to draw from Bishop Latour's observation, see Robert Nozick, *Anarchy, State, and Utopia*, p.95.

[17] For an implicit claim to that effect, see the axiomatization of self-ownership with external resource equality offered by John Roemer in section 3 of his unpublished "Public Ownership and the Private Property Externalty," November 1984.

over JO *given* that people are regarded as sovereign over their own powers.

Where there is unanimous preference for the other constitution, either of JO and ED may readily be converted into the other. If everyone under JO wants ED, they will simply divide the jointly owned resources. And if everyone under ED wants JO, they will simply pool what they seperately own. Neither system has a convertibility advantage over the other under unanimous preference for the alternative system, when transaction costs are ignored (as they surely should be at the present level of reflection). But what if some but not all under ED want JO, or some but not all under JO want ED?

Under ED the some who want JO will not get it. They will not, that is, get full joint ownership of everything by everybody, since some will keep their separate shares. But those who want JO could join with all those who want to join with them in a less than comprehensive joint ownership: call it VJO (V for voluntary). Now, not all of those who want JO will want VJO as much as they do JO, or even at all. Do they therefore have a grievance against the ED starting point? Can they say that those who want ED get what they want but those who want JO do not? No, for the proper parallel to someone who wants comprehensive JO is someone who wants comprehensive ED, and he is not guaranteed what he wants under ED either (since ED makes VJO possible). If those who want JO go into VJO, then neither they nor those who want comprehensive ED get what they want. But both groups fail to get what they want because others make choices which a believer in substantive self-ownership would defend their right to make.

If, on the other hand, there is JO at the beginning, then it persists as long as just one person wants it to, and that seems inconsistent with regarding the others as self-owners. One could, of course, begin with a JO under which anyone would be entitled to leave with an aliquot share of total external resources. But to add such an entitlement to JO is, when transaction costs are ignored, to turn it into ED: JO with the right to contract out is equivalent to ED, since ED permits each to contract into JO or VJO.

The conclusion seems to be that, if one begins with a commitment to both self-ownership and equality of external resources, and one has to choose between JO and ED, then the natural way to realize external resources equality is through ED rather than through JO. To go for JO would probably reflect a belief, prejudicial to self-ownership, that people should be endowed with rights which enable them to benefit from (the fruits of) the personal powers of others.

IV. DWORKIN ON STEINER

9. The Steiner constitution unites self-ownership with an equal division of external resources (only), and therefore implements what Ronald Dworkin calls "the starting gate theory of justice," which he wrongly supposes may readily be dismissed.[18]

Before I address Dworkin's case against the starting gate theory, it will be useful to relate the concerns of the present paper to those of his magisterial articles on equality.[19] The Dworkin articles define a distinction between equality of welfare, which Dworkin rejects, and equality of resources, which he favors. That distinction is orthogonal to the one which has exercised me here, which is between personal and worldly endowments. An egalitarian view of worldly resources may be attached to an egalitarian view of personal powers, or, instead, as in Steiner, to a view which represents them as self-owned. If one takes, as Dworkin does, a doubly egalitarian view, then one may, as he shows, develop that view either as an egalitarianism of welfare or as an egalitarianism of (all) resources. Whichever way one develops it, no one owns anything as of basic moral right, and things and persons are so arranged as to equalize either welfare or share in total resources. But if, like Steiner, one restricts one's egalitarianism to worldly resources, then, too, one might develop the egalitarian component either as an egalitarianism of welfare or as an egalitarianism of resources. One way to implement the second alternative is to divide external resources equally[20] and then let people do what they want with them. The first alternative, to wit, welfare egalitarianism with respect to external resources only, might seem incoherent, but John Roemer has provided a compelling axiomatic sketch of it in a recent inventive paper.[21]

Thus, Dworkin's distinction between welfare and resources egalitarianism, and my distinction between comprehensive egalitarianism and egalitarianism with respect to external resources only, generate, when they are put together, the following four-fold classification of views:

---

[18] See Dworkin, *op. cit.*, pp. 309–10.
[19] "Equality of Resources" was preceded by "Equality of Welfare," *Philosophy and Public Affairs*, vol. 10, no. 3 (Summer 1981).
[20] By means, for example, of the initial auction described by Dworkin at pp.286–90 of "Equality of Resources·"
[21] See footnote 17 above. Two of Roemer's axioms are that (1) Nobody's welfare declines if all retain the same skill as before and the amount of land increases and (2) If A has at least as much skill as B, then he has at least as much welfare as B. Such axioms are, intuitively, pretty evident, on a welfarist interpretation of self-ownership and worldly resource equality.

	Welfare Egalitarianism	*Resources Egalitarianism*
with respect to all resources	comprehensive welfare egalitarianism (e.g., as described by Dworkin)	comprehensive resources egalitarianism (e.g., as espoused by Dworkin)
with respect to external resources only	partial welfare egalitarianism (e.g., as axiomatized by Roemer)	partial resources egalitarianism (e.g., as espoused by Steiner)

Dworkin empahsizes the distinction separating the columns of the above table, but he gives short shrift to the distinction which separates its rows. He does not bring the bottom row into clear focus, and he therefore does not deal successfully with its right-hand side, which is tantamount to what he calls the "starting gate theory," a theory whose fairly obvious rationale eludes him. The starting gate theory "holds that justice requires equal initial resources" and "laissez-faire thereafter." It says that "if people start in the same circumstances and do not cheat or steal from one another, then it is fair that people keep what they gain through their own skill." This, says Dworkin, is "hardly coherent political theory at all." It is "an indefensible combination of very different theories of justice": for Dworkin, an initial equality is justifiable if and only if it is justifiable to perserve equality throughout.

But Dworkin misjudges the motivation for the starting gate theory. He is wrong that the laissez-faire component depends on "some version of the Lockean theory that people acquire property by mixing their labor with goods or something of the sort," and that a similar approach should, therefore, apply at the beginning, that consistency requires Lockean or Nozickian acquisition then, rather than an equal division of resources. It is, I shall argue, false that "the moment when the immigrants first land is . . . an arbitrary point in their lives at which to locate any one-shot requirement that they each have an equal share of any available resources."[22]

The laissez-faire component in the starting gate theory cannot be grounded in Locke's theory that people acquire property by mixing their labor with things, since starting gate's laissez-faire begins only once all external resources have been distributed, and it is then too late to acquire title in something by mixing one's labor with it. Labor mixture secures title, for Locke, only in what is not yet owned, and there is nothing unowned with

---

[22] All quotations in the foregoing two paragraphs are from "Equality of Resources," p.309.

which to mix one's labor once the initial equal division external resources has been effected.

Dworkin represents Locke as holding that labor secures title because it joins what the laborer works on to something he already owns, to wit, his labor. I think that is a correct exegesis of Locke. But some think that, for Locke, laboring on something makes it one's own not (only) for the stated reason, but when and because, by laboring on it, one thereby enhances its value.[23] And *some* such consideration might indeed be used to justify the laissez-faire component in the starting gate theory. But one who drew upon it would not, I shall argue, be thereby committed against an initial equal division.

Note that what I shall call the "value argument" is truly different from the argument from labor mixture, even though many (and sometimes, perhaps, Locke[24]) are prone to confuse the two. If you own what you labored on because your labor is in it, then you do not own it because you have enhanced its value, even if what deserves to be called "labor" necessarily creates value. And, for the value argument, it is the conferring of value itself, not the labor by which it is conferred, which is essential: if you magically enhanced something's value without laboring, but, say, by wishing that it was more valuable, then, on the value argument, you would be entitled to whatever that argument justifies you in having.

Locke's principal labor mixture paragraphs do not, in my view, invoke the consideration that labor enhances the value of that to which it is applied.[25] And Karl Olivecrona may be right that when, in later paragraphs, Locke does bring value enhancement to the fore, he is not trying to justify the initial appropriation of private property.[26] According to Olivecrona, Locke is there, instead, justifying the extensive inequality of goods that comes to obtain long after original appropriation has ceased. His justification is that almost all of the value of what is now so unequally distributed is due not to any unequal initial appropriating but to the labor which followed long after initial appropriation.

So construed – not, that is, as a justification for original appropriation – the value argument might indeed be used to justify the inequality generated by laissez-faire, the justification of it being that labor is responsible for (almost all of) the value difference in which that inequality inheres. But it is perfectly consistent to propound that defense of laissez-faire inequality while

---

[23] For an extended discussion of Locke on labor's value-creating power, see my *Marx and Locke on Land and Labour*, forthcoming.

[24] See *ibid.*

[25] See *ibid.*

[26] See Karl Olivecrona, "Locke's theory of Appropriation," *Philosophical Quarterly*, vol. 24 (July 1974), pp.231–233.

yet insisting on an equal division at the outset of the resources for whose value no one's labor is responsible. Indeed, if labor's value-creating power is the basic justification of the inequality brought about by laissez-faire, then an initial equal division of external resources is not merely consistent with, but also a natural prelude to, laissez-faire, since no one creates the value of raw natural resources.

To conclude: if what matters about labor is that it annexes something already owned to something unowned, then labor plays no part in justifying the laissez-faire component in the starting gate theory, since everything is already owned once laissez-faire begins. And if what matters about labor is that it adds value, then it might indeed justify the laissez-faire component, but without having inegalitarian implications for the distribution of raw resources. To be sure, one *might* contrive a (not very good) argument for original appropriation by reference to labor's value-creating power, but one is not *committed* to endorsing such an argument when one justifies inequalities which arise *after* appropriation by arguing that labor brought them about. It is, then, false that

> the theory of Lockean acquisition (or whatever other theory of justice in acquisition is supposed to justify the laissez-faire component in a starting gate theory) can have no less force in governing the initial distribution than it has in justifying title through talent.[27]

Now, the true foundation of the starting gate theory is the contrast between persons and worldly resources as possible objects of rights and egalitarian dispensation. When no external resources have as yet been acted upon by anyone, it is reasonable to think that no one has more right to them than anyone else does, and one compelling way of instituting equal rights in them is by conducting Dworkin's auction. But it is not so evidently reasonable to suppose, similarly, that no one has, to begin with, more right than anyone else over the powers of given people. And if one also thinks that each individual has the right to decide what to do with his own powers, and one then – surely not inconsistently – combines that thought with external resources egalitarianism, the upshot is the "starting gate theory."

The fundamental distinction for the starting gate theory is not between what is appropriate at the beginning and what is appropriate later. The theory gets framed that way only on the supposition that all external resources are to hand at the outset. If that is false, and some of them come forward later, by rising out of the sea, or as a consequence of exploration,

[27] Dworkin, "Equality of Resources," p.309.

then the so-called (and essentially misnamed) starting gate theory requires a supplementary equal division rather than a Nozickian free-for-all. "The moment when the immigrants first land" is not, therefore, "an arbitrary point" at which to insist on equality. It is unarbitrary in virtue of the auxiliary assumption that all the external resources that there are going to be are already available.

The combination of initial equality and subsequent unequalizing competition which, Dworkin claims, "cannot hold together a political theory," makes sense, he thinks, in the game of Monopoly, "whose point is to allow luck and skill a highly circumscribed and, in the last analysis, arbitrary role."[28] Now, whatever Dworkin means (I find the statement baffling) when he says that part of the point of Monopoly is to allow skill to play an arbitrary role, consider instead a different game, which models the "starting gate theory" rather more accurately, and indeed gives it its name, to wit, some sort of track race. One may find a political theory which takes that as a suitable model for distributive justice repugnant. One may think that the Coes and Ovetts and Chamberlains in the game of life should not receive high rewards because of their God- or nature-given talents. But then one must contend with intelligible qualms about people's rights over their own powers, which Dworkin ignores. The normative stance of the left would be easier to sustain if the starting gate theory were simply incoherent. But it is not.

IV CONCLUSION

10. It is a familiar right-wing claim that freedom and equality are conflicting ideals, and that, to the extent that they conflict, freedom should be preferred to equality. Robert Nozick presses a particular version of the claim when he argues that people's rights over themselves exclude any kind of equality of condition.

I have shown, in section 6 above, that Nozick's version of the claim that freedom and equality are inconsistent cannot be sustained. Under joint ownership of the world's resources, everyone can enjoy the rights constituting Nozickian self-ownership without prejudice to the maintenance of equality of condition.

I have not, however, shown that there is *no* conflict between freedom and equality for leftists to worry about. Socialists can preserve the freedom offered by Nozick and also promote equality, but that is because Nozick does not offer real freedom. If we set Nozick aside, then we must admit that some

[28] *ibid.*, p.310.

(not necessarily drastic) limitation of people's rights in their own powers, or to the fruits of their exercise, is necessary to maintain (even rough) equality of condition. I hope to discuss the needed limitations in future work.

Philosophy and Politics, Oxford University

SELF-REALIZATION IN WORK AND POLITICS:
The Marxist Conception of the Good Life

JON ELSTER

I. INTRODUCTION

In arguments in support of capitalism, the following propositions are sometimes advanced or presupposed: (i) the best life for the individual is one of consumption, understood in a broad sense that includes aesthetic pleasures and entertainment as well as consumption of goods in the ordinary sense; (ii) consumption is to be valued because it promotes happiness or welfare, which is the ultimate good; (iii) since there are not enough opportunities for consumption to provide satiation for everybody, some principles of distributive justice must be chosen to decide who gets what; (iv) the total to be distributed has first to be produced. What is produced depends, among other things, on the motivation and information of the producers. The theory of justice must take account of the fact that different principles of distribution have different effects on motivation and information; (v) economic theory tells us that the motivational and informational consequences of private ownership of the means of production are superior to those of the various forms of collective ownerships.

In the traditional controversy over the relative merits of capitalism and economic systems, the focus has been on proposition (v). In this paper, I consider instead propositions (i) and (ii). Before one can even begin to discuss how values are to be allocated, one must consider what they are – what it is that ought to be valued. I shall argue that at the center of Marxism is a specific conception of the good life as one of active self-realization, rather than passive consumption.[1] It is a conception that, with various qualifications and modifications, I am also going to defend by arguing that self-realization is superior to consumption both on welfarist and on nonwelfarist grounds.[2]

* I am grateful to my colleagues in the project "Work and social justice" at the Institution for Social Research for their comments on earlier drafts of this paper. Special thanks are due to Fredrik Engelstad for his guidance in the literature on work satisfaction.
[1] The broader interpretation of Marx that sustains this assertion is set forward in my *Making Sense of Marx* (Cambridge: Cambridge University Press, 1985).
[2] For the notion of welfarism, see Amartya Sen, "Welfarism and Utilitarianism," *Journal of Philosophy*, vol. 76 (1979), pp.463–488.

It ought to be noted, before I proceed, that it is far from obvious that political theory ought to be concerned with determining the proper conception of the good life. John Rawls argues, for instance, that the goal of political philosophy is to determine the just distribution of "primary goods," i.e., the goods that everyone would want in order to realize his or her own conception of the good life.[3] It would be unjustified paternalism if the state were to intervene in order to promote a special conception of the good by influencing the availability of various options or trying to foster the desire for some rather than others.

I have much sympathy for this liberal argument. The idea that someone else than the persons concerned knows what is best for them has a long and unsavory history whose lessons should not be forgotten. Yet liberalism is also and obviously incomplete, in that it totally neglects the *endogeneity of preferences*.[4] Liberalism advocates the free choice of life-style, but it forgets that the choice is to a large extent preempted by the social environment in which people grow up and live. These endogenously emerging preferences can well lead to choices whose ultimate outcome is avoidable ruin or misery.[5] Although this resistible preemption is vastly preferable to a dictatorially imposed conception of the good life, it casts a long shadow on the presumed sovereignty of individual preferences. The political question remains, however, even granting that people do not desire that which would be best for them; how, except in a dictatorial or paternalist fashion, could a change for the better come about? The solution must be a form of self-paternlism: if people do not want to have the preferences they have, they can take steps – individually or collectively – to change them.[6]

Hence, the thrust of the paper is twofold. Substantively, it argues for a certain conception of the good life. Methodologically, it argues that such substantive questions are not outside the scope of political theory. The structure of the argument is as follows. Section II exemplifies and defines the notion of self-realization, argues for the superiority of self-realization over consumption, and tries to explain why people may nevertheless resist its attractions. The following Sections discuss the two main vehicles of self-

---

[3] John Rawls, *A Theory of Justice* (Cambridge, MA: Harvard University Press, 1971), p.90ff. I ought to add that there is much in Rawl's book that goes beyond the simple consideration of primary goods. In particular, his discussion of what he calls the Aristotelian Principle (p.424ff.) has many affinities with the present analysis of self-realization. Yet his argument for the design of basic social institutions does not go beyond primary goods.

[4] See my *Sour Grapes* (Cambridge: Cambridge University Press, 1983), Ch. III, for the importance of endogenous preference formation to political philosophy.

[5] For an extreme example of how one can "improve oneself to death," see Carl Christian von Weizsacker, "Notes on Endogenous Change of Tastes," *Journal of Economic Theory*, vol. 3 (1971), p.356.

[6] On the notion of individual and collective self-paternalism, see my *Ulysses and the Sirens* (Cambridge: Cambridge University Press, rev. ed., 1984) Ch. II.

realization that have been discussed in the Marxist and neo-Marxist tradition. Section III considers the concept of *work* and argues that in spite of the apparent disutility of work, it can be a channel for self-realization. Section IV discusses the neo-Marxist idea that *politics* can provide an outlet for self-realization, through participation in political discussions and decision making. Section V considers both of these vehicles in the light of the Marxist view that the value of self-realization ought to be implemented jointly with that of *community*, i.e., self-realization for others or with others. Section VI, finally, looks more closely at ways in which the desire or opportunity for self-realization could be promoted or blocked by various institutional arrangements. I conclude with some tentative remarks on "how to get from here to there."

II. THE CONCEPT OF SELF-REALIZATION

(a) *Some examples and a preliminary classification*

Here is a list of some activities that can lend themselves to self-realization: playing tennis, playing piano, playing chess, making a table, cooking a meal, developing software for computers, constructing the Watts Towers,[7] juggling with a chain saw, acting as a human mannequin,[8] writing a book, discussing in a political assembly, bargaining with an employer, trying to prove a mathematical theorem, working a lathe, fighting a battle, doing embroidery, organizing a political campaign, and building a boat.

Activities that for various reasons do not lend themselves well to self-realization can be roughly divided into spontaneous interpersonal relations, consumption, and drudgery. The first class of activities range from talking with friends to making love; they do not lend themselves to self-realization because they are not defined by some further goal or purpose. Consumption activities include eating a meal, reading a book, or paying for the services of a prostitute; the reason why they do not lend themselves to self-realization is spelled out in detail below. Drudgery includes sweeping the streets, working on an assembly line, or (with the qualifications discussed in Section IV) voting in an election; it does not lend itself to self-realization because it very soon becomes trivial or boring.

---

[7] The Watts Towers in Los Angeles were constructed single-handedly by an Italian immigrant, Sam Rodia, over a period of 33 years, out of debris and bric-a-brac that he collected from the streets of the city. (For information see the *Los Angeles Times* for August 12, 1984.) They are beautiful in conception and execution, unlike, say, conceptual art, which has mainly the freakish value of stunning novelty, soon fading into boredom. For a discussion of the conditions for self-realization in art, see *Sour Grapes*, Ch. II. 7.

[8] This example and the preceding one were observed at Venice Beach in Los Angeles. They are included to remind us that self-realization is not always channeled into activities that in some substantive sense are socially useful, beyond the value of stunning the spectators.

These classes of activities can also be compared along the dimensions of *purposiveness* and *satisfaction*. In consumption, the purpose of the activity is to derive satisfaction. In self-realization, the purpose is to achieve something, and satisfaction is supervenient upon the achievement rather than the immediate purpose of the activity. Spontaneous interpersonal relations can be deeply satisfying but have no purpose beyond themselves. Drudgery has a well-defined purpose, but is inherently unsatisfying. One should add that the purpose of drudgery normally is to produce something that is satisfying, i.e., a use-value. A final class of activities, therefore, would be those which are inherently unsatisfying and produce nothing or little that is of value. Punishment which took the form of digging ditches and filling them up again would be an example. Some forms of "community work" for the unemployed also approach this category, in that the unemployed are set to do work that society normally does not value enough to pay for.

As these examples indicate, a particular kind of activity may not be confined to a single category. Raising children or having sexual relations, for example, can be drudgery under certain conditions, consumption under others, self-realization under still different circumstances, and spontaneous interaction in some cases. The central features that turn an activity into a potential vehicle for self-realization are that it has an external goal and that it can be performed more or less well – i.e., the goal can be realized to a higher or lower degree – according to independently given criteria. If an activity is to be an actual vehicle for self-realization, its goal must be of suitable complexity – neither so simple as to produce boredom, nor so difficult as to produce frustration. The activity must offer *a challenge that can be met.*

Although self-realization can be deeply satisfying, the satisfaction must not be the immediate purpose of the activity. Self-realization belongs to the general class of *states that are essentially byproducts,*[9] i.e., states that can only come about as the side effect of actions undertaken for some purpose, such as "getting it right" or "beating the opposition." In Section IV below, I discuss how the quest for self-realization through political participation is self-defeating if the political system is not oriented towards substantive decision making. The same danger can arise in self-realization through creative work, if the artist becomes too preoccupied with the process of creation itself.

The main argument of this paper is built around the comparison between consumption and self-realization in terms of their inherent benefits and disadvantages. This approach can be justly criticized as too narrow, since the choice between the two forms of activity ought also to be considered in terms of their impact on spontaneous interpersonal relations, which are an impor-

---

[9] For a general discussion of this notion, see *Sour Grapes* Ch. II.

tant part of the good life on most people's conception. On the one hand, for instance, the tendency for self-realization to expand into all available time, because of the economies of scale that characterize it, is a threat both to consumption and to friendship. On the other hand, one could argue that friendships based on joint self-realization are more rewarding than those which are rooted in common consumption. I am unable to assess the net effect of these opposed tendencies.

(b) *Towards a definition*

In the Marxist tradition, self-realization is the full and free actualization and externalization of the powers and the abilities of the individual. I shall discuss the four components of this definition in the order in which I have just mentioned them. The full motivation behind the definition will only become clear in subsection *(c)* below, where the reasons for valuing self-realization are set out.

(i) *The fullness of self-realization.* The idea that the individual can *fully* bring to actuality *all* the powers and abilities he possesses is one of the more utopian elements in Marx's thought, and certainly not one that I am going to defend.[10] One is constrained to choose between being a jack-of-several-trades and a master of (at most) one. I shall argue that the latter option ought to be chosen, because of the economies of scale that characterize self-realization. It is, however, an important question exactly how a "trade" or skill is to be defined. I argue in Section III below that self-realization through work in a constantly changing society may require the development of general skills that can be harnessed to widely different tasks.

(ii) *The freedom of self-realization.* Even though an individual cannot develop *all* his abilities, he ought to be free to develop *any* of them. The notion that self-realization must be free but cannot be full is captured in a "putty-clay" model of human nature.[11] *Ex ante* the individual should be free to choose which of his many powers and abilities to develop, but *ex post* the roads he did not take become closed to him. The reason why the choice of a vehicle for self-realization must be freely made by the individual is that otherwise it would not be *self*-realization. The individual is both the designer and the raw material of the process. Hence, self-realization presupposes self-ownership, in the weak sense of the right to choose which of one's abilities to develop. If I want to write poetry but also have the potential to become a doctor or engineer, there could be no justification for society to

---

[10] Well-known passages in which Marx insists on the fullness of self-realization are found in *The German Ideology*, in Marx and Engels, *Collected Works*, vol. 5 (London: Lawrence and Wishart, 1976), pp.47, 394.

[11] For this approach to production see Leif Johansen, "Substitution versus Fixed Production Coefficients in the Theory of Production," *Econometrica*, vol. 27 (1959), pp.157–176.

force me – e.g., by means of an ability tax – to choose one of the latter options. It would, however, be justified in creating incentives to channel my desire for self-realization into socially desirable occupations, so long as I am not punished if I choose otherwise. Negative and positive incentives ought to be linked to the activities actually performed, not to potential activities.

Note, however, that self-realization does not entail self-ownership in the stronger senses of (a) the right to choose when to deploy one's (trained) abilities, or (b) the right to retain the full income one can derive from that deployment. It does not impinge on the doctor's self-realization if he is forced to treat patients in a disaster area or to pay taxes on his income. One may or may not think that some of his other rights would be violated, but that is not the issue here.

The formal or negative freedom to choose any given line of self-actualization ought, not to be confused with the positive freedom or opportunity to do so. If I want to realize myself by making epic technicolor films, I may be unable to do so because I lack the material resources, even if nobody actively tries to block my desire. A society cannot guarantee that all individuals get what they need in order to carry out their preferred project of self-realization, since it might then be impossible to match the demand for resources with the supply. It can, however, try to create a large variety of opportunities for self-realization, and good mechanisms for matching desires with opportunities. In doing so, however, it will be constrained by the need to favor (i) forms of self-realization that do not require excessive amounts of material resources, and (ii) forms that lead to the creation of material resoures.

(iii) *Self-actualization.* I decompose the notion of self-realization into self-actualization and self-externalization. Self-actualization itself can be analytically depicted as a two-stage process, although in reality the two stages proceed *pari passu*. The abilities and powers of the individual are two steps removed from actuality: they must first be developed and then be deployed. Being able to (learn to) speak French is a condition for knowing how to speak French, and this, in turn, is a condition for speaking French.[12] The actual deployment of the ability is, of course, the *raison d'être* for its development and that which gives value to self-realization.

(iv) *Self-externalization.* The individual has many powers and abilities which may be deployed in ways that cannot be observed by others. One may

---

[12] For a conceptual analysis of abilities and their actualization, see Anthony Kenney, *Action, Emotion and Will* (London: Routledge and Kegan Paul, 1963), Ch. VIII. Kenny's is an Aristotelian concept of self-actualization, to be distinguished both from the Freudian notion of liberating one's repressed thoughts and desires and the Nietzschean one of identifying with one's deeds. For a useful discussion, see Alexander Nehamas, "How One Becomes What One Is," *The Philosophical Review*, vol. XCII (1983), pp.385–417.

train one's ability to enjoy poetry or wine, but the use of this power is not a part of the public domain. It is consumption rather than self-realization. One may, however, externalize the power by interpreting poetry for others or taking up the occupation of wine taster, in which case the activity becomes a potential vehicle for self-realization. To enjoy wine is not an activity that can be performed more or less well, although one may enjoy the wine more or less. By contrast, professional wine-tasting lends itself to evaluation by external criteria.

(c) *Why value self-realization?*

I shall argue that both the self-actualization and the self-externalization aspects of self-realization provide reasons for desiring it. Both of these arguments are welfarist in character, the first directly and the second more indirectly. In addition, I shall argue that even under conditions in which the desire for self-realization does not lead to increased satisfaction, it can be a desirable desire to have on grounds of autonomy.

(i)*The need for suspension of tranquillity.* Leibniz wrote that "l'inquiétude est essentielle à la félicité des créatures."[13] This premise also has a central place in Marx's argument for self-realization.

> It seems quite far from [Adam] Smith's mind that the individual, 'in his normal state of health, strength, activity, skill, facility', also needs a normal portion of work and of the suspension of tranquillity. Certainly, labor obtains its measure from the outside, through the aim to be attained and the obstacles to be overcome in attaining it. But Smith has no inkling that this overcoming of obstacles is in itself a liberating activity. [Labor] becomes attractive work, the individual's self-realization, which in no way means that it becomes mere fun, mere amusement, as Fourier, with grisette-like naiveté, conceives it. Really free working, e.g. composing, is at the same time precisely the most damned seriousness, the most intense exertion.[14]

The central intuition behind this passage can be stated in terms of the Solomon-Corbit theory of "opponent process."[15] A rough diagrammatic statement of their theory is provided in Fig. 1, which allows us to compare

---

[13] Leibniz, *Nouveau essais sur l'Entendement Humain*, in G. W. Leibniz, *Die Philosophischen Schriften*, ed. Gerhardt, (Hildesheim: Olms, 1966 reprint) vol. 6, p.175.

[14] Marx, *Grundrisse* (Harmondsworth: Pelican Books, 1973), p.611.

[15] Richard L. Solomon and J. D. Corbit, "An Opponent-Process Theory of Motivation," *Psychological Review*, vol. 81 (1974), pp. 119–145. See also my "Sadder but Wiser? Rationality and the Emotions," *Social Science Information* vol.24 (1985), pp. 375–406.

the utility streams derived from episodes of (at least some types of) consumption and self-realization. Let us first define an episode AC – of either kind – as the time from the beginning of the activity to the time when utility is back to the pre-activity level. Any given consumption episode, then, has the pattern that it is initially pleasurable, but includes painful withdrawal symptoms when the activity ceases. The "main process" AB has the opposite sign of the "opponent process" BC. Conversely, in self-realization the main process is painful – "Aller Anfang ist schwer" – and the payoff comes at the end of the episode. If we consider repeated episodes, of qualitatively the same kind, the theory postulates that the opponent process comes to dominate the main process. The pleasures of consumption tend to become jaded over time, while the withdrawal symptoms become increasingly more severe. The consumption activity remains attractive not because it provides pleasure, but because it offers release from the withdrawal symptoms.[16] Conversely, the attractions of self-realization increase over time, as the start-up costs diminish and the gratification from achievement becomes more profound.[17] There are economies of scale in self-realization, while consumption has the converse property.

If this rough model is accepted, several observations follow. First, to derive maximal benefit from consumption, one should search for variety and diversity in order to enjoy the high initial benefits from many different activities. Self-realization, on the other hand, requires concentration on one line of activity in order to exploit the economies of scale. Since variety soon becomes expensive, people with limited means (i.e., most people) do better if they choose self-realization. Second, self-realization has the pattern of "one step backwards, two steps forwards," both within and across episodes. The initial stage AB of any given episode is always painful, although it becomes less painful over time. Moreover, the first times the net effect of the whole episode AC may be negative, while episodes with a positive net effect only

[16] It might be objected that this is a model of addictive consumption, not of consumption generally. With nonaddictive consumption, one cannot assume an increasingly strong opponent process, although the idea of decreasing strength of the main process remains plausible. Since the latter is all I need for my argument, it is not affected by the objection. In any case, there may be an element of addiction (in the sense of an increasingly strong opponent process) in all forms of consumption, although it is usually less dramatic than in the use of drugs, tobacco, and alcohol. The objection might then be rephrased as a question about whether the net effect of a given episode always becomes negative as the number of episodes increases.

[17] There are two exceptions to this statement. First, some abilities might not be susceptible to indefinite development; second, some persons might not be able to develop their abilities indefinitely. Tic-tac-toe, unlike chess, soon becomes boring; a person with poor motor reflexes might find out the hard way that he was not made for chain saw juggling. Economies of scale obtain only if abilities and tasks are suitably matched so as to avoid either of the extremes of boredom and frustration.

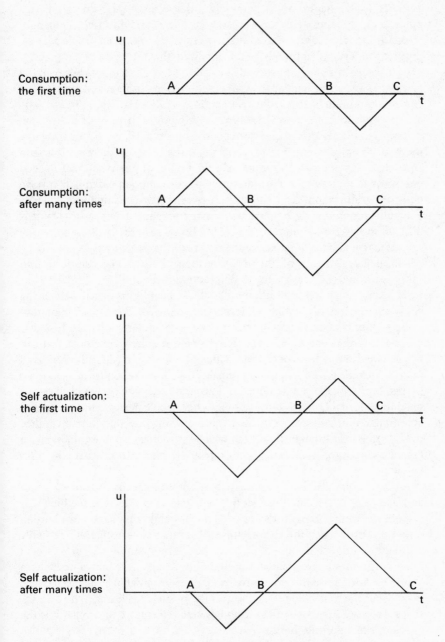

Figure 1. Temporal Patterns of utility corresponding to single episodes of consumption or self actualization, at early and later stages.

emerge at later stages. Many people find that writing their first article for publication is a largely painful process, with a small and uncertain element of pleasure. At later career stages, the net effect of writing an article may be positive, but even then usually on the condition that the beginning is painful.

(ii) *The self and others.* I asserted above that there is a contrast between the temporal patterns of utility corresponding to self-realization and *some types of consumption.* Other forms of consumption, vis., those which represent self-actualization without self-externalization, exhibit the pattern of the bottom diagrams of Fig. 1. Learning to read poetry, for instance, is a painful process; the payoff comes later. Moreover, on any given occasion there are start-up costs that may deter one from picking up a book of poetry, so that instead one turns to a crime novel. Some forms of consumption essentially involve deferred gratification. The similarity between such consumption activities and self-realization will be obvious to many parents. The reason why it is difficult to make children take, say, piano lessons is exactly the same as the reason why it is hard to persuade them to read the first fifty pages of a book which, one feels sure, will then capture their interest. The culprit in both cases is myopia, i.e., resistance to delayed gratification.

To explain why self-realization ranks above such forms of self-actualizing consumption, I shall invoke a Hegelian argument.[18] The most important value for human beings is self-esteem. Self-esteem derives largely from the esteem accorded one by other people. Esteem requires something that can be esteemed, some form of externalization of one's inner self. It is of no avail to be a "beautiful soul" if the soul remains ineffable and mute; the self must be made part of the public domain. This argument is closely linked to the need for external criteria of evaluation. Other people perform the indispensable function of assessing, criticizing, and praising one's performance; they provide the "reality control" without which self-actualization would be like a "private language," a morass of subjectivity. (I return to this issue in V (b) below.)

Drudgery can also be a form of self-externalization that provides esteem and, hence, self-esteem. The fact that one does or produces something that someone is willing to pay for shows that one is being useful and not a burden on others, even when the task itself is inherently uninteresting. This is only indirectly a welfarist argument. It would be simplistic to say that self-esteem is a source of welfare, happiness, or utility. It is, more fundamentally, a condition for the ability to derive welfare from anything. Self-esteem is needed for the motivation to go on with the business of living. When we say that a depressed person suffers from low self-esteem, we mean that it is the cause of the suffering, not its object.

[18] See G.W.F. Hegel, *Phenomenology of Spirit* (Oxford: Oxford University Press, 1977), pp.118, 193, 395ff.

(iii) *Self-realization and autonomy.* In Section VI below, I argue that the lack of desire for self-realization may be due to "adaptive preferences," i.e., to the adjustment of desires to what is possible. In a society with few opportunities for self-realization, it may *for that reason* not be highly valued. With more opportunities, the desire might emerge. Yet we ought to consider the possibility that increased opportunities for self-realization might generate more desires than can be satisfied.[19] If so, the increase in opportunities might make people on the whole worse off in terms of welfare, and yet we might want to say on nonwelfarist grounds that the change was a good thing. For reasons of autonomy, it is better to desire things because they are desirable than to do so because they are available. Many people would agree with this if one used freedom rather than self-actualization as an example, but the argument applies no less to the latter case. To bring the point home, consider an example used by Ronald Dworkin in his rebuttal of welfarist conceptions of equality.[20] Imagine a gifted artist or scientist who, despite his great achievements, is desperately unhappy because he is acutely aware of his shortcomings. Indeed, it is precisely because of his great gifts that he, better than others, can perceive how far his achievement falls short of the ideal. When the circle of light expands, so does the surrounding circle of darkness. It would be simplistic to say that this person should go into another occupation, where he can set his sights lower and not think of himself as a fraud. The achievements of such people are inseparable from their total dedication to what they are doing. Although the darkness makes them depressed, they cannot live without the light. Theirs are lives worth living, though not on grounds of welfare.

(d) *The resistance to self-realization*

Yet there are other reasons, beyond that of adaptive preferences, why people might not desire self-realization. Even when there are available opportunities, people might not take them because of myopia, risk-aversion, or free-riding.

(i) *Myopia.* The fact that self-realization involves deferred gratification, both within and across episodes, must enter importantly into the explanation of why it is not chosen even when its superiority is clearly recognized. As I have argued elsewhere,[21] this is not simply a question of time discounting. It can also, more centrally, be a question of weakness of the will. People may desire a life of self-realization and take the first, relatively costless steps towards it, and yet not bring themselves to undergo the painful learning process that is required.

---

[19] For a more detailed exposition of a similar argument, see *Sour Grapes*, pp.124, 133ff.
[20] Ronald Dworkin, "What is Equality? Part 1: Equality of Welfare," *Philosophy and Public Affairs*, vol. 10 (1981), p.222.
[21] "Weakness of will and the free-rider problem," *Economics and Philosohy*, vol. 1 (1985) pp. 231–265.

(ii) *Risk-aversion.* I have emphasized that self-realization requires a matching of abilities and tasks to avoid boredom and frustration. It is not, however, a question of choosing a task that is optimally suited to given and known abilities. The situation, unfortunately, is one in which one of William Blake's Proverbs of Hell finds ample application: "You never know what is enough unless you know what is more than enough." The only way for the individual to find the limits of his abilities is, often, to come up against them.

To model the problem decision-theoretically, let us assume that the individual confronts the following situation:

		Task	
		Easy	Complex
	High	30	100
Ability			
	Low	50	10

The numbers indicate the satisfaction that the individual derives under the different combinations of ability level and task complexity. They assume that matching ability and skill is always preferable to nonmatching, that high-level matching is better than low-level matching, and that the frustration from having chosen a task which is too difficult is worse than the boredom from having chosen one that is too easy. Let us first assume that the choice involves risk, with, say, equal probability that one's ability will be high or low. A risk-neutral individual would choose the complex task, but a risk-averse one might well choose the easy task. Next, assume that the situation is totally clouded in uncertainty, so that no probabilities can be assigned to the various ability levels. In that case, many people would use the maximin strategy of choosing the task which guarantees the highest minimal satisfaction, which again is the easy task. In either case, the conclusion follows that people individually might be deterred from choosing the course of action that would make them better off on the average. In theory risk-pooling could overcome the problem, but it is hard to see how any viable insurance system could be set up.

(iii) *Free-riding.* It must be emphasized that if risk aversion makes people eschew the more demanding vehicles for self-realization, they do not in any way act irrationally. The need for security is not an objectionable one. Yet before we conclude that risk-aversion is an insuperable obstacle to self-realization, we must consider another aspect of the problem. Self-realization is not only rewarding for the individual who engages in it. It also provides gratification for those who consume the output of the activity. To the extent that people choose to realize themselves by engaging in scientific or technological activities, they produce medicines that save lives and innovations that make available to everybody and at low cost products that formerly were reserved for an elite. Even those whose efforts at self-realization are frustrated because they overestimated the level of their ability benefit from the activities of those who correctly estimated their ability to be high.

This shows that self-realization is also a problem of collective action. It is probably better *for everybody*, and not just on the average, if all act as if they were risk-neutral, even if they are risk-averse. Yet for each individual, it is always tempting to be a free rider and benefit from the risk-taking of others, while acting in a risk-averse manner. To overcome the free-rider problem, self-realization would probably have to become a social norm, although various other solutions are also possible.[22]

I add two further remarks on this problem. First, it is not clear that even risk-neutral behavior would bring about the socially desirable outcome if the subjective probabilities are correctly formed. Either risk-loving or over-estimation of one's own abilities may be required. The following passage from a book by two cognitive psychologists is well worth reflecting upon:

> People sometimes may require overly optimistic or overly pessimis-tic subjective probabilities to goad them into effective action or prevent them from taking dangerous action. Thus it is far from clear that a bride or groom would be well advised to believe, on their wedding day, that the probability of their divorce is as high as .40. A baseball player with a batting average of .200 may not be best served, as he steps up to bat, by the belief that the probability that he will get a hit is only .2. The social benefits of individually erroneous subjective probabilities may be great even when the individual pays a high price for the error. We probably would have few novelists, actors or scientists if all potential aspirants to these careers took action based in a normatively justified probability of success. We also might have few new products, new medical procedures, new political movements, or new scientific theories.[23]

Second, we may use this occasion to dwell on the distinction between the self-realization of men and that of Man.[24] It is part and parcel of the ethical individualism of Marxism (further discussed in Section V below) that communism ought not to be justified by the prospect of great achievements

[22] For a survey of ways in which free-riding can be overcome, see the article cited in the previous note and also my "Rationality, Morality and Collective Action," *Ethics*, vol. 96 (1985), pp.136–155.

[23] Richard E. Nisbett and Lee Ross, *Human Inference: Strategies and Shortcomings of Social Judgement* (Englewood Cliffs, NJ: Prentice Hall, 1980), p.271.

[24] For this distinction, see G.A. Cohen, "Karl Marx's Dialectic of Labour," *Philosophy and Public Affairs*, vol. 3 (1974), pp.235–261.

for Mankind, but by what it offers to each and every individual. It is characteristic of class societies that they allow for the self-realization of Man at the expense of that of most individual men, by enabling scientific and cultural achievements by the few at the expense of the drudgery of the many, while communism in Marx's conception will allow the full and free self-realization *of each individual*. We can retain both the ethical individualism of Marx and the emphasis on self-realization without accepting this utopian conception. The revised version of the ideal is the free and partial self-realization of some, as a result of the attempted self-realization of all, justified by the fact that the benefits of success also accrue to those who fail in the attempt.

III. WORK AS A VEHICLE FOR SELF-REALIZATION

The main tradition in economic thought has looked at work as largely unpleasant, justified only by what it produces.[25] Marx, as we saw in the passage from the *Grundrisse* cited above, had a different view. While he dissociated himself from Fourier's view that work could be made into "mere amusement," he also took exception to Adam Smith's view that work was, necessarily, "a curse." Work, according to Marx, is rewarding *and* painful; moreover, it could not be rewarding without being painful.

Contemporary industrial psychologists have also, from a very different perspective, considered the intrinsic benefits of work. They have almost exclusively discussed the comparative benefits and hardships associated with different forms of work, without asking themselves whether and when work is preferable to its absence, even if income is kept constant. This focus is understandable, whether the concern is with empirical testing or industrial reform, since the option of gaining a full income while not working is not feasible. Yet, from the present perspective, this option can enter usefully into various thought experiments designed to bring out the distinction between motivation and welfare – between what people prefer to do and what is best for them. I argue first that, for several reasons – one of which is self-realization – people may be better off working even if they would prefer not to. I then consider the extent to which the argument from self-realization applies to industrial work in modern societies.

(a) The "disutility of work"
The very definition of work constitutes a problem. I shall use the term in a broad and somewhat loose sense, to refer to any organized and regular

---

[25] For a full survey, see Ugo Pagano, *Work and Welfare in Economic Theory*, (Oxford: Blackwell 1984).

activity whose purpose is to produce use-values or intermediate goods for the production of use-values. It is sometimes made part of the definition of work that it involves some pain or cost, even if only opportunity costs, to the worker. For reasons to be made clear below, I do not follow this usage. Nor is it essential for the definition that work be remunerated.

Why do people work? Serge Kolm has offered the following list of reasons.

- Because of direct coercion, as in forced labor
- In exchange for a wage
- Because of a desire to help and serve others
- Out of a sense of duty or reciprocity
- Out of interest for the work itself
- For the sake of social relations at the workplace
- To show others that one is making a contribution to society or that one possesses certain skills
- Because of the social status associated with work
- To escape boredom
- As play
- Out of habit[26]

The notion of the disutility of work may be considered in the light of some of these reasons for working. Independently of the income from work, a person is usually made worse off by never working than by holding a regular job. Yet given the choice of whether to work or to abstain, with the same income, he might prefer to abstain. This may also be true even if it is rephrased in marginalist terms. For all n, it may be true that, if given a choice between working n hours per week and working $n-1$ hours, a person would always prefer the latter option, yet would be worse off from never working than from working a full week. This situation arises because the person neglects the positive externalities of work or, what amounts to the same, the negative externalities of unemployment. These externalities are not effects on other people, but on the person himself at later times. The situation is an intrapersonal, intertemporal Prisoner's Dilemma.[27]

To understand the precise character of the externality, consider the workplace as a source of friendship and self-esteem. For any n, a reduction in working hours from n to $n-1$ will have little immediate impact on these benefits. A person would not lose his friends or their esteem by working slightly less, and he would gain some leisure. He might well prefer the reduction. Yet the cumulative long-term damage to his social life may be

[26] S.C. Kolm, *La Bonne Economie* (Paris: Presses Universitairs de France, 1984), pp.119–120.
[27] For discussion, see the article cited in note 21.

more substantial, and outweigh the short-term gain in leisure. Each hour he is absent from work creates negative externalities for future periods, by loosening his insertion in the web of social relation and reducing his sense of his own worth.

A similar argument applies to the benefits derived from work as self-realization. As I made clear towards the end of Section II, myopia can be a major cause of resistance to self-actualization. Hence, the "marginal utility of work" would have a very different value if it were measured at the beginning of a given task and again when the task approaches completion.[28] Even if one considered the marginal utility of the task as a whole, the value would depend heavily on whether one considered an earlier or a later performance. I conclude that the marginalist approach to the utility of work is ill-conceived, since work tasks are not made up of homogeneous bits, but have a complex temporal structure.

(b) *The scope for self-realization in industry*
Can work in modern societies provide a mode of self-realization? Marx usually cites art and science as paradigm for self-realization, which is not very helpful. Even though he insisted that communism would be based on large-scale industry and argued against conceiving of work on the model of the artisan, his examples of self-realization fit the latter better than the former. Recent work in industrial psychology is more useful, although it does not, for several reasons, fit my purposes perfectly. For one thing, it takes for granted the property relations and incentive structures of capitalist firms; for another, the central concept of "job satisfaction" is much broader and vaguer than the concept of self-realization (as it is used here).[29] Reasons of space and competence prevent me from trying to summarize these studies here, but I shall try to restate and discuss some of the findings in terms of the framework set out in Section II above.

A recent survey lists work, pay, promotion, verbal recognition, and working conditions as the main causes of job satisfaction. The first of these is further specified in terms which are quite close to my present approach: "Work attributes that have been found to be related to work interest and satisfaction include: opportunity to use one's valued skills and abilities;

---

[28] In some cases, it would also give a different result if measured very close to completion; cp. Byron's "Nothing so difficult as a beginning/In poesy, unless perhaps the end."

[29] In the literature on job satisfaction the notion of self-realization is usually discussed with reference to the writings of Abraham Maslow, and dismissed as hopelessly confused. See, for instance, Edwin A. Locke, "Nature and Causes of Job Satisfaction," Marvin D. Dunnette, ed., *Handbook of Industrial and Organizational Psychology* (Chicago: Rand McNally College Publishing Company, 1976), pp.1307–1309. Although I agree with the criticism of Maslow, I hope that the present discussion shows that the notion is not inherently unamenable to precise analysis.

opportunity for new learning; creativity; variety; difficulty; amount of work; responsibility; non-arbitrary pressure for performance; control over work methods and work pace (autonomy); job enrichment (which involves increasing responsibility and control); and complexity. While each of the above factors is conceptually distinguishable from the others, there is one element which they share in common, the element of *mental challenge*."[30]

Similarly, one influential writer argues that "Work redesign can help individuals regain the chance to experience the kick that comes from doing a job well, and it can encourage them to once more *care* about their work and about developing the competence to do it even better. These payoffs from work redesign go well beyond simple job satisfaction. Cows grazing in the field may be satisfied, and employees in organizations can be made just as satisfied by paying them well, by keeping the bosses off their backs, by putting them in pleasant rooms with pleasant people, and by arranging things so that the days pass without undue stress or strain. The kind of satisfaction at issue here is different. It is a satisfaction that develops only when individuals are stretching and growing as human beings, increasing their sense of competence and self-worth." He further decomposes the conditions for job enrichment into five elements: skill variety, task identity, task significance, autonomy, and feedback.[31] Clearly, this is a pie that can be cut many ways. There seem to be, nevertheless, some common assumptions and problems that can be related to my concerns here.

(i) *Routine, variety or complexity?* Monotonous, repetitive tasks, by and large, are not conducive to job satisfaction. Monotony can be alleviated by increasing either task variety or task complexity. Increasing task variety can take the form of job rotation in semiautonomous groups, but there seems to be some skepticism about this solution.[32] In terms of the framework used here, the skepticism can be justified by observing that job rotation does not permit one to exploit the economies of scale of self-realization. Variety is a desideratum in consumption, not in work. True, it is better to rotate between several simple tasks than to devote oneself full-time to one of them, but full-time concentration on one complex task is better still.

J. Richard Hackman argues, however, that "not all jobs are suited to all people. Some individuals prosper in simple, routinized work, while others prefer higly complex and challenging tasks .... What percentage of the workforce actually desire higher order need satisfaction and so are likely to

---

[30] Locke, *ibid.*, p.1319.

[31] J. Richard Hackman, "Work Design," in J. Richard Hackman and J. Lloyd Suttle, eds., *Improving Life at Work* (Santa Monica: Goodyear, 1977), pp.96–162.

[32] Gordon E. O'Brien, "The Centrality of Skill-Utilization for Job Design," K.D. Duncan, Michael M. Gruneberg and Donald Wallis, eds., *Changes in Working Life* (New York: Wiley & Sons, 1980), p.180. See also Hackman, "Work design," pp.115, 120.

respond positively to enriched jobs? Some observers estimate that only about 15 percent of rank-and-file employees are so motivated."[33] From the argument in Section II, two objections to these statements follow immediately. First, instead of saying that some people like challenges and others do not, one should say that what *is* a challenge differs across people. Second, the fact that many people do not desire challenging work does not mean that they would not "prosper" in it, once they got over the initial hurdles.

(ii) *Matching workers with jobs.* G.E. O'Brien distinguishes between several strategies for achieving this match.[34] First, one can adapt the tasks to the workers by reform at the workplace. This strategy has the most central place in the literature. O'Brien raises the question of whether economic democracy could be geared to this purpose. In his opinion, this will not be a sucessful strategy, for the reason, among others, that "The less skill-utilization and influence people have in their jobs, the more likely it is that they see their lives as being determined by others . . . . This expectation makes it difficult for them to respond initially to changes in jobs or power structures which provide them with more autonomy." I return to some aspects of this problem in Section VI (a) below.

Conversely, one may try to fit the worker to the task by suitable hiring criteria. According to O'Brien, "selection psychologists have done well in rejecting applicants with below required skill levels but have been less careful about rejecting applicants whose skill repertoire exceeds the job descriptions." If it is correct, this observation could be explained by the fact that a capitalist firm has no incentive – or may not think it has an incentive – to avoid hiring overqualified workers. If an underqualified worker is hired, both the firm and the worker suffer, but only the worker suffers if he is overqualified.[35]

One may also attack the problem by long-term strategies of planning rather than short-term strategies of adaptation. One of these is to design new factories and organizations so as to facilitate the matching of workers and tasks. The other is "to promote an educational policy which encourages students to have a realistic assessment of their own abilities and the probability of obtaining jobs which match these abilities." The idea is presumably that with a more realistic assessment, students will decide not to develop abilities the deployment of which will meet no demand. The argument may or may not be valid, depending on the further assumptions

[33] Hackman, "Work design," pp.115, 120.
[34] O'Brien, "The Centrality of Skill-Utilization," pp.180ff.
[35] Hackman, "Work design," p.117, argues that overqualification also causes loss of productivity via the lack of motivation. This may well be true for some workers and some tasks, but sometimes a higher level of qualification probably leads to superior performance.

made about individual motivation.[36] In any case, one must distinguish between two problems. As I mentioned earlier, no society can provide a guarantee that there will be a demand for a given ability. On the other hand, a good society ought to ensure that for each individual there is some ability he can develop that will meet an effective demand.

(iii) *Autonomy and feedback*. These requirements from the literature on job satisfaction reflect the interaction between the self and others in self-realization. On the one hand, the task, to be satisfying, must be freely chosen and performed. "An employee will not automatically like a task simply because it is challenging or because he has mastered it. He also has to like it for its own sake. This means that a man must choose the line of work *because he likes it*, not because someone else told him to like it, or because he is trying to prove something."[37] On the other hand, the individual needs the recognition and evaluation of competent others, both to know how well he is performing and to give substance to his self-esteem. The most satisfactory feedback is provided by co-workers and clients rather than supervisors, since the latter are paid to use profitability rather than quality as the criterion for evaluating work.

The last observation points to a possible conflict between economic efficiency and self-realization. Tocqueville recounts in *Democracy in America* that he "met an American sailor and asked him why his country's ships are made so that they will not last long. He answered offhand that the art of navigation was making such quick progress that even the best of boats would be almost useless if it lasted more than a few years."[38] With rapid technical change, the careful attention to detail that characterizes most forms of self-realization is pointless; conversely, pride in craftmanship may block innovation. The way out of this dilemma would have to be in the development of *adaptable skills* that can be harnessed to a variety of concrete tasks and, in fact, be enhanced by such variety. This would differ from job rotation in that each task would be an aplication and extension *of the same skill*, so that the economies of scale would not be lost.

---

[36] Raymond Boudon, *Effets Pervers et Ordre Social* (Paris: Presses Universitaries de France, 1977), Ch. IV, argues that this can turn into a problem of collective action: it may be individually rational for each student to seek higher education, although all would be better off if all flipped a coin to decide. This presupposes, however, that students are motivated by expected income rather than by expected satisfaction, which would also take account of the disappointment and frustration generated by getting a low-education job at the end of higher education. Boudon himself (*ibid.*, Ch. V) has the best treatment of this problem, although, surprisingly, he does not bring his analysis to bear on the problem of educational choice.

[37] Locke, "Nature and Causes," pp.1320–1321.

[38] Alexis de Tocqueville, *Democracy in America* (New York: Anchor Books, 1969), p.453.

IV. POLITICS AS A VEHICLE FOR SELF-REALIZATION

Marx did not believe that there would be room or need for conflictual politics in communism; *a fortiori* he could not promote politics as a channel for individual self-realization. Later Marxists have thought differently, notably Jürgen Habermas. He suggests that Marx overemphasized *work* at the expense of *interaction*, both in his theory of history and in his philosophical anthropology. The development of moral competence through rational discussion is a form of self-realization that ought to be valued as highly as self-realization at the workplace.[39]

Since I have discussed this claim at some length elsewhere,[40] the present discussion will be more summary. It will be organized around two distinctions. On the one hand, politics may be conceived either as a *private* activity, or as one that essentially takes place in the *public* domain. On the other hand, it may be valued either as a *means to some nonpolitical end* or as an *end in itself*. The latter distinction is not an exclusive one: politics may be valued both as a means and as an end. Indeed, the thrust of my argument is that to be an end in itself, it must also be a means to something beyond itself.

(a) *Private politics*

According to this conception – memorably stated by Anthony Downs – the essential and almost only mass political activity is that of voting.[41] In Section II, voting was classified as drudgery, i.e., as inherently unrewarding, to be valued only for the outcome it produces.This characterization hides a paradox, however, since it is hard to see how the outcome – an infinitesimally small chance of casting the decisive or pivotal vote – could motivate the act of voting (assuming that it is not compulsory).[42] Where the secret ballot is used, it is not plausible to argue that voting has any consumption value.[43] Nor does it offer any scope for self-realization, since it is not something that can be done more or less well. True, the decision to vote for one party or candidate rather than another may be the outcome of a process of deliberation which can be evaluated according to independent criteria, but to expose oneself to such evaluation is already to take leave of private politics. It is hard to see how voting could be anything else than drudgery, but equally hard to see what motivation it could have as drudgery.

[39] Jurgen Habermas, *Theorie des kommunikativen Handelns* (Frankfurt aM: Suhrkamp, 1981).
[40] In my "The Market and the Forum," in Aanund Hylland and Jon Elster (eds.), *Foundations of Social Choice Theory* (Cambridge: Cambridge University Press, 1986), pp.103–132; see also *Sour Grapes*, Ch. II. 9.
[41] Anthony Downs, *An Economic Theory of Democracy* (New York: Harper, 1957).
[42] See notably Brian M. Barry, *Economists, Sociologists and Democracy* (Chicago: University of Chicago Press, rev. ed., 1979).
[43] For a brief discussion and rejection of this possibility, see Howard Margolis, *Selfishness, Altruism and Rationality* (Cambridge: Cambridge University Press, 1982), p.86.

The solution to the paradox is found in a class of motivations that include duty, fairness, internalized social norms, and sheer magical thinking.[44] These attitudes are not easily categorized along the dimensions of purposiveness and satisfaction introduced in Section II. Voting, under normal conditions, cannot be justified by any purpose and does not produce any satisfaction – except that of doing what one believes one ought to do. Then we must ask, however, why one should believe one ought to do something that neither has an extrinsic purpose nor produces intrinsic satisfaction. I am not going to pursue this question here, except to note again that behavior guided by duty or social norms is somewhat recalcitrant to the conceptual scheme used here.

(b) *A controversy over ancient politics*
The argument that politics is mainly or even exclusively to be valued as a form of self realization has been put forward in discussions of the ancient *polis*. Hannah Arendt, especially, championed the view that politics in the ancient city states was about the agonistic display of excellence and individuality, and nothing else: "Without mastering the necessities of life in the household, neither life nor the 'good life' is possible, but politics is never for the sake of life. As far as the members of the *polis* are concerned, household life exists for the sake of the 'good life' in the *polis*."[45] In plain language, economics is a condition for politics, but not the object of politics. Nor, as far as one can glean from her text, did ancient politics have any other goal which could lend it value as a vehicle for self-realization.

A more ironic version of Hannah Arendt's argument is provided by Stephen Holmes who, when summarizing the views of Benjamin Constant on ancient politics, also appears to deny that ancient politics had any nonpolitical end: "Participatory self-government in the *polis*. . . was an improvised solution to the hoplite's awful problem: a surfeit of leisure time and the terrifying threat of ennui."[46] The goal – escape from boredom rather than self-realization – is more lowly, but the denial of any instrumental value to politics equally explicit.

This view may be challenged on factual grounds, as well as on grounds of consistency. For the first, we may look to the work of Moses Finley. He turn Arendt's view around and argues that: "In the city-states the premise, one might say the axiom, was widespread that the good life (however that was

---

[44] For further discussion, see my "Rationality, Morality and Collective Action." More instrumental attitudes, such as altruist and utilitarian motivations, might also enter into the explanation of voting, but I believe that their importance is smaller than the ones mentioned in the text.
[45] Hannah Arendt, *The Human Condition* (Chicago: University of Chicago Press, 1958), p.37.
[46] Stephen Holmes, *Benjamin Constant and the Making of Modern Liberalism* (New Haven: Yale University Press, 1984), p.60.

conceived) was possibly only in the *polis*; that the regime was expected to promote the good life; that therefore correct political judgments, the choice between conflicting policies within a *polis*, or, if matters reached such a stage, the choice between *polis* regimes, should be determined by which alternative helped advance the good life . . . . The good life, it should be stressed, had a substantial material component."[47] Elsewhere, asking why the Athenian people claimed the right of every citizen to speak and make proposals in the Assembly, yet left the exercise of the right to a few, he finds that "one part of the answer is that the *demos* recognized the instrumental role of political rights and were more concerned in the end with substantive decisions, were content with their power to select, dismiss and punish their leaders."[48]

My claim is that of these two assertions – most people did not value politics as a vehicle for self-realization; they did value politics as a means to nonpolitical ends – the second would be true even if the first were not. It is inconsistent to value political participation if it is not *about* something. It follows from the argument in Section II that political discussion must have an independently defined goal if it is to provide an outlet for self-realization. The goal must be to make good decisions about what must ultimately be nonpolitical matters. To arrive at a good decision, political discussion must be guided by the norms of rationality; hence, the powers and abilities brought to actuality by discussion are those of rational deliberation. The more urgent and important the decision to be made, the greater the potential for self-realization.

It follows that ancient politics as conceived by Arendt or Constant would be self-defeating. To escape boredom, one must be motivated by some other goal than that of escaping it. What is also – and somewhat inconsistently – emphasized by Holmes and Constant, however, is that constant threat of *war* provided the indispensable, externally given object of ancient politics. The urgency of war concentrates the mind wonderfully, and lends to politics the proper degree of seriousness without which it could neither be a remedy for boredom nor provide a vehicle for self-realization.

Mass political participation, then, can be a form of self-realization, if it takes the form of rational public discussion and decision making about substantive matters. National politics in modern societies involves too many people to provide an occasion for participatory self-realization, while mass demonstrations and similar activities suffer from not being oriented towards decision making. The most promising arenas for this form of self-realization

[47] Moses I. Finley, "Authority and Legitimacy in the Classical City-State," *Det Kongelige Danske Videnskapernes Selskab. Historisk-Filosofiske Meddelelser* 50:3, (Kobenhavn: Munksgaard 1982), p.12.
[48] Moses I. Finley, "The Freedom of the Citizen in the Ancient Greek World," in his *Economy and Society in Ancient Greece* (London: Chatto and Windus, 1981), p.83.

are local government, economic democracy, and democracy within organizations more generally. The conditions under which they lend themselves to self-realization are further discussed in the next Sections.

V. SELF-REALIZATION AND COMMUNITY

According to Hegel and Marx, pre-capitalist societies were characterized by community without individuality. The modern period, conversely, has seen the emergence of frenetic individuality and the widespread disintegration of community. Marx believed that communism would bring about a synthesis of the two values. Although I cannot argue in any detail for this view here, I believe that his conception was inspired by the philosophy of Leibniz, who argued in a similar vein both that each monad differs from all others and that each monad reflects all others from its point of view.[49] On the one hand, people will tend to choose vehicles of self-realization that correspond to their "individual essences," to use a phrase from Leibniz. "Milton produced *Paradise Lost* for the same reason that a silkworm produces silk. It was an activity of *his* nature."[50] The ethical individualism of Marxism requires that "Above all we must avoid postulating 'society' again as an abstraction *vis-à-vis* the individual."[51] On the other hand, the self-realization of the individual must not be an agonistic and antagonistic process, but should take place in and for the sake of the community. According to Marx, self-realization is integrated with community when it is *production for others*. I shall first consider this idea, and then the alternative proposal that the two values might be reconciled in *production with others*.

(a) *Self-realization for others*
This ideal is most clearly stated in a passage from Marx's early manuscripts.:

> Let us suppose that we had carried out production as human beings. Each of us would have *in two ways affirmed* himself and the other person. (1) In my *production* I would have objectified my *individuality*, its *specific* character, and therefore obtained not only an individual *manifestation of my life* during the activity, but also when looking at the object I would have the individual pleasure of knowing my personality to be *objective, visible to the senses* and hence a power *beyond all doubt*. (2) In your enjoyment or use of my product

[49] Cp. my "Marx et Leibniz," *Review Philosophique*, vol. 108 (1983), pp.167–177.
[50] *Theories of Surplus-Value* (London: Lawrence and Wishart, 1963), vol. 1, p.401.
[51] *Economic and Philosophical Manuscripts*, Marx and Engels, *Collected Works* (London: Lawrence and Wishart, 1975), vol. 3, p.299.

I would have the direct enjoyment both of being conscious of having satisfied a *human* need by my work, that is, of having objectified *man's* essential nature, and of having thus created an object corresponding to another *man's* essential nature . . . . Our products would be so many mirrors in which we saw reflected our essential nature.[52]

The text is not transparently clear. It may, perhaps, be read as suggesting a distinction between two ways in which the appreciation of other people enhances the satisfaction I derive from work. On the one hand, I may derive pleasure from the pleasure they derive from my product. This will be the case only when I produce for people I know well, e.g., when I cook a meal for my family. The idea that one can derive pleasure from knowing that one provides a service to "society" is, in my opinion, unrealistic.[53] On the other hand, the critical assessment of other people is needed to tell me whether I am performing well or not. For this purpose, it is crucial that the assessment could be – and sometimes is – negative; "sans la liberté de blâmer il n'y a pas d'éloge flatteur." Family members and friends cannot easily perform this function, since spontaneous interpersonal relations do not go well with this coolly evaluative attitude. Cooking for strangers is more satisfactory. Hence, I suggest that Marx was wrong *if* he intended to suggest – but it is far from certain that he did – that one and the same reference group could perform both functions.

Even if cooking is drudgery rather than self-realization, one might prefer to cook for strangers. Doing or producing something that others are willing to pay for is a source of self-esteem even when the work itself is not challenging or interesting. This may be among the reasons why women often feel the need to escape the close and sometimes suffocatingly ambiguous atmosphere of the family. To repeat, it is not a question of deriving pleasure from the fact that one does something which is socially valued, but of creating the conditions for deriving pleasure from other activities.

(b) *Self-realization with others*
An alternative synthesis of self-realization and community would be producing *with* others rather than *for* them. It would be embodied in the work collective rather than in the producer-consumer community. I do not have in mind what one could call *common* self-realization, in which each of several people would perform separate tasks under shared conditions. (Think of a group of scholars working together in a library.) Rather, I refer to

---

[52] "Comments on James Mill," *ibid*, pp.227–28.
[53] The idea is central in Kolm, *La Bonne Economie*. Although Kolm is right in arguing that such "general reciprocity" would overcome some of the defects of ordinary reciprocity, it would also lose the main virtue of the latter, viz., the warmth and spontaneity of personal relations.

joint self-realization, in which "the free development of each is the condition for the free development of all."[54] (Think of the players in an orchestra or the participants in a political discussion.) Following the discussion in Sections III and IV, we may distinguish between joint self-realization in work and in decision making. (The players in an orchestra, in addition to playing together, may also decide together which pieces to play and what to do with the proceeds from the concert.)

Consider, first, joint self-realization in the production process. Historically, the trend in the division of labor has been towards greater integration and independence of tasks on the one hand, and ever-simpler tasks with reduced scope for self-realization on the other. The mode of interdependence in modern industry is such that, if A does not do his job, B cannot do his – but it need not be true that the better A does his job, the better B can do his, and certainly not that B's good performance conversely enhances the conditions for A's good performance. And even if this is also the case, it need not be true that both tasks offer indefinite scope for improvement and growth. The conditions for joint self-realization may be observed on a small fishing vessel or in joint authorship, but do not seem to be favored by the nature of industrial work.

Consider, next, participatory democracy at the workplace. The first question that arises is that of efficiency. It is trivial to observe that any implementation of direct economic democracy would have to strike a compromise between the values of participatory self-realization and efficiency. A similar compromise might have to be struck between self-realization in work and efficiency, and in general between any two values one might want to promote. A less trivial statement is that participatory self-realization may actually depend on efficiency. As argued above, the value of participation depends on the degree to which the object of participation is to make good decisions. In the present case, the goal is not to find the decision that would be best if found costlessly, but to make the best decision all things considered, *including the cost of decision making itself.* If enterprises run by direct democracy make a mess of it, the workers will get neither the benefits from efficiency nor from self-realization. Hence, maximal self-realization occurs with a less-than-maximal degree of participation; total direct democracy would be self-defeating.

The market is a device for telling firms how well they perform. Hence, an argument for market socialism, as distinct from state socialism, is that the threat of bankruptcy, like the threat of war, concentrates the mind wonderfully. I would like to illustrate this argument with a piece of personal history. Around 1970, I was somewhat involved with two work collectives, a

[54] Marx and Engels, *Manifesto of the Communist Party*, Marx and Engels, *Collected Works* (London: Lawrence and Wishart, 1976), vol. 6, p.506.

publishing firm that depended on market success for survival and an academic institution that did not. Although the participatory democracy was much more strenuous and demanding in the first, it was also more rewarding. We gained much insight into the various sub-processes of publishing, and the way they come together in the final product: a book that is bought by someone. After a time, however, strain took its toll and the collective abdicated for a leader. In the second group, the lack of an independent goal and of well-defined performance criteria led to make-believe democracy. Discussion about who had the right to vote on what issues took up an increasing amount of time. The process of self-government turned inward upon itself, with boredom rather than self-realization as the predictable result.

We may contrast direct participatory democracy with representative economic democracy. Direct democracy is strenuous but rewarding, provided that the efficiency constraint is respected. Representative democracy retains the virtue of justice, but does not provide scope for self-realization for the rank and file of workers. The worst system is that which exists when direct democracy degenerates into activist rule, because too many people think the strains of participation exceed the rewards. Activists are not subject to the normal low-cost checks and controls of representative systems, only to the high-cost control of co-participation.

There are two possible ways of coping with the instability of participatory democracy. One is to base the direct democracy on compulsory participation. My view is that, unless it is chosen unanimously as a form of collective self-control, reflecting the fact that self-realization is strenuous and subject to weakness of will, this system would be unjustifiable. It would involve using other people as means to one's own self-realization, and undermine the essentially free nature of rational discussion. The other solution is to have automatic transformation from direct to representative democracy when the level of participation drops below a certain level. If the activists are people for whom decision making is a central form of self-realization, they could offer themselves as candidates in the representative elections. If they simply like untrammeled power, they would not thus offer themselves, which is as it should be.

These remarks apply to political democracy no less than to economic democracy. Under suitable conditions, both can be arenas for joint self-realization. Although in economic democracy the collectivity is one of workers rather than of citizens, it is not oriented toward self-realization in the actual work, but to self-realization in the process of making work-related decisions. This does not mean that the workers perform managerial functions. They engage in a rational, knowledgeable discussion which issues in instructions to the managers. Managers may achieve self-realization individually, by developing and deploying their administrative skills. The self-realization of the workers would, like that of the musicians in an orchestra, be a genuinely joint one. If some of the participants deviate from the rules of a rational discussion, they thereby make it difficult or pointless for others to follow them.[55]

VI. INSTITUTIONS, DESIRES, AND OPPORTUNITIES

What are the institutional conditions that could promote or block self-realization? More precisely, how are the desire and the opportunity for self-realization in work and politics affected by institutional relations within and between firms? This is a question that involves two independent variables and four dependent ones, and in addition we may expect there to be relations between the dependent variables. Here I shall only speculate about some of the connections that may obtain. I first raise the issue of adaptive preferences, already broached in Section II above. I then consider how relations within the firm may affect the opportunity for self-realization, and how relations between firms may affect both the desire and the opportunity. I conclude with some comments on "how to get from here to there."

(a) *Adaptive preferences*
The absence of self-realization may be due to the absence of a desire for self-realization or to the absence of opportunities. If, in a given society, we observe that there are few opportunities for self-realization and that people do not much seem to want it, it would be tempting to explain the first of these facts by the second. The causal chain could, however, go the other way. Because most people have few opportunities for self-realization, their desires and aspirations might unconsciously adjust to this limitation, to avoid cognitive dissonance. In particular, a high rate of time discounting and a high degree of risk-aversion might emerge endogenously, to make the best elements in the feasible set appear to be optimal even within the wider set that includes opportunities for self-realization as well as for consumption. The idea that self-realization is too strenuous and demanding may be tainted by an element of "sour grapes."[56] On the other hand it may well reflect a respectable, autonomous preference for a quiet life or a life devoted to friendship. We would be able to tell the difference if more opportunities for self-realization were available, for if they were still not chosen, it would show that the desire for a different life style was an autonomous one, or at least one not shaped by the feasible set.

---

[55] Habermas, *Theorie des kommunikativen Handelns*; see also Knut Midgaard, "On the Signifi-cance of Language and a Richer Concept of Rationality," Leif Lewin and Evert Vedung, eds., *Politics as Rational Action* (Dordrecht: Reidel, 1980), pp.87–93.
[56] For a more detailed exposition of this argument, I again refer to Ch. III of my *Sour Grapes*.

(b) *Democracy and size*

Oliver Williamson and others have argued that there are inherent advantages of hierarchy over peer group organization.[57] Hierarchy economizes on the costs of diffusion of information, which is channeled through the leadership instead of being exchanged between all members in pairwise interactions. It imposes a solution on trivial allocation problems that might otherwise have been the object of protracted bargaining. It is more consistent with the monitoring of labor productivity which, although not impossible in the peer group, violates its spirit. These advantages, finally, increase more than proportionally with the size of the group.

To assess these claims, the problem must be stated more precisely. I am concerned with evaluating economic institutions in terms of justice, the scope allowed for self-realization, and psychological stability. Efficiency is not explicitly an issue, but it enters indirectly as a requirement for self-realization, as I argued above. Recall, moreover, that the peer group is only supposed to make major policy decisions, not to supervise the day-to-day activities of all members. It appears to me that all the advantages of hierarchy cited above could be preserved by having some members of the peer group perform managerial functions in accordance with these policy decisions. The difficulty, it would seem, arises at the level of these decisions themselves. Direct democracy is vulnerable to attrition and to plain lack of interest in decision making, e.g., if the workers are fully engaged in self-realization through work. Moreover, with large numbers of workers, it is technically inefficient and hence self-defeating *on its own terms*. To preserve efficiency and economic justice, delegation of decision making to elected representatives then becomes necessary. This arrangement would allow self-realization for these representatives, but not for the rank and file. In the best of all possible worlds, the latter would then be able to achieve self-realization in the work process itself.

Firm size depends largely on technology. To the extent that it is possible to channel technical change in the direction of smaller productive units, it is most urgent to do so in firms where the productive tasks themselves do not offer much scope for self-realization. Because of the economies of scale in self-realization, it is less important to insist on direct democracy where the work itself already offers sufficient challenge. Musicians in an orchestra may well prefer a dictatorial leader, even if he sometimes makes decisions with which they disagree, since this leaves them with more time to concentrate on their work.

[57] Oliver E. Williamson *Markets and Hierarchies* (New York: The Free Press, 1975). For a recent survey, see M. McPherson, "Efficiency and Liberty in the Productive Enterprise: Recent Work in the Economics of Work Organization," *Philosophy and Public Affairs*, vol. 12 (1983), pp.354–368.

(c) *Market or planning?*

The macroeconomic institutions of a society will have a profound influence on both the desire and the opportunity for self-realization. What I shall have to say about the impact on desires will be largely speculative, but I believe the comments on opportunities are somewhat more robust.

Central planning is not favorable to the two modes of self-realization under discussion. To imagine participatory economic democracy in a centrally planned economy is almost a logical contradiction, since it would involve having the same decisions made by two different sets of people. (Imagine, moreover, the complications that would follow from participatory democracy in the planning agencies!) I have also argued that the market performs a useful function for self-realization through work by providing independent external criteria of evaluation, whereas Soviet-type economies have been plagued by the difficulty of finding similarly nonmanipulable criteria. On the other hand, the "market mentality" might work against self-realization by providing incentives to produce profitable junk rather than high-quality products that meet no effective demand. The problem is analogous to the conflict between technical change and self-realization mentioned above, and the solution would also have to be similar: to offer scope for self-realization through general skills of tinkering and improvising.

"Market socialism" with direct economic democracy might also be thought to be, if not a contradiction in terms, at least psychologically unstable. Will not the competition between enterprises be incompatible with the solidarity within the enterprise that is needed to make self-management work? The role of solidarity is twofold. On the one hand, all workers must be motivated to work steadily without shirking. On the other hand, the more qualified workers must accept that the salary gap cannot be too large, i.e., that the labor market must be regulated, since otherwise the motivation of the less qualified might be impaired. I do not know of any evidence that these requirements are incompatible with the spirit of competition. Without going so far as to say that solidarity cannot work unless it is solidarity *against others*, it appears to be a fact of life that intergroup competition and intergroup solidarity often coexist stably.

(d) *How to get from here to there (and remain there)*

Consider some possibilities:

		Workers under capitalism prefer	
		Capitalism	Socialism
Workers under socialism prefer	Capitalism	(i)	(ii)
	Socialism	(iii)	(iv)

Scenario (i) corresponds to a dominant capitalist ideology: workers don't want to move to socialism, and if they got there they would want to leave it. Scenario (ii) can be seen as an expression of "counteradaptive preferences," created by the fact that both capitalism and socialism have many unattractive and ugly features, so that each of them would generate a desire for its opposite.[58] Scenario (iii) need not similarly be an expression of adaptive preferences. If socialism retains all the options of capitalism, while adding that of self-realization, the desire in socialism for socialism would not be an adaptive one. The preference for capitalism in capitalism would, however, be adaptive. Scenario (iv) would seem totally utopian in the light of recent history. Note, however, that from the observed resistance to moving towards socialism one cannot infer a lack of preference for socialism, since the former might also be due to the costs of transition and the free-rider problem in revolutionary action.

I argued in Section II that the resistance to self-realization is largely due to myopia and free-riding. We now see that the same two obstacles arise in the path towards socialism. I believe that the two problems and the solutions to them are closely related, but that is the topic of another paper.[59,60]

Political Science,
University of Chicago and Institute for Social Research,
Oslo

[58] For the idea of counteradaptive preferences, see *Sour Grapes*, p.111–12. For the idea that capitalism and socialism cyclically generate desires for each other, see John Dunn, *The Politics of Socialism* (Cambridge: Cambridge University Press, 1984).

[59] See the paper cited in note 21 above.

[60] Note added in proof: I was both elated and depressed (as is usual in such cases) to find that a central argument of this article had been anticipated by Frank J. Landy, "An opponent-process theory of job satisfaction," *Journal of Applied Psychology*, vol. 63 (1978), pp. 533–547.

THE MARXIST CONCEPTUAL FRAMEWORK AND THE ORIGINS OF TOTALITARIAN SOCIALISM

ALLEN BUCHANAN

1. *Causes and Reasons*

One of the few things modern liberals, classical liberals, and conservatives can agree on is the charge that some of the worst features of totalitarian socialist regimes have their origins in the writings of Karl Marx and Friedrich Engels.[1] Nevertheless, the nature of this claim, and therefore the reasons for accepting or rejecting it, are often left obscure.

If it is understood simply as a causal statement, then it must be confirmed or disconfirmed by empirical social science. The political philosopher can at most assist by providing a clear characterization of the conceptual content of the beliefs which constitute the independent variable in the alleged causal relation: those beliefs concerning Marx's and Engels's thoughts which are said to have exerted the causal influence in question. Even if empirical research did show that beliefs about Marxist theory were a significant causal influence in the rise of certain features of totalitarian socialism, this would be of limited *philosophical* interest if the beliefs in question were misunderstandings of the theory and if the correct explanation of why these misunderstandings occurred appealed to factors external to the theory itself. However, it would be of considerable philosophical interest if correct beliefs about Marxist theory exerted a causal influence on some of the more undesirable aspects of totalitarian socialism, or if incorrect beliefs did *and* the existence of these misunderstandings could be traced to ambiguities or gaps in the Marxist theory itself.

The political philosopher has a legitimate interest in the relationship between the writings of Marx and Engels on the rise of totalitarian socialism, not because he is interested in articulating and testing causal connections between beliefs and social phenomena in general, but because Marxist theory is supposed – by its authors – to inspire and guide change toward a better society. Indeed, the founders of Marxism insist that a social theory is to be judged by its practical fruits.

Whether or not certain elements of Marxist theory *did in fact* play a significant causal role in the rise of some of the more unattractive features of

---

[1] Too often, critics of Marxism have failed to distinguish clearly between abuses of Marxist theory and deficiencies of the theory itself.

totalitarian socialism is not of primary concern to the philosopher. But it will count heavily against Marxist theory if it can be shown that a system with precisely those deficiencies that are observed in totalitarian socialism is just the sort of system one would reasonably expect to come about through the efforts of persons who relied upon the Marxist conceptual framework for inspiration and guidance. Of course, if such conceptual deficiencies can be demonstrated, and if a better alternative explanation is lacking, then the most reasonable causal hypothesis will be that existing totalitarian socialist systems have these deficiencies because their development was in fact influenced by adherence to the defective conceptual scheme advanced by Marx and Engels.

Virtually any social theory, from Marxism to libertarianism, can, with sufficient perversity, be twisted so as to justify almost any policy. The egalitarianism of the French Revolution provided ideological resources for rampant imperialism masquerading as liberation, and the United States invoked a similarly distorted appeal to individual rights in 1847 when it fought to free Americans (who happened to be living in Mexico) from Mexican domination. To show that the evils of totalitarian socialism have conceptual origins in deficiencies of Marxist theory, then, it is not sufficient to show that Marxist theory can, if sufficiently abused, support such regimes. Instead, it must be shown that the evils of totalitarian socialism are a natural, if not a thoroughly predictable development, given the character of Marxist doctrine. This way of stating the issue has an important virtue: it allows us to ask not only whether certain features of totalitarian socialism can be traced to positive theses or concepts that are distinctive of the Marxist framework, but also whether there may be omissions or lacunae in Marxist thought which encourage the abuses of totalitarian socialism. I shall argue that some of the relevant deficiencies in the Marxist conceptual framework are omissions rather than commissions.

In what follows, I focus on what I take to be the most serious evils of totalitarian socialism: its anti-democratic, elitist character; its violation of individual civil and political rights; and its thorough "politicization" of life, the breaking down of the division between the political and private spheres and the correlative unlimited expansion of the state's control over all aspects of human life. I shall argue that these characteristics of totalitarian socialism are linked to three basic features of Marxist theory: (1) a simple rational self-interest theory of revolutionary action, (2) the lack of a theory of efficient, democratic social coordination, and (3) an impoverished understanding of the circumstances of justice and of the value of rights. Mainly for stylistic reasons, I will refer to Marx's views, rather than Marx's and Engels's, but this should cause no difficulty. Although it is true that the two founders of Marxism held different views on some subjects. I know of no evidence to suggest that they disagreed significantly on any of the matters I shall discuss.

2. The Simple Rational Self-Interest Theory of Revolutionary Motivation

The main elements of Marx's theory of how a successful proletarian revolution will come about can be briefly outlined. At a certain stage in the development of capitalism, what Marx calls the "contradictions" of the system become so extreme that they become plain to any but the most abject bourgeois hypocrite. A shrinking minority of propertied nonworkers stands in undisguised opposition to an expanding majority of propertyless workers. Caught in the toils of worsening business cycles, workers are laid off because they have been too productive. Wealth accumulates in the hands of the minority, while accelerating impoverishment and mental and physical degradation are the lot of the majority. Once the proletarian, aided by the work of the revolutionary leadership, recognizes these basic facts of the class struggle (which Marx articulates and systematizes in his materialist conception of history and his analysis of capitalism), he will realize that his own interest, as well as that of every other proletarian, requires the overthrow of the system. As the capitalists continue to exert more pressure on the proletarians, extracting ever more surplus value, it becomes more apparent to the proletarians that the system must be overthrown. When enough proletarians achieve this recognition of their interests, they will act together to overthrow the system.[2]

Perhaps the most distinctive feature of Marx's theory of revolution is its claim that any significant motivational role for moral principles, including principles of justice that refer to individual rights, is unnecessary for the success of the revolution. According to Marx, communist leaders need not appeal to anyone's sense of justice, and there is no need to work out a theory of rights to inspire and guide successful proletarian revolutionary activity. Marx even goes so far as to say that talk about justice and rights is "obsolete verbal rubbish" and "ideological nonsense," and to emphasize that communists "preach no morality."[3] He seems instead to have espoused what may be called a simple rational self-interest theory of successful revolutionary action, assuming that once the proletarians come to know that it is in their interest to overthrow the capitalism system, they will act together to take the necessary means to achieve their collective end. The role of the revolutionary leadership (those Marx calls "the communists") is to educate the proletarians as to their best interests and to provide tactical and strategic guidance.

---

[2] For a fuller discussion of Marx's theory of revolutionary action, along with citations of key texts in Marx, see A. Buchanan, "Revolutionary Motivation and Rationality," *Philosophy & Public Affairs*, vol. 9, no. 1 (1979) pp. 59–82, and A. Buchanan, *Marx and Justice: The Radical Critique of Liberalism* (Totowa, NJ: Rowman & Allanheld, 1982), Chapter Five. Much of my discussion of Marx's theory of revolution in the present essay is drawn from these two sources.

[3] K. Marx, "Critique of the Gotha Programme," in *Karl Marx: Selected Writings*, ed. D. McLellan (Oxford UK: Oxford University Press, 1977), p.565.

Elsewhere I have argued that the simple rational self-interest theory of successful revolutionary action is subject to a serious objection. Concerted revolutionary action on the part of the proletariat is a public good which, like other public goods, may be blocked by the familiar free-rider and assurance problems. A public good is any desired object or state of affairs which has these characteristics: (1) producing it requires the contribution of a group of people; (2) if it is produced it will be available to everyone in the group including those who did not contribute to its production; (3) it would be either impossible or too costly to exclude noncontributors from partaking of the good; (4) each individual's contribution is a cost to him; and (5) the benefit each individual will gain if the good is produced will outweight the cost of his contribution. When these conditions obtain, individuals may refrain from contributing to the public good either in order to take a free-ride on the efforts of others and reap the benefit without incurring the cost, or because they are unwilling to contribute unless they have assurance that others will reciprocate (even though they would contribute if they had such assurance and have no intention of taking a free-ride on the efforts of others).

For economy of exposition I shall concentrate on the free-rider problem, but most of what I say will apply to the assurance problem as well. The free-rider problem arises for public goods such as population control, clean air, energy conservation, preventing wage-price spiral inflation, and national defense, and can be represented by a simple decision-matrix.

	Others	
	Contribute	Don't Contribute
Contribute	Benefits of G 2 Costs of Contribution	No Benefits of G 4 Costs of Contribution
Individual		
Don't Contribute	Benefits of G 1 No Costs of Contribution	No Benefits of G 3 No Costs of Contribution

The numbers in the four cells of the matrix represent the individual's preferences among the possible outcomes: the lower left cell (the individual doesn't contribute, others do) is his first preference, the upper left cell his second preference, etc. As the matrix shows, the public good will not be produced if individuals act rationally in the sense of maximizing expected individual utility.

Public goods problems, however, are not limited to groups *individual* utility maximizers. The matrix can be used to represent the free-rider problem for individuals who seek to maximize *group* rather than individual utility. Each individual may reason in the following way. "Regardless of whether I contribute or not, either enough others will contribute so that the good will be produced or they will not. If enough others do contribute, then my costs of contribution will have done no good, but they will constitute a subtraction from the utility the group gains from the good. If not enough others contribute to produce the good, then my costs of contribution again will have been wasted and again will constitute a subtraction from the group's utility. In either case I should not contribute, in order to maximize group utility."

Derek Parfit and Brian Barry have raised an interesting objection to the group-utility maximizing version of the public goods problem.[4] Since the expected utility of an option is the product of the net benefit that would result and the probability that the benefit will occur, contributing to the public good will maximize expected utility even through the probability that one's contribution will make the difference between success and failure is extremely small, *if the net expected benefit is very great.* But if the benefits from the public good in question will accrue to *extremely large numbers of people,* then this latter condition may be satisfied. So, even if one believes that the probability that one's own contribution will make or break the revolution is extremely small, one may nonetheless believe that success would produce so much good (because so many people would reap the fruits of the revolution, both now and in future generations) that one *will* contribute, if one is a group-utility maximizer.

One might reply to the Barry-Parfit point by arguing that, as a matter of fact, most people who generally behave as group-utility maximizers simply are not successfully motivated by the thought of such extremely remote possibilities for gain. And one might even go further, claiming that such behavior is not irrational, even for those who are committed to maximizing group utility.

However, to blunt the force of the Barry-Parfit argument as a reply to the charge that Marx's theory of revolution is subject to a public good problem, one need not deny that thoroughgoing group-utility maximizers would contribute to the proletarian revolution. Instead, one can argue that the group-utility maximizing solution is simply not available to Marx for two reasons. First, the claim that proletarians will act out of devotion to maximizing expected group utility, even when the probability that success

[4] B. Barry, *Sociologists, Economists, and Democracy* (London: Collier-MacMillan, 1970), p.32. D. Parfit, *Reasons and Persons* (Oxford: Oxford University Press, 1984), pp.73–78.

depends upon any one person's contribution is vanishingly small, seems to run contrary to Marx's refusal to rely upon moral motivation and, in particular, upon altruism. But second, and perhaps more important, a main feature of Marx's theory of worker alienation is his thesis that capitalism pits worker against worker, erecting formidable barriers to altruism or group-utility-maximizing motivation. Indeed, one of the great appeals of Marx's simple rational self-interest theory is that it purports to show how revolution will come about in the absence of altruism or group-utility-maximizing motivation.

Marx himself seems uncomfortably aware of the implications of his theory of worker alienation for his simple rational self-interest theory of revolution in the following passage:

> Competition separates individuals from one another, not only the bourgeois but still more the workers, in spite of the fact that it brings them together. Hence, it is a long time before these individuals can unite, apart from the fact that for the purpose of this union – if it is not merely local – the necessary means, the big industrial cities and cheap and quick communications, have first to be produced by large-scale industry. Hence every organized power standing over and against these isolated individuals, who live in conditions daily reproducing this isolation, can only be overcome after a long struggle.[5]

In this passage the problem of how competing, alienated, self-interested individuals can act together is recognized but not solved. Advances in communication and concentration of workers may be necessary conditions for effective collective action, but as the public good problem shows, they are not sufficient.

Once the process of revolution gets underway, individuals may come to be motivated by gains that are intrinsic to the process itself – a sense of community, solidarity in the face of adversity, etc. And, as Marx predicts, the alienated, self-interested individual might, through the process of revolution, begin to be transformed into a communal being who identifies directly, as it were, with the interests of the group. But, of course, none of this explains how alienated workers, as Marx describes them, could be motivated to begin the process by the desire to maximize group utility, especially when the probability that any one individual's action would make a difference is pitifully small.

[5] K. Marx and F. Engles, *The German Ideology*, in *Collected Works: Marx and Engles*, vol. 5 (New York: International Publishers, 1976), p. 75.

The weakness of Marx's theory of revolution becomes more apparent once we attend to his assumptions about the role of the capitalists in the revolutionary process. Marx believed that successful revolutionary action by the proletariat will occur *only* if the capitalists continue to exert increasing pressure upon the workers, presumably because he thought that only then will a sufficient number of workers come to see clearly that their interest requires the overthrow of the system. Now, each capitalist is said to be driven by the incentive structure of the capitalist system to extract ever more surplus value from his workers. Marx maintains that to avoid his own extinction through competition each capitalist must continue to do that which will eventually result in the extinction of the capitalist class, even if he knows that if other capitalists act as he does the proletariat will find its condition unbearable and a revolution will occur. What is rational for each capitalist is collectively irrational.

Stemming the pressure they are exerting on the workers is, for the capitalist class, a public good. And according to Marx, what we now call the free-rider problem prevents the capitalists from achieving that public good, and failure to achieve it is a necessary condition for successful proletarian revolution.

Thus, Marx himself not only was aware that the free-rider problem may block collective efforts to provide public goods, but also made the insolubility of the capitalists' public good problem a cornerstone of his theory of revolution. It seems more than appropriate, therefore, to conclude that Marx must show why the workers' public good problem can be solved, while the capitalists' cannot, and that he must do so in a way that is consistent with the main elements of both his theory of revolutionary motivation and his theory of alienation. In other words, defenders of Marx cannot simply dismiss the public goods objection to Marx's simple rational self-interest theory of revolution on the grounds that such problems are alien to Marx's conceptual framework.

The task for the Marxist, however, is onerous. The most common and obvious solution to a public good problem is to enforce contribution by the threat of coercion, so that noncontribution will become more costly than contribution. But if this path is taken, all the advantages lie on the side of the capitalists. According to Marx, they already control the dominant coercive apparatus, the state, while the worker's goal is to gain control of the state (and then destroy it). Indeed, perhaps the most plausible explanation of the failure of proletarian revolution in almost all industrialized countries includes the hypothesis that capitalists have in fact solved their public goods problem by making the condition of the workers tolerable through welfare programs, including health and unemployment insurance financed by tax contributions from capitalists, enforced by the state.

Quite aside from Marx's difficulties in explaining why the capitalists cannot solve their public goods problem, Marx's failure to recognize that his own theory of revolutionary motivation poses a public goods problem for the proletariat can have serious practical consequences for how Marxist revolutionaries respond to those who refuse to join the revolutionary struggle.

Indeed, once these deficiencies of Marx's theory of revolution are clearly understood, the emergence of two of the worst features of totalitarian socialist regimes is hardly surprising. The first feature is the tendency, exhibited in both the Soviet Union and China, to reclassify as 'small capitalists' (or 'kulaks') some of those previously regarded as proletarians, and then to suppress or annihilate them for the sake of the revolution. For if one uncritically assumes the simple rational self-interest theory, then one will be tempted to reason as follows: "These persons, whom we have previously considered proletarians, steadfastly refuse to join the revolutionary struggle, in spite of the fact that our educational efforts, as well as the deepening crises of capitalism, have made it abundantly clear that revolution is in the interest of the proletarians. Therefore, these individuals must not really be proletarians."

Now, it is no doubt true that the reclassification strategy sometimes has been used in socialist revolutions by unscrupulous leaders as a rationale for their own efforts at personal aggrandizement. But the explanation I have given for it shows why it is an almost predictable development, even if we assume the purest of motives for those who control the revolution.

The second tendency often goes with the first and is perhaps most clearly exhibited in the Russian and Vietnamese revolutions. It is the emergence of an authoritarian revolutionary elite, a minority willing to use coercion and terror, not only against the class enemies of the proletariat, but also against recalcitrant proletarians in order to ensure their contribution to the revolution. Once we recognize the failure of the simple rational self-interest theory to respond to the proletarians' public goods problem, the use of coercion by a dedicated revolutionary vanguard against proletarians makes perfectly good sense. It would be surprising if a rational Marxist revolutionary leader did not avail himself of this strategy, since the capitalists' effective use of the coercive solution to their public goods problem would serve as a model, and since Marx's admonition to dispense with moral principles in the revolutionary process removes moral constraints against paternalism toward the proletariat. And granted Marx's own frequent insistence that the new communist society develops organically out of the revolutionary process, it again should not surprise us if post-revolutionary socialist regimes should continue to exhibit authoritarian elitism and to classify as bourgeois (or as mentally ill) those who oppose the leadership. In this sense, some of the most reprehensible features not only of the socialist revolutionary process but also of the post-revolutionary socialist state, have their conceptual origins in deficiencies of the Marxist simple rational interest theory of revolution.

It might be replied on Marx's behalf that even though there are passages in which he seems to subscribe to the simple rational self-interest theory, there are also scattered remarks in which he at least leaves open the possibility for developing a more complex and plausible Marxist theory of revolutionary motivation. In particular, it might be argued, a refined Marxist theory could consistently place greater emphasis on what were referred to earlier as in-process benefits and upon leadership by example. Indeed, a significant role could also be recognized for loyalty to and solidarity with one's fellow workers, since it is not at all clear that doing so would contradict Marx's claim that successful revolution does not depend (at least primarily) on *moral* motivation. (Even if loyalty, for example, is in some sense a moral notion, it still seems quite different from what Marx took to be the paradigmatically moral notions of justice and rights.)

This reply on Marx's behalf is hard to assess. This much seems clear, however. Even if Marx could have or even implicitly did endorse a more complex and plausible view of revolutionary motivation, he failed to develop it and at least conveyed the impression that the simple rational self-interest theory was a distinctive element of his overall position. If this is so, then there is a sense in which Marx's writings do provide an explanation of some of the tragic practices which the simple rational self-interest theory encourages.

3. *The Lack of a Theory of Efficient Democratic Social Coordination*

Marx is committed to the prediction that communist society will achieve *highly efficient, nonexploitative, democratic* social coordination. Though he has remarkably little to say about the democratic nature of communist social coordination, he seems to mean that each individual, at least over time, is to have an equal share of control in the process by which rational, comprehensive decisions for allocation, production, and distribution are made and implemented. This process may be described roughly as 'centrally planned socialism', since there is no suggestion in his writings that Marx ever seriously contemplated the relatively decentralized system known as market socialism. Moreover, he strenuously condemned two features of market socialism – its dependence upon competitive motivation (competition among firms) and its reliance upon market supply and demand rather than upon a deliberate decision-making process for the entire economy. Marx is committed to a very strong prediction, namely, that communism will achieve even greater productivity than capitalism but without exploitation, that it will distribute what is produced much more efficiently, that it will do so through a process which is democratic, and that all of this will be achieved without reliance upon markets but, rather, through comprehensive, and presumably centralized, planning. Further, all of this is to be achieved without the state as a coercive apparatus, as it is in a 'command economy' of the sort found in existing nonmarket socialist systems such as the U.S.S.R. and China.

It would be an exaggeration to say that no theory of an efficient, non-market, planned social coordination exists. At the turn of the century, Pareto and Barone argued that a system of input-output equations could be used to make allocation decisions that would achieve the efficiency of the ideal market at equilibrium, but without the use of markets. In other words, a non-market theory capable of generating an efficiency theorem is available. However, as Hayek has pointed out[6] and as most economists now agree, use of this theory requires the solving of many millions of simultaneous equations, and even with steady advances in computer technology, actually using this theory to coordinate social activity for a large-scale society would not be feasible in the foreseeable future, if ever.

As I already noted, Marx and most later Marxists (including G.A. Cohen and Allen Wood) assume not only that a highly productive and efficient alternative to the market is feasible, but that it can be achieved by a system of *democratic* decision making.[7] At least in the dominant Marxist tradition, then, justifying predictions about the superiority of communism requires *a theory of democratic social coordination* whose explanatory power is comparable to that of the ideal market model. Such a theory, if it were available, would have to address a number of well-known arguments against democratic decision making on grounds of inefficiency.

Among the most important sources of inefficiency in democratic decision making for the allocation of resources and the production and distribution of goods in a large-scale economy are (1) time costs and (2) information costs of the procedure itself.[8] In a democratic process, the ever-scarce resource of time is consumed lavishly: first, in articulating issues and presenting an agenda to voters; second, in discussing the issues; and third, in actually achieving a decision (where this may involve rounds of voting). Even if the use of electronic mass-media technology could reduce the first source of time costs, the second and third may still result in great inefficiency,

---

[6] F. Hayek, "The Present State of the Debate," F. Hayek, ed., *Collectivist Economic Planning* (New York: Augustus M. Kelley, 1967), pp.208–210. For a critical discussion of the Socialist Calculation Debate to which Hayek's essay was a contribution, see A. Buchanan, *Ethics, Efficiency, and the Market* (Totowa, NJ: Rowan & Allanheld, 1985), Chapter 4.

[7] A detailed discussion of Marx's views on communism as a democratic form of social organization is presented in A. Buchanan, *Marx and Justice: The Radical Critique of Liberalism*, pp.169–175.

[8] For a more detailed discussion, see A. Buchanan, "Marx on Democracy and the Obsolescence of Rights," South African *Journal of Philosophy*, Marx Centenary Issue, Vol. 2, No. 3 (1983), pp. 130–35.

especially where decisions are interdependent and must be made quickly or in a definite, time-ordered sequence. Time costs are particularly trouble-some where the unaminity rule is used, but they are also present in all other forms of majority rule.

The exorbitant information costs of democratic procedures are no less grave. For complex, large-scale allocation decisions, the information required for a rational decision may not be available or may be available only at great cost, or will often be so complex that it will be very difficult if not impossible for any individual or group of individuals to integrate and apply it. There may also be motivational impediments to the gathering, integration, and application of information. In many cases the individual will reasonably believe that his vote will not be decisive. The individual may then reason that either enough others who share his preferences will vote on a given issue to achieve the outcome he prefers, even if he does not vote, or that not enough others will vote to achieve the outcome he prefers, even if he does vote. Thus, he may conclude that regardless of how others vote, the rational thing for him to do is not to vote, since voting (as well as becoming sufficiently informed on the issues) is a cost. This is just to say that informed voter participation is a public good, and may be subject to the free-rider problem.

Further, in many cases the individual will lack an incentive to expend time and resources in order to become informed and to vote simply because the issue in question will be of little consequence to him. Hayek has correctly stressed the enormous amount of ever-shifting information required for making allocation and distribution decisions for a large-scale economy and how little information individuals need in the market system by comparison.

The use of representatives, of policy packages, and of centralization in the process of gathering, integrating, and disseminating information can all be viewed as attempts to reduce the time and information costs of democratic decision making. Efficient (i.e., Pareto-optimal outcomes) are hardly likely, however, if the voter must choose a package of policies (some of which he does not endorse) or must rely upon a representative (who will at best vote in accordance with some but not all his preferences). Moreover, centraliza-tion of the information process, even if it is done efficiently, threatens to undermine the *democratic* character of the decision-making process by concentrating power in the hands of those who control the data upon which others vote their decisions.

But even if we set aside inefficiencies due to time and information costs, there is another important source of inefficiency in democratic decision making. Pareto-sub-optimality is a direct consequence of the fact that majority decisions are incapable of taking into account the *intensity* of an individual's preferences. Suppose Jones favors policy P very strongly, while Smith opposes P, but not strongly. If Jones were able to engage in vote bargaining to trade his vote on some other issue about which Smith does care strongly, or if Jones were able to give Smith a 'side payment' in exchange for Smith's favorable vote on P, then both Jones and Smith would be better off than if they simply were to vote their preferences. Vote bargaining, either in the form of trading or of selling votes, allows individuals to express the intensity of their preferences, while majority rule voting does not. As with representatives, policy packages, and centralization of information, avoiding inefficiency through vote bargaining comes at a steep price. Vote bargaining undermines the ideal of equal control that animates the insistence on democratic control over allocation and distribution, because it is equivalent to giving some individuals more votes than others on a given issue by giving the former fewer votes on other issues. Vote bargaining, then, is not a device for achieving efficient democratic social coordination; it is a way of achieving efficiency at the expense of democracy.

Of course, the decision to allow vote bargaining for certain types of decisions might itself be arrived at by some form of democratic, i.e., majority rule. But to admit this is not to deny that vote bargaining erodes the fundamental commitment to equal control over decisions – it is only to recognize that a procedure which is democratic may be used to undermine democracy.

It is not my aim here to demonstrate that an efficient democratic alternative to the market is impossible. Instead, I only hope to have established that a *theory* of efficient democratic social coordination must be developed to support Marx's predictions about communism.

The point is not simply that Marx (like subsequent Marxists) failed to provide a workable theory of efficient, nonexploitative, democratic, non-market social coordination. More surprisingly, Marx seems to have felt that *no such theory was needed.* Marx proudly stated that he offered no "recipes for the cook-shops of the future," and his followers have rather smugly taken his refusal to say much about the actual workings of social coordination in communism to be an example of the epistemological superiority of Marxist 'scientific socialism' over 'utopian socialism'. But this vaunted agnosticism about the specifics of social coordination in communism is one of Marxism's deepest flaws, not one of its greatest virtues.

What could have led Marx to predict so confidently that social coordination in communism would satisfy such strong and potentially conflicting constraints – that it would be highly productive and efficient and democratic and nonexploitative, and would rely neither upon markets nor the coercive power of the state – without so much as a sketch of a theory of communist social coordination?

My suggestion is that Marx, like many other Marxists, including most recently Allen Wood, subscribed to what may be called the 'impediment theory' of democratic social coordination. According to this view, any problems of democratic social coordination serious enough to require recourse to a theory of social coordination are simply artifacts of the class system. As soon as the impediment of the class system is removed, democratic social coordination exhibiting all the features that Marx attributed to communism will emerge.

> Fundamentally . . . [Marx] does not see the problem as a procedural problem at all. For Marx, the chief obstacle both to individual freedom and social unity is the division of society into oppressing and oppressed classes. Of course as long as we tacitly assume a class society, the goals of freedom and community will look both separately unattainable and diametrically opposed. In a society where one individual's freedom is not necessarily another's servitude, and where people have no motives to use community as a pretext for advancing some people's interests at the expense of others, questions of social decision making will not appear to people in the form of theoretical paradoxes or insoluble technical problems.[9]

This response by Wood simply begs the question. Without confronting the growing and sophisticated literature on the subject, Wood has simply dismissed all the familiar problems of democratic decision making on the basis of the unargued assumption that they would not arise in a classless society. Not only is this assumption unargued and far from self-evident; it is on its face implausible. The need for a theory of democratic decision making seems only to presuppose conflicting preferences, not egoism or class interests. And even members of a classless society who all sincerely seek the common good may have serious disagreements over how to specify the common good or how best to achieve it.

We have seen that, on the one hand, Marx is self-righteously agnostic about *how* communist social coordination will come about, while on the other, he is marvelously confident *that* it will come about and that it will have all of the desirable features he attributes to it. But this particular combination of professed ignorance and professed knowledge is far from scientific. If the error were limited to the realm of theory, it would not be so serious. But in Marxism, theoretical error encourages practical disasters, and Marx himself stresses that his theory is to be judged by the practical consequences of adherence to it.

If one remains steadfast in the belief that highly efficient, democratic, nonexploitative social consideration will emerge once class division are

---

[9] A. Wood, *Karl Marx* (London: Routledge & Kegan Paul, 1981), p.58.

eradicated and egoism is abolished or diminished, but recognizes that in fact the desired form of social coordination has not yet come about, a reasonable conclusion to be drawn is that class divisions have not yet been fully overcome and that egoism still flourishes. Once we see that Marx either subscribed to or at the very least strongly encouraged the impediment theory, it is not at all surprising that the ruling elite in totalitarian socialist regimes have frequently blamed the failures of their economic plans on 'wreckers', 'residual bourgeoisie', and 'outside agitators' from the West. Thus, the tendency to find scapegoats for the failure of the state's economic policies, and the ensuing violations of these individuals' rights, can be traced to fundamental deficiencies in the conceptual resources available to the Marxist. This is not to deny, of course, that the phenomenon of scapegoating has other roots as well.

4. *The Impoverished Conception of the Circumstances of Justice and the Value of Rights*

We have seen that Marx denied any important role for moral concepts generally and for concepts of justice and rights in particular in the revolutionary process, and I have already suggested that this tendency could hardly be expected to contribute to the development of adequate principles of justice or rights to be implemented in the post-revolutionary society.

This latter conclusion, however, would not trouble Marx. As I have argued in great detail in *Marx and Justice*,[10] Marx seems to have held that principles of justice, at least those which specify individual rights, simply will not be needed in communism because that form of society will have eliminated the sources of those sorts of conflicts which make individual rights valuable. Though my aim in this essay is to draw implications from this interpretation rather than to rehearse the complex arguments that support it, the main reasons for ascribing such a radical view to Marx can at least be sketched.

The hypothesis that Marx believed there would be no need, or at least no important social role, for rights-principles in communism provides the best explanation of three important features of his theory. The first is the fact that Marx not only heaped scathing criticism on the appeals which non-Marxist socialist made to notions of justice and rights, but also cast derision and scorn on discourse about rights and justice in general. As we have seen, Marx went so far as to say that talk about justice and rights is "out-dated verbal rubbish" and "ideological nonsense." The second is the total absence in Marx's writings of any indication that in communism there will be a role for rights-principles or concepts of justice, either in institutional arrangements or in individuals' practical attitudes towards themselves and others.

[10] A. Buchanan, *Marx and Justice: The Radical Critique of Liberalism*, Chapter Four.

The third reason for concluding that Marx thought communism would be a society beyond the need for concepts of justice and principles specifying rights is more complex. Marx's criticisms of civil and political rights in "On the Jewish Question" and of rights of distributive justice in *Critique of the Gotha Program* indicate that he subscribed to a very narrow view of what Hume and Rawls call 'the circumstances of justice' or, more precisely, the conditions under which rights-principles are valuable. In "On the Jewish Question" Marx advanced, or at the very least strongly suggested, the following argument for the obsolescence of basic civil and political rights:

(1) Rights, as (legal) guarantees for freedoms specified under the rights of man (and the citizen), are needed only where there is a potential for serious infringements of these freedoms.

(2) Serious infringements of the freedoms specified under the rights of man (and the citizen) can arise only from clashes of class interests and the egoism to which class conflict gives rise.

(3) In communist society there will be no classes, hence no clashes of class interest, and no egoism arising from class interest.

Therefore:

(4) In communism there will be no need for the rights of man (or of the citizen, if, as Marx suggests, these are correlatives of the rights of man) as legal guarantees.

Notice that the argument I attribute to Marx does not saddle him with the highly implausible view that there will be no conflicts in communist society. Instead, the argument only says that in communism there will be no conflicts arising from class interests or from the egoism which class interests generate. The crucial premise, of course, is (2) – a very simple and sweeping empirical hypothesis about the sorts of conflicts which make basic civil and political rights valuable protections for individual freedom. Marx describes the "rights of man" (which include the rights to freedom of expression, freedom of religious belief, equality before the law, and freedom of the person) as ". . . nothing but the rights of the member of civil society, i.e., egoistic man, separated from other men and from the community."[11]

In the *Critique of the Gotha Program*, Marx not only makes the very general remark that talk about justice and rights is "obsolete verbal rubbish" and "ideological nonsense," but he also voices a more substantive criticism that seems to be directed to what he takes to be the very concept of a right.

[11] K. Marx, "On the Jewish Question," D. McLellan, ed., *Karl Marx: Selected Writings* (Oxford: Oxford University Press, 1977), p.52.

But one man is superior to another physically or mentally and so supplies more labour in the same time, or can labour for a longer time, and labour, to serve as a measure, must be defined by its duration or intensity, otherwise it ceases to be a standard of measurement. This equal right is an unequal right for unequal labour. It recognizes no class differences, because everyone is only a worker like everyone else; but it tacitly recognizes unequal individual endowment and thus productive capacity as natural privileges. It is, therefore, a right of inequality, in its content, like every right. Right by its very nature can consist only in the application of an equal standard in so far as they are brought under an equal point of view, are taken from one definite side only, for instance, in the present case, are regarded only as workers and nothing more is seen in them, everything else being ignored. Further, one worker is married, another not; one has more children than another, and so on and so forth. Thus, with an equal performance of labour, and hence an equal share in the social consumption fund, one will in fact receive more than another, one will be richer than another, and so on. To avoid all these defects, right instead of being equal would have to be unequal.[12]

This passage indicates that Marx believed that the very concept of a right is defective – that rights as such are flawed, not just that certain forms of rights are.

We have already seen that Marx does little to support his prediction that the communist mode of production will be highly productive and efficient. The lack of support for this prediction has dire consequences for Marx's view that communism will not rely upon principles of justice specifying individuals' rights, because Marx seems to think that egoism and class conflict are all but inevitable until significant progress is made in overcoming scarcity of material goods. To the extent that Marx's predictions of increased productivity and efficiency are unsupported, his thesis of the obsolecence of rights rests on inadequate foundations. So even if Marx were correct in his conception of the circumstances which make rights valuable, he would still not be entitled to reject any significant role for rights in communism.

Marx's view, however, is subject to a much more radical criticism. His conception of the conditions under which rights are valuable is itself flawed. Rights can and do usefully serve the following functions, none of which presupposes class conflicts or even egoism. They can serve:

---

[12] *ibid.*, pp.568–69.

(1) as constraints on democratic procedures (e.g., for the protection of minorities) or as guarantees of access to participation in democratic procedures, i.e., as safeguards against anti-democratic, elite control;

(2) as constraints on paternalism, i.e., as limits on when and how we may interfere with a person's liberty for the sake of benefiting that person (where benefit is understood as welfare or freedom or some combination of these);

(3) as constraints on what may be done (and how it may be done) to maximize social welfare, or some other specification of the common good, such as freedom;

(4) as safeguards constraining the ways in which coercion or other penalties may be used in the provision of public goods; and,

(5) as a way of specifying the scope or limits of our obligations to provide for future generations.[13]

Further, each of these functions might still be needed even in a society which had a greater abundance of material goods than ours.

Hence, even if Marxists could make good the prediction that the overthrow of capitalism will result in a highly productive and efficient, democratic, nonexploitative, nonmarket system of social coordination, we would still have no good reason to believe that such a system could come into being, much less maintain itself, without a significant role for rights, including rights of democratic participation.

It is important to be clear about exactly where the burden of proof lies. On my interpretation, it is Marx who must defend a very sweeping empirical claim – the claim that a highly productive and efficient, nonexploitative, democratic, nonmarket society, can be established and maintained without reliance on rights (or upon the state). The burden of proof is clearly on the Marxist to substantiate this claim by showing that all of the functions that rights can serve will either not be needed in communism or will be taken care of in other ways. In the absence of a theory of communist social coordination (subject to all the strong and potentially conflicting constraints Marx places on that system), this task cannot even be begun.

Thus, Marx not only failed to provide conceptual resources that might have proved useful weapons in combatting rights violations during and after the revolution, but his writings also actively discouraged his followers from attempting to adapt old ways of thinking about justice and rights or to develop new ones better suited to socialist or communist social systems.

[13] A. Buchanan, *Marx and Justice: The Radical Critique of Liberalism*, pp.165–66.

Those who are convinced, as Marx was, that rights which demarcate the political from the private sphere are merely boundary fences to separate warring egoists and protect them in their selfish pursuits are precluded in principle from appealing to rights as protections against the thoroughgoing politicization of life and the relentless expansion of state authority that are characteristic of totalitarian socialism.

Marx is often criticized for denigrating individual personality and individual freedom. This criticism is grievously unjust. Marx dedicated his life to revolution precisely because he valued individual personality and individual freedom above all else and because he believed that they could flourish only in a system of democratic control over the means of production. Marx is not a villain contemptuous of individuality. He is a tragic figure who valued the individual but succeeded all too well in promulgating a theory that not only lacked the conceptual resources needed for building a society in which the individual is free to develop, but that also discouraged others from recognizing, much less attempting to remedy, its shortcomings.

Philosophy, University of Arizona

MARXISM, DICTATORSHIP, AND THE ABOLITION OF RIGHTS

DAVID GORDON

Is a Marxist society liable to be an oppressive one? To ask this question is immediately to pose two others: what is meant by Marxism; and what counts as an oppressive society? To take these questions in reverse order, by an oppressive society I shall mean one in which, *other things being equal*, people do not possess basic civil liberties. Examples of basic civil liberties (I intend here to be fairly uncontroversial) include, but are not limited to, freedom of religion, freedom of speech, freedom of assembly, and, if the society has a political system, the freedom to participate in that system. An example of what I mean by basic civil liberties is the system of basic liberties discussed by Rawls; the United States Bill of Rights is another example.

Before turning to what I mean by Marxism, three points of clarification are in order. First, I am referring to "oppressive" rather than "totalitarian" societies because the term "totalitarian," as, e.g., in the influential model of Friedrich and Brzezinski, often has as a criterion one-man rule;[1] I do not intend to discuss one-man rule, as I have no interesting arguments on whether or not a Marxist regime tends in this direction. Second, I should explain the "other things being equal" clause in my definition of an oppressive society: Marxists contend that civil liberties, as they exist in bourgeois society, are "purely formal"; it is only when a socialist society is established that human beings realize their true nature.[2] The establishment of socialism is more important than the existence of formal civil liberties. The *ceteris paribus* clause is meant to allow the possibility that this view is correct. If it is, then a society deficient in civil liberties that realized the goals held "more important" than them would not count as oppressive. (I do not myself think that this position is correct, but I do not wish to beg the question against proponents of it.) Third, I have not listed the right of individuals to

* I should like to thank the editors of *Social Philosophy and Policy* and Robert Nozick for very helpful suggestions.

[1] Carl J. Friedrich and Zbigniew K. Brzezinski, *Totalitarian Dictatorship and Autocracy* (Cambridge: Harvard University Press, 1956), pp.31f.

[2] Marx, in *On the Jewish Question*, states that the rights of men are "nothing but the rights of the member of civil society, i.e., egoistic man, separated from other men and from the community"; Karl Marx, *Selected Writings*, ed. David McLellan (Oxford: Oxford University Press, 1977), p.52

acquire property as a basic right. I in fact believe that it is one but once more do not wish to appeal at the start to a contention the socialist rejects.[3]

The question of how to define Marxism has aroused enormous controversy. Preferring, in Russell's phrase, "the advantages of theft over honest toil," I propose to stipulate a set of positions to be considered as necessary conditions for a Marxist view. (1) At some point in the development of a capitalist economy, transition to socialism is both possible and desirable. (I shall not consider cases of establishing socialism without the prior existence of a developed capitalist economy and take no position on whether one can support such change on a Marxist basis.) (2) A socialist society is characterized by public ownership of the means of production and a planned economy. (3) The form of the transition to socialism is the "dictatorship of the proletariat." (4) After the transitional period, a stage will ensue in which at least the major reasons for social conflict will cease to exist: "the free development of each will be the condition for the free development of all." (A Marxist might also hold, although this is not essential to Marxism, that at least one stage, called by Marx the "first stage of communism," intervenes between the dictatorship of the proletariat and the final stage of communism.) (5) The establishment of the dictatorship of the proletariat and subsequent stages is of supreme importance to human society.[4]

At last we can directly consider the question posed at the outset, but to do so, a division is necessary. The question must be asked separately for the dictatorship of the proletariat and the final stage of communism (as well as any intervening stages): is either liable to be oppressive? Further, in each case, we must distinguish between the defining criteria of the stage and the results of attempting to establish the stage. People often fail to achieve what they aim at, and the possibility that attempting to establish either stage will in fact establish something else must be considered. Additionally, if the answer to the question posed differs for each stage (e.g., suppose one concludes that the dictatorship of the proletariat is oppressive but the final stage of

---

[3] Rejecting the right of individual acquisition of property has more consequences than one might think. G.A. Cohen has argued (see his essay in the present volume) that self-ownership does not necessitate a libertarian position on property ownership. But the alternatives he gives are not socialist systems as Marxism understands socialism. It may be that if one accepts Marxism, one must reject self-ownership.

[4] I have not included as one of the conditions of Marxism that the change from capitalism to socialism will be accomplished through a revolution, since it is a much-controverted point whether Marx thought that the need for revolution in the transition to a socialist regime was invariable or only very likely. If he thought the former (as I think he did), then the case presented below that a Marxist regime will suppress civil liberties is strengthened. Revolutions and civil liberties mix poorly. Lenin makes a very good case for the view that Marxism teaches inevitable revolution in *State and Revolution*. He argues that seeming exceptions in Marx and Engels's works refer to conditions that no longer apply. See V. I. Lenin, *State and Revolution*, in *Selected Works in One Volume* (London: Lawrence and Wishart, 1969), p.274f.

communism isn't), we must determine which response is more important in assessing the likelihood that Marxism will lead to oppression.

One last preliminary matter. Several economists, most notably Ludwig von Mises and Friedrich Hayek, have argued that an economically developed socialist economy is either impossible in principle (Mises) or in practice (Hayek).[5] Although I find their arguments convincing, I shall not use them here as I wish to use only contentions that I can prove within the confines of this paper.

To begin, then, with the dictatorship of the proletariat, which Marx, in a letter to Wedemeyer, declared to be one of his most important social discoveries.[6] This dictatorship consists of rule by and in the interests of the proletariat, i.e., the working class. (Difficulties in defining "proletariat" will be resolutely ignored here.) Marx believed that capitalist society is dominated by the bourgeoisie, which uses the state as a means of enforcing its position as the ruling class. The proletariat must now "smash the existing state machinery" and establish a new state in which *its* interests prevail. The state remains what to Marx it must always be, an instrument of class domination: but now the proletariat is the ruling class.

From this brief characterization, we can at once see a possible area of conflict between proletarian dictatorship and civil liberties. A society in which civil liberties obtain is one in which the whole population has them. But if the purpose of the proletarian state is to secure and maintain the position of the proletariat as a ruling class, the bourgeoisie will possess civil liberties only to the extent that this is consistent with the state's purpose. (It will not suffice to reply that not everyone has civil liberties in capitalist society: even if this were true, it does not show that the dictatorship of the proletariat is unoppressive or less oppressive than capitalist society.) The state must smash the bourgeoisie: how, then, can this class possess civil liberties guaranteed to its members by right?

Marx himself left no room for doubt on this score. Writing immediately after the 1848 revolutions, he stated:

> With the victory of the 'red republic' in Paris, armies from the countryside will pour over the frontiers, and the real power of the contending parties will emerge clearly. Then we will remember June and October, and we too will cry out: *Vae victis* . . . there is only

---

[5] Ludwig von Mises, *Socialism* (New Haven: Yale University Press, 1951), pp.128–145; and *Human Action* (New Haven: Yale University Press, 1963), pp.698–715. F.A. Hayek et al., *Collectivist Economic Planning* (London: George Routledge, 1935). See the discussion of this issue in John Gray's essay in the present volume.

[6] Karl Marx, Letter of March 5, 1852 to Joseph Wedemeyer in Karl Marx and Friedrich Engels, *Selected Correspondence* (Moscow: Foreign Languages Publishing House, 1956), p.64.

one way to shorten, to simplify, to concentrate, the murderous death pains of the old society and the bloody birth pains of the new society: only one way – revolutionary terrorism.[7]

Nor can this be dismissed as a youthful effusion. In a letter of 1881, Marx stated: "One thing you can at any rate be sure of: a socialist government does not come into power in a country unless conditions are so developed that it can above all take the necessary steps for intimidating the mass of the bourgeoisie sufficiently to gain time – the first desideratum – for lasting action."[8] As an example of a "necessary step," Marx approved the Commune's execution of a hostage, the Archbishop of Paris.

Elsewhere Marx satirizes Proudhon's anarchistic misgivings about the proletarian state. In an article appearing in January, 1873, he characterizes the anarchist's objections, with obvious disdain, in this way:

> If the political struggle of the working class assumes violent forms, if the workers substitute their revolutionary dictatorship for the dictatorship of the bourgeois class, they commit the terrible crime of violating principle; because, in order to satisfy their wretched, profane everyday needs, in order to crush the resistance of the bourgeois class, instead of laying down arms and abolishing the state they give it a revolutionary and transitional form . . .[9]

Engels, in a letter of March, 1875 to Bebel, showed himself Marx's faithful collaborator on this point. Engels stated: "it is pure nonsense to talk of a free people's state: so long as the proletariat still *uses* the state, it does not use it in the interests of freedom but in order to hold down its adversaries, and as soon as it becomes possible to speak of freedom the state as such ceases to exist." He criticized the Commune for not resorting to terror against the bourgeoisie. Unless it had been willing to use "the authority of the armed people" against the bourgeoisie, it could not have survived a day: "Should we not, on the contrary, reproach it for not having used it freely enough?"[10]

The remarks of Marx and Engels in praise of drastic action were not confined to generalities. At the close of Chapter II of the *Communist*

---

[7] Karl Marx, "Victory of the Counterrevolution in Vienna," *Neue Rheinische Zeitung*, November 7, 1848 in Karl Marx, *On Revolution* ed. S.K. Padover (New York: McGraw-Hill, 1971), p.42.

[8] The passage is quoted from Robert Tucker "Marx as a Political Theorist," in *Marx and the Western World*, ed. N. Lobkowicz (Notre Dame: University of Notre Dame Press, 1967), p.342.

[9] The passage is as quoted from Hal Draper "Marx and the Dictatorship of the Proletariat," *New Politics*, vol. 1 (Summer, 1962), p.99.

[10] Friedrich Engels, as quoted in Tucker, "Marx as a Political Theorist," p.342.

Manifesto, Marx and Engels themselves raise the objection against communism that "it abolishes eternal truths, it abolishes all religion, and all morality, instead of constituting them on a new basis." They do not meet this difficulty by denial: on the contrary, declaring that the development of the communist revolution "involves the most radical rupture with traditional ideas," they bluntly assert: "But let us have done with the bourgeois objections to communism." They spell out what their "radical rupture" involves by calling for "despotic inroads on the rights of property and on the conditions of bourgeois production." Those benighted enough to wish to avoid these despotic inroads by departing for other shores would find a slight obstacle confronting them in the fourth point in the list of specific measures given as "pretty generally applicable" in the "advanced countries": "Confiscation of the property of all emigrants and rebels." Forced labor would be the order of the day, according to point eight: "Equal liability of all to labor. Establishment of industrial armies, especially for agriculture." (I assume that disapproval of the regime would not be grounds for exemption from the draft.) The proletariat, in sum, "makes itself the ruling class and, as such, sweeps away by force the old conditions of production."[11]

One possible response to my argument is to claim that any society must punish lawbreakers. The bourgeoisie must be terrorized because it opposes by force the transition to socialism. To deal harshly with sabotage is not by that fact to be oppressive. But this does not get to the heart of the matter. It is not only specific crimes that are proscribed: the entire social power of the former ruling class must be eliminated. As Richard Miller accurately notes, in his essay in this volume, the bourgeoisie occupies many networks of power built up over a long period of time. Smashing the power of the previous state and setting up a new ruling class will require much stronger measures of suppression than merely not allowing armed revolt.

I should like to go out on a limb by saying that if the proletarian dictatorship thought it would promote socialism to exterminate all members of the bourgeoisie, I can see nothing in the Marxist view of morality that would rule this out. I do not say that doing this *would* promote the growth of a socialist society. Yet it seems to me a strong indictment of a system that it does not in principle rule out such a policy of mass murder.

An argument by Richard Miller also addresses the points I have been making. He contends that a society that takes strong measures of suppression against certain groups need not count as oppressive. Suppose, for example, that laws are passed forbidding the publication of fascist or racist

---

[11] All quotations in this paragraph are from "Manifesto of the Communist Party" in Karl Marx and Friedrich Engels, *Basic Writings on Politics and Philosophy*, ed. Lewis S. Feuer (New York: Anchor Books, Doubleday & Company, 1959), pp.27–29.

views. Or suppose that certain racist organizations are suppressed and their members subject to summary judgment.[12] Is such a society oppressive?

I am less ready to answer no to this question than Professor Miller. But suppose that he is correct that the society he has described is unoppressive. It does not follow that if a society suppresses a large section of the population, particularly a section that is not doing anything obviously morally wrong, it still can count as unoppressive.[13] On the Marxist view, the bourgeoisie by its mere position of social influence, dating from its prominence under the old order, threatens the stability of the new regime. If, merely on such grounds, people may be dealt with harshly, the society *is* oppressive, other things being equal.

It can be objected to this entire line of analysis that Marx and Engels sometimes speak of the dictatorship of the proletariat as democratic. Engels, for example, writing to Karl Kautsky about the Erfurt program, said: "One thing that is absolutely certain is that our party and the working class cannot achieve rule except under the form of the democratic republic. This latter is even the specific form of the dictatorship of the proletariat, as the Great French Revolution already showed."[14] Marx, in his pamphlet *The Paris Commune*, praises the fact that the Commune's officials were removable at will by the people and that all decisions of the Commune were subject to popular approval. Perhaps, then, the proletarian dictatorship is not a dictatorship in any bad sense.

I find this approach inadequate. A government may be democratic, in the sense that its policies have majority support, and still be oppressive. The passages about democracy I have just quoted are entirely consistent with the passages about revolutionary terrorism. They cannot, then, be used to counter the argument that the dictatorship of the proletariat is oppressive. (This same problem seems to me fatal to the arguments of Alan Gilbert and Richard Miller that the problems of oppression in existing socialist societies are principally caused by insufficient participation of the proletariat in running the states. For them, lapses into hierarchy must be avoided: they are at the root, for example, of many of the bad aspects of Stalinism. This argument exhibits precisely the confusion between democracy and freedom from oppression that I am challenging.)

We can see by the use of the word "dictatorship" that a dictatorship of the proletariat would be, on the Marxist conception, something other than just a

---

[12] See his essay in this volume.

[13] If a Marxist claimed that former members of the bourgeoisie, by their mere lack of enthusiasm for the new regime, were acting in a morally bad way, this obviously would beg the question. (I do not think most Marxists *would* say this.)

[14] *Karl Marx and Friedrich Engels: Selected Correspondence 1846–1895*, ed. Dona Torr (New York: International Publishers, 1942), p.486.

democratic state run by workers. At first glance, this appears paradoxical: how can an entire social class be a dictator? But the sense of dictatorship in classical political theory (which was the main way the term was used in the nineteenth century) is not "tyranny." Instead, it means a temporary delegation of control to one man in an emergency, giving him power to suspend ordinary laws. By speaking of "*dictatorship* of the proletariat" Marx must have intended to mean that the entire proletariat now assumes emergency power. To deny this is to assume that Marx spoke without purpose.[15]

We may go further. To say that the estabishment of socialism is of supreme importance is to say that any moral claims in conflict with the socialist goal cannot be accepted. To the extent, then, that civil liberties of *proletarians* conflict with the socialist end, they too fall by the wayside. The dictatorship of the proletariat cannot recognize "side constraints" on anything that would best promote socialism: to deny someone's freedom of speech, for instance, if that would be helpful in the necessary promotion of socialism, is required by morality, not prohibited by it.[16]

It may be replied that this objection amounts to very little. Civil liberties *may* sometimes conflict with the socialist goal (how could such conflicts in principle be ruled out?) but this does not show that a socialist regime is inconsistent with a great deal of liberty for proletarians. Perhaps interference with civil liberties does not help very much in the establishment of socialism; if so, there will be little need for it.

But this counter fails once we examine specific liberties. Is socialism aided by a large measure of freedom of speech? Rather, does not allowing such freedom open the possibility that people (including some members of the proletariat) will be convinced by anti-socialist arguments? And a weakening of conviction in the desirability of socialism is hardly a project on the agenda of a Marxist government. Perhaps it will be objected that such interference will be counterproductive; what if most members of the proletariat *want* unlimited freedom of speech?

But, given the commitment of the dictatorship of the proletariat to the supreme importance of the establishment of socialism, freedom of speech must bow to this goal. By hypothesis, we assume that the majority of the proletariat supports Marxism as defined at the beginning of this paper. (Also to be taken into account here is the fact that vigorous suppression of the bourgeoisie might result in "spillovers" against recalcitrant proletarians.)

---

[15] For the use of the term dictatorship in classical political theory, see Alfred Cobban, *Dictatorship: Its History and Theory* (New York: C. Scribner, 1939).

[16] Someone who accepts moral side-constraints on his behavior is prohibited from doing certain things. He may not violate the constraints to achieve some moral goal, even if the goal is greater observance of the side-constraints by himself or others. See Robert Nozick, *Anarchy, State, and Utopia* (New York: Basic Books, 1974), pp.29ff.

The likelihood of restrictions of civil liberties becomes even stronger when one recalls that in a socialist society all means of communication (at least of large scale) are under governmental control. Dissenters from the prevailing system are directly dependent on the agents of the view they oppose to secure a hearing. Additionally, as a famous remark by Trotsky points out, dissenters depend on the state to secure employment.[17] It is an inadequate reply to this criticism to imagine institutions to alleviate this problem, e.g., some newspapers which are under the control of persons not connected with the state. Such devices can readily be constructed; but, given that allowing certain types of dissent impedes the growth of socialism, why should a socialist state be interested?

The same conclusion follows when one considers freedom of religion. Unlike classical liberalism, Marxism does not regard religious conviction as a matter purely of private conscience. On the contrary, religion is regarded as a product of alienated consciousness, the result of a class-divided society. But the dictatorship of the proletariat intends to abolish classes. As it does so, the need for religion will vanish: no longer will the "opium of the people" fulfill any purpose. Religion is a case of what Volume I of *Capital* terms "fetishism": it has no place in a fully developed socialist society.[18] (By religion, I here intend "supernatural" religion. I do not deny that some reconstructions of religion on this-worldly basis, for example, some versions of liberation theology, might be compatible with Marxism.)

Given this view of religion, one cannot reasonably expect a Marxist state to be neutral toward churches. Active efforts to discourage religious practice and to promote atheism are to be expected. All the more so is this on the agenda when one recalls that Marxists hold religion to be ideological in character: it encourages the proletariat not to give full attention to the class struggle. It does not follow from this that a Marxist regime must at once proceed to destroy all churches and synagogues: which measures are taken will obviously be a matter for prudence to decide. However this may be, no right of religious freedom need stand in the way of the proletarian state.

A possible counter is that no measures of state coercion are required. If Marxist theory is correct, then as the alienation of labor lessens with the development of socialism, religion will automatically lose its appeal. But this reply ignores the Marxist contention that history does not operate inde-

---

[17] Trotsky remarks: "In a country where the sole employer is the State, opposition means death by slow starvation. The old principle, who does not work shall not eat, has been replaced by a new one: who does not obey shall not eat." Leon Trotsky, *The Revolution Betrayed* (Garden City, N.Y.: Doubleday, 1937), p.76. I have benefited from reading an unpublished essay by Williamson Evers on freedom on speech under socialism.

[18] There is a valuable brief treatment of Marx's view of religion in G.A. Cohen, *Karl Marx's Theory of History: A Defence* (New York: Oxford University Press, 1978), pp.115f.

pendently of people's wills. Even if religion *were* doomed to *automatic* extinction (and Marxist theory doesn't say that it is), it might be helped along the path by human action. And on the Marxist view, this is what religion deserves. Why *not* take measures against it?

More generally, in a Marxist regime education is in the hands of the state. The *Manifesto* calls for "free education for all children in public schools."[19] Once more, given that the supreme end of the state is the development of socialism, why should the proletarian state allow nonsocialist schools to function? It is a commonplace, unquestioned so far as I know, that the ideas of the younger generation play an important role in the future development of a society. Surely no socialist society could neglect to secure that *its* views were taught to the young, not those of some other social ethic. (Again, the reply that capitalist schools indoctrinate misses the point. In a socialist society no one need be allowed to establish schools in opposition to the prevailing ideology.) Given, further, the importance of education for the inculcation of belief, any freedom granted to nonsocialists to propagate their views must over the course of several generations be considered virtually nugatory. Once more the question arises, why *shouldn't* a socialist state exercise such control, given its standards?

The argument deployed here, if it is valid so far, applies as well to the freedom of association and assembly. Groups of proletarians opposed to the fundamental aims of the proletarian dictatorship have no recourse in Marxist thoery to which they can appeal if they wish to argue that their suppression is unjustified.

I have argued that since Marxists hold that the establishment of socialism is of supreme importance, measures helping to secure this end must override obligations that are otherwise morally binding, e.g., not interfering with freedom of speech. A Marxist view cannot be a "side-constraints" position. (The case as I have presented it parallels an objection raised against J.S. Mill's philosophy. Just as utilitarianism seems incompatible with strict adherence to rights, because one cannot be sure that not violating rights will always promote the general happiness, so one cannot always know that preserving civil liberties will best promote socialism. And if I am right, one has good grounds for thinking the reverse.) I have *not* assumed that Marx reduced all moral obligations to class interest. If this more radical view (strongly argued for by Richard Miller) is correct, then the case is even stronger. Unless one could show that it is in the interest of the proletariat to give members of the bourgeoisie or dissident proletarians civil liberties, there is no moral reason to do so and every reason not to. On the weaker view I have been attributing to Marxists, one can hold that there are moral

[19] Marx and Engels, *Manifesto of the Communist Party* in *Basic Writings*, ed. Feuer, p.29.

obligations to preserve civil liberties, even though these are overriden by an imperative of greater importance.

As I indicated in this paper's introduction, there is a separate question we must now ask. Regardless of what Marxist theory predicts, is it in fact likely that establishing socialism will involve so much difficulty that an oppressive state will be required? What will the effects of implementing the dictatorship of the proletariat actually turn out to be? In support of the view that they might not turn out to be *that* bad, reference may be made to statements by Marx and Engels that a peaceful transition to socialism was in some cases possible. (Professor Shlomo Avineri is one recent student of Marx who has strongly emphasized this possibility.)[20]

But I think that on the point of whether or not strong measures are necessary, Marxist theory as understood by the nonrevisionists is correct: the bourgeoisie is indeed liable to prove a tough nut to crack. Its members are unlikely to be very compliant in surrendering their influential position. (Note that accepting this does not entail accepting the rest of Marxist views about the bourgeoisie, e.g., that it is an oppressive ruling class under capitalism.) The case is even stronger if, as has actually been the case, the dictatorship of the proletariat is established only in some countries. If other, nonsocialist countries perceive revolutionary socialist societies as a threat, then there is every reason to think such a society will have to resort to severe procedures to prevent foreign countries from allying with dissidents at home to topple the regime. (Once more, it need not be the case that members of the bourgeoisie are actually doing anything criminal, at least in any sense that is not question begging: their only "crime" need be that they would throw their weight behind another regime if given the chance.) Perhaps one can get around this point by holding that a socialist revolution should take place only simultaneously, in the powerful countries of the world. But this seems an unlikely contingency.

As far as I can see, the only escape from this conclusion is to hold that the transition to socialism will result in a regime of so great immediate benefit that everyone, including the bourgeoisie, will enthusiastically support it. But this was not what Marx himself expected. He thought the transitional period would be a long and difficult one, and he seems to have been right. Why should the transition to socialism *immediately* result in a society of which all approve? Even if one thinks that socialism is immensely more productive than capitalism, it does not follow that it must be so at once or within a short time.

Further, the question of whether the dictatorship of the proletariat must

[20] Professor Avineri's views are found in *The Social and Political Thought of Karl Marx* (London: Cambridge University Press, 1968), pp.217ff.

use oppressive measures differs from the issue of whether it must be established by revolutionary violence. Even if a Marxist regime were established by peaceful means, it would not follow that it could avoid using oppressive measures to eliminate the power of the bourgeoisie. Indeed, as Lenin was quick to point out, Marx and Engels stated exactly the contrary.[21] Even if a socialist regime took power democratically, there would still be immense resistance from the bourgeoisie which would require violence to overcome. Only if one holds that Marx was wrong about this would the criticism about oppression fail to apply. (Perhaps, however, a democratic transition might make *some* difference to how much violence was actually required during the transitional stage.)

Even if everything I have said is correct, I have not proved that the dictatorship of the proletariat is oppressive by the terms of my definition. It might be the case that even if there were few civil liberties under such a regime, this is outweighed by compensating advantages. What would these be? According to Marxist theory, proletarians are exploited under capitalism: they are unable, or at best able only with difficulty, to avoid having to sell their labor power. Further, the work of proletarians is alienated in capitalist society. What that much-used word alienation means I shall not attempt to canvass; but obviously something very bad is supposed to be present under capitalism that is not present, or present to a lesser extent, under socialism. Also, a socialist economy is supposed by its advocates to be more productive than a capitalist economy. Or it is supposed *at least* that a socialist economy is better able than a capitalist one to provide for genuine human needs.

Before considering these claims, note that there is a general weakness in the argument which uses them to show that a socialist society that suppresses civil liberties need not be oppressive. It is insufficient just to enumerate certain advantages of socialism to show that it is not oppressive. It also has to be shown that these advantages outweigh the costs. Even if the socialist is right about all his claims, more needs to be done to prove his case. And to my knowledge, no socialist has done anything toward proving such a claim.

The rejoinder here is obvious. Why is it up to the socialist to prove that what he favors outweighs any losses owing to diminished civil liberties? Why can't a socialist say that, given the advantages of the new regime inaugurated by the dictatorship of the proletariat, it is up to the critic to show that other things outweigh them? But, of course, this misses the point. The socialist needs to be able to show that the advantages of socialism outweigh the losses in civil liberties in order to show that the society he favors is not oppressive. The fact that we need to show the contrary to demonstrate that it

---

[21] Lenin, *State and Revolution*, in V.I. Lenin, *Selected Works in One Volume* (London: Lawrence and Wishart, 1969), pp.283ff.

is oppressive says nothing against this. In the absence of a method of weighing, all we can say is that we don't know whether a socialist society with the indicated advantages is oppressive.

Concerning the alleged compensating advantages of socialism, space permits me to offer only a few remarks. These do not pretend to be anything approaching a rigorous argument. But it seems to me that socialists have failed to show that there *are* any compensating advantages of socialism. They generally argue only that capitalism possesses various oppressive qualities (exploitation, alienation of labor) without showing that socialism does not have these features. Instead, socialism is simply defined or described so that it does not have them.

For example, Marx claims that proletarians under capitalism are forced to sell their labor power to capitalists. A capitalist has by definition a substantial amount of capital enabling him to impose terms on the proletarian which are contrary to the latter's interests. (A recent, careful statement of the Marxist case has been given by G.A. Cohen, who contends that it is extremely difficult for the proletarian to leave the proletariat and collectively impossible for the members of the class to leave.)[22] I do not myself think that this charge has been made out. But suppose that it has. This gives us no reason to think that the society established by the dictatorship of the proletariat would lack an analogous feature. Quite the contrary, under socialism all workers are forced to accept terms from the state, whose resources dwarf those of any individual workers *or* capitalists. Because the economy is socialist, workers *cannot* get out of the system and set up capitalist enterprises of their own.

If it is replied to this that the system is not oppressive because, under the dictatorship of the proletariat, the workers choose who is to administer the economy and how this task is to be performed, the answer is that this is insufficient. Even if there is virtually unanimous proletarian support for the government's policies, it is still the case that each individual worker has nothing but his labor power to offer. If the situation of having to offer this labor power makes workers oppressed under capitalism, why are they unoppressed under socialism? (Notice, the Marxist case for exploitation is not dependent on proletarian disapproval of capitalist policies.)

About alienation I can say but little. But why should one suppose that alienation will be less under socialism than capitalism (unless, of course, one defines the term so that little or no alienation can occur under socialism)? Perhaps it will be said that under socialism workers will enjoy more of a sense of participation in their work and will have a chance to do more creative work, as opposed to the drudgery of much work under capitalism.

[22] G.A. Cohen, "The Structure of Proletarian Unfreedom," *Philosophy and Public Affairs*, vol. 12, No. 1 (Winter, 1983), pp.3–33.

But merely to describe various desirable features of a society is not to show why a socialist economy would be more apt to promote these than a capitalist one. It is not enough to answer that with proletarian control, workers could set up conditions of work to their satisfaction. Could they do so and also have an efficiently organized economy? Socialists cannot solve this problem by fiat, i.e., by simply asserting without proof that better working conditions, far from being inimical to productivity, will vastly improve it.

Many socialist claims are based on just this assumption of the greater productivity of socialism over capitalism (or, at least, greater productivity as regards genuine human needs). Once again, what evidence is there for this? To say, as some do, that socialist revolutions cannot take place until capitalism has expanded productivity so that there is a large surplus,[23] is not to say that socialism could maintain, much less expand, the surplus. Given Marx's explicit statement that he was not engaged in making blueprints for the future, how can we know that the optimistic view taken by Marxists is correct?

I have dealt briefly and inadequately with the topic of alienation. But there is an explanation I should like to suggest that, in part, explains both why Marxists consider socialism superior to capitalism and why they think that any losses in civil liberties are outweighed by other factors. I think that they assume that practically all proletarians favor the overthrow of capitalism and the establishment of socialism. They will, further, not regard work as alienating under socialism and will tend to think restrictions of civil liberties are unimportant. But, first, no evidence that workers *do* have these beliefs has been presented. And even if most workers did hold these views, what about those who did not? Also, even if workers are opposed to capitalism, it does not follow that they will favor socialism. Finally, if it is argued that workers oppose capitalism because that system is not in their interests, it still remains to be shown that some other system *is* in their interests. (And it is not clear why setting up a system in which there is national planning by committees of workers is sufficient to establish a system in the interests of the workers.)

So much for the dictatorship of the proletariat. But what of the "higher" stage in which the free development of each is the condition for the free development of all? This is imagined as a society in which general abundance prevails. Or, if this is going too far, there is at least far greater abundance than exists under capitalism. I certainly do not argue that a society of great abundance in which everyone develops as he or she pleases is oppressive.

---

[23] Cohen, *Karl Marx's Theory of History: A Defence*, pp.129f. See also G.V. Plekhanov, *The Development of the Monist Conception of History* (Moscow: Foreign Languages Publishing House, 1956) for the classic Marxist statement of the importance of the development of the forces of production.

But the mere description of this ideal form of society has in itself nothing to do with socialism. Why believe that if such abundance prevailed, it would come about as the result of a socialist economy? Further, what reason is there to think that this sort of society can best be achieved via the dictatorship of the proletariat? No mechanism for transition to this paradisiacal society has ever been sketched by Marxists.

In any event, some problems exist in the conception of the "higher" stage. First, given the improbable assumption that a socialist system of national planning could achieve such a level of abundance, is there reason to believe that it is the only system that could do so? If not, would there be restrictions on people attempting to establish some other system? Also, what if some people preferred *less* abundance under some other regime than was available under socialism? Would they be forcibly suppressed? It is too quick to answer this by saying that since the state would not exist, they would not be suppressed. Marx defines the state as existing only when there are class antagonisms and thinks that most social conflict arises as a result of such antagonisms.[24] But there is still an apparatus of administration which could be used to suppress dissidents. (In Engels's phrase, "The government of men will be replaced by the administration of things.") Also, suppose a society first eliminates all those who oppose it and conditions all children to accept the assumptions on which it operates. If *this* were needed to establish communism and everybody who was left liked the system enthusiastically, then although it would not be oppressive by my definition (there could be civil liberties but no one would want to use them against the regime), something would be wrong. Perhaps in addition to ending up non-oppressive, a society has to get to this goal in the right way to count as non-oppressive.

My remarks about the "higher stage" have been very sketchy. But this is not my fault. Marx himself had next to nothing to say about it. His most extended comment on it, as far as I am aware, occurs in the *Critique of the Gotha Program*:

> In a higher phase of communist society, after the subordination of the individual to the division of labor, and therewith also the antithesis between mental and physical labor, has vanished, – after labor has become not only a means of life but life's prime want; after the productive forces have also increased with the all-round development of the individual, and all the springs of cooperative wealth flow more abundantly – only then can the narrow horizon of

[24] Karl Marx, *The Civil War in France*, in Karl Marx and Friedrich Engels, *Selected Works* (New York: International Publishers, 1968), p.289.

bourgeois right be crossed in its entirety and society inscribe on its banners: "From each according to his ability, to each according to his needs!"[25]

That Marx saw no need to give a detailed portrayal of his ideal society is not surprising. He believed that to do so would be to anticipate history: in the *Manifesto*, he satirizes the "duodecimo editions of the New Jerusalem"[26] put forward by utopian socialists. Marx's reluctance to offer a blueprint for the future is to some extent reasonable. But his virtual silence, apart from a few rhetorical remarks, may lead one to question whether the "higher stage" held much importance in his thought. Indeed, it seems to me the argument can be pressed one step further. Has Marx succeeded at all in defining a society? It does not appear so: rather, he has merely lavished a number of terms of praise on an unknown quantity. If someone remarks, "London is by far the most remarkable city in England," he has not given a definition of London. The application to the "higher stage" is obvious. If I am right, consideration of the "higher stage" in our evaluation of whether Marxism is oppressive can be dropped entirely. This, however, is speculative, and I do not insist on it.

I conclude, therefore, that perhaps a higher stage socialist society would be oppressive, although it need not be. But as the undesirable features of the dictatorship of the proletariat can much more easily be achieved than the desirable features of the "higher" stage, if these latter can be attained at all, I conclude that the former is more important in evaluating Marxist socialism's liability to lead to oppression.

Where, then, are we? A dictatorship of the proletariat would very probably have to take severe measures against "class enemies" and very likely have to take them against dissident proletarians as well. There is little reason to think that the society established under socialism would offer compensating advantages, though I do not claim to have proved this. There is also little reason to expect that there will be any transition to a "higher" stage or that if such a stage were achievable, it would also be socialist. A Marxist regime, then, would most probably be oppressive. And this is granting that a developed socialist economy could exist at all.

History, Institute for Humane Studies

---

[25] Karl Marx, *Critique of the Gotha Program*, in *Basic Writings*, ed. Feuer, p.119.
[26] *Manifesto of the Communist Party*, p.39.

MARXIAN FREEDOM, INDIVIDUAL LIBERTY, AND THE END OF ALIENATION*

JOHN GRAY

Introduction

It is a commonplace of academic conventional wisdom that Marxian theory is not to be judged by the historical experience of actually existing socialist societies. The reasons given in support of this view are familiar enough, but let us rehearse them. Born in adversity, encircled by hostile powers, burdened with the necessity of defending themselves against foreign enemies and with the massive task of educating backward and reactionary populations, the revolutionary socialist governments of this century were each of them denied any real opportunity to implement Marxian socialism in its authentic form. Nowhere has socialism come to power as Marx expected it would – on the back of the organized proletariat of an advanced capitalist society. For this reason, the historical experience of the past sixty years can have no final authority in the assessment of Marxian theory. The failings of Marxist regimes – their domination by bureaucratic elites, their economic crises, their repression of popular movements and of intellectual freedoms, and their dependency on imports of Western technology and capital – are all to be explained as historical contingencies which in no way threaten the validity of Marx's central conceptions. It is not that Marxian socialism has been tried and found wanting but, rather, that it has never been tried.

For all its familiarity, this standard argument has a curiously paradoxical aspect. According to all its major exponents, Marxism exemplifies a unity of theory with practice. This is to say that, in the last resort, practice must for Marxism be the test of theory. There is an incongruity in the conventional interpretation of twentieth century Marxian regimes as aberrations from the purity of Marxian socialism, since in the self-image of Marx and Lenin the central ideas of the Marxian system were not Platonic entities, immune to revision by historical experience, but distillations from history and summaries of its lessons. For Marx and Lenin, historical practice is not conceived as a degenerate form of theory but, instead, as theory's only legitimate source. Neither Marx nor Lenin could have endorsed the insulation from

* For their comments on an earlier draft of this paper, I am indebted to Alan Buchanan, Gerry Cohen, Steven Lukes, and Ellen Paul.

the criticism of history which the Marxian system is accorded in the conventional academic interpretation of twentieth century Marxist regimes and movements.

In one of its aspects, the upshot of this paper is to return Marxian theory to history and to subject it to the criticism of common experience. My strategy of argument, however, will be one which seeks to exhibit the structural necessity of the chief defects of actually existing socialist societies as unavoidable results of the serious attempt to realize Marxian socialism in a concrete historical form. My more specific argument will be that the totalitarian outcome of Marxian socialism in practice is an intelligible and predictable implication of fundamental flaws in its theoretical foundations. Thus, I will focus on Marx's system – in both of its interrelated aspects as a critique of capitalism and a projection of socialism – from a perspective which takes its impact on human liberty as centrally important. In this emphasis, I claim to be faithful to Marx's own intentions – for whatever else he may have been, he was an avowed apostle of human freedom, and conceived socialism as the realization of freedom – and to the concerns of his liberal critics. One cost of this restriction on my argument is that I do not address Marx's theory of class and exploitation. This I aim to do on another occasion.

My argument has three phases. First, I shall consider two versions of the Marxian claim that capitalism renders the proletariat unfree: the version advanced by G.A. Cohen and Marx's own version. I will conclude that Cohen's reconstruction of the Marxian argument fails on its own terms and is unfaithful to Marx's central intentions. I shall argue that, for Marx, the unfreedom of proletarians in capitalist society derives from their subjection to unplanned economic forces. Contrary to Cohen's version of the Marxian thesis, the unfreedom of proletarians and capitalists alike is found in their domination by an economic system – that of commodity production – which has its own laws and logic and in which there is no systematic connection between the motives and intentions of producers and the ultimate outcome of their labor. Capitalist unfreedom, accordingly, is in the alienation of labor by the market process itself. It can be transcended only by the abolition of commodity production and its replacement by production for direct use. This latter requirement is the central element in Marx's conception of socialism.

In the second part of the paper, I consider the character of Marxian communism and develop a number of arguments for its impossibility. The impossibility of Marxian communism does not lie principally in the demands it makes on human motivation, and it presupposes nothing about the constancy or variability of human nature. Rather, the impossibility of Marxian communism is epistemological: the project of a communist mode of production from which market relations have been extirpated neglects the vital informational functions of market pricing as a discovery procedure for the utilization of dispersed knowledge. The epistemological impossibility of communism is no less disabling for Marxian socialism, which I construe as a system of economic coordination by democratic central planning. If communism is defective in virtue of the fact that it contains no mechanisms for economic coordination, the socialist command economy (democratic or not) confronts the insuperable task of concentrating dispersed knowledge in planning institutions which cannot recover it. The history of socialist economies everywhere – which is a history of waste, malinvestment, and all-pervasive shortage – becomes intelligible when we understand it in the context of the debate on socialist calculation of the 1920s and 1930s, in which Mises, Hayek, and Polanyi achieved a clear intellectual victory over their opponents (a victory which the conventional history of economic thought has consigned to oblivion). It is in this debate, and particularly in Polanyi's insights into the role of tacit personal knowledge in social and economic life, that we find a compelling theoretical explanation of the universal failures of actually existing socialist economies. It is as a response to these comments that some of the most self-critical of socialist theorists, such as Jon Elster, whose views I consider below, have lately come to acknowledge market socialism as the only form of socialism left in the field. This second section of the paper concludes with a brief consideration of market socialism, its relations to Marxism, and its internal contradictions as an economic system.

In the third and final phase of my argument, I attempt to exhibit the political consequences of the socialist command economy. Here, I shall argue for the structural necessity of totalitarian political control in any genuine socialist economy, invoking chiefly the contributions of public choice theory to the understanding of political life. Once again, a body of theory provides a compelling explanation of a tract of historical experience for which the Marxian system can find no convincing explanation. In this connection I make a brief digression to consider the Russian experience, which has been almost universally misinterpreted in culturalist terms which invoke the supposed peculiarities of Russian political traditions to account for the stability of the Soviet totalitarian system. Against these interpretations, I shall argue that the central factor in explaining Soviet totalitarianism is one that recurs everywhere Marxian socialism is attempted, namely, the absence in Marxian thought of any plausible proposals for the protection of individual freedom. Nor is this absence accidental, since it flows from the authentically Marxian project of transcending the civil condition.

The conclusion of my argument is that, whereas Marx's thought is pervaded by an inquiry into the conditions of freedom in advanced industrial societies, his central conception of social freedom as collective planning of production for direct use encompasses an impossibility. Further, the serious attempt to embody this impossibility in concrete historical form has ineluctably led to the consequences we have witnessed in all actual Marxian regimes. Since these consequences – in particular, the totalitarian suppression of civil freedoms – are explicable by defects in the theory, we do not need to seek for *ad hoc* hypotheses which represent them as historical contingencies. On my account, we understand the historical experience of Marxist regimes best if we see it as a criticism of Marx's most fundamental conceptions. Insofar as Marxian thought does embody a unity of theory with practice, the historical experience of our time constitutes Marxism's successful self-refutation. Though the self-destruction of the Marxian system in political practice is the best way of stating the fate of Marxism in the real world of human history, the argument I develop is not an immanent criticism of Marx's system but rather an argument that should be accessible to Marxists and non-Marxists alike. It is, in effect, an attempt to apply to recent historical experience the insights of a range of neglected theorists who anticipated and explained the self-defeat in practice of Marxism and its prodigious consequences for the prospects of individual freedom in the modern world.

I. *Why Capitalism Makes the Proletariat Unfree: Two Views*

The most powerful argument for the unfreedom of workers under capitalism that has been advanced in recent Marxian writing is that of G.A. Cohen.[1] It appears to have two moves, or phases. The first is the claim that capitalism, or free enterprise, cannot constitute or be identified with liberty (even economic liberty). This is because capitalist institutions rest upon, or encompass, private property, and private property, Cohen maintains, necessarily restricts liberty. As he puts it: "free enterprise economies rest upon private property: you can sell and buy only what you respectively own and come to own. It follows that such economies pervasively restrict liberty. They are complex structures of freedom and unfreedom. The sentence 'free enterprise constitutes economic liberty' is demonstrably false."[2] Capitalism cannot be equated with liberty because one of its central institutions necessarily restricts liberty.

The second move of Cohen's argument turns on the claim that any member of a group may be free to do something which every member of the group is not free to do. Thus, whereas it may be true that any worker may

[1] G. A. Cohen, "Capitalism, Freedom and the Proletariat," A. Ryan, ed., *The Idea of Freedom* (Oxford and New York: Oxford University Press, 1979), pp. 8–25.
[2] *ibid.*, p. 12.

become a capitalist, it does not follow that the *class* of workers is thereby free. This is because capitalism as a system depends for its existence upon a substantial hired labor force which would not exist if more than a few workers exercised the option of upward ascent to the status of capitalists. The unfreedom of workers under capitalism, for Cohen, is in the fact that "each is free only on condition that the others do not exercise their similar freedom":[3] this gives Cohen the result that "though most proletarians are free to escape the proletariat, indeed even if all are, the proletariat is an imprisoned class."[4] If the freedom of any worker to leave his class depends in this way on the fact that most others do not also do so, then the class of workers is unfree even if every worker has the freedom to become a capitalist.

What are we to make of Cohen's argument? It is worth remarking, to begin with, that its first move depends upon invoking a conception of freedom whose source is standard liberal discourse. I do not mean by this that Cohen commits himself to a liberal view of freedom – no systematic conception of freedom is defended in his paper – but that the first move of his argument derives all its force from certain formal claims about the idea of freedom which are taken from liberal discourse. One of these claims – defended with great penetration in the writings of Isaiah Berlin – is that freedom is one value among many.[5] Restrictions of freedom, no matter how justified, remain just that: restrictions of freedom. We are to avoid, as conceptually incoherent, the moralized view that justified restraint of liberty is no loss of liberty: everything is what it is, and not another thing. Further, on this liberal view, having or exercising freedom always presupposes or entails restraint of freedom: if anyone has a freedom to do something, this means at least that others do not prevent him from doing it. Taken together, these two features of the standard liberal view amount to the claim that freedom to do wrong is still freedom, and anyone's freedom depends upon the correlative unfreedom of others.

It is clear that the correlativity of freedom with unfreedom,[6] which is a central feature of liberal discourse, has no special connection with property;

---

[3] *ibid.*, p. 23.

[4] *ibid.*, p. 24.

[5] See Isaiah Berlin, *Four Essays on Liberty* (Oxford and New York: Oxford University Press, 1969); I have myself discussed Berlin's value-pluralist defense of negative liberty in "Negative and Positive Liberty," John Gray and Z. A. Pelcynski, eds., *Conceptions of Liberty in Political Philosophy* (London and New York: Athlone Press and St. Martin's, 1984), pp. 321–348.

[6] Hillel Steiner has argued from this correlativity (that social freedom is gained whenever it is lost) that social freedom can be neither increased nor diminished, but only redistributed. Steiner's conception of freedom as a zero-sum value rests on an unsound inference from the premise that freedom is gained where it is lost to the conclusion that it is the same freedom that is lost and gained. But see Hillel Steiner, "Individual Liberty," *Proceedings of the Aristotelian Society*, vol. 75 (1974–5), pp. 35–50.

but it is the only consideration I can find in the first part of Cohen's argument which supports his claim that capitalism necessarily involves unfreedom. That any man's freedom has as its shadow the unfreedom of others is a truism within the liberal conception of freedom, and not a truth about property. All systems of property, capitalist or socialist, are embodied in legal and moral rules which create opportunities and impose constraints on those who live within them, and these opportunities and constraints will have an important bearing on the freedom of the various social groups that live within any such system of rules. This says nothing about the tendency of different systems of rules about property to promote or restrict freedom on balance. Cohen acknowledges this, when he says that his argument thus far does not tell us which property institutions do best for freedom. In fact, his argument tells us still less than this: it tells us nothing about the bearing of property on liberty, save perhaps that property is not liberty, though it always restricts liberty. We are not told why the liberties conferred and restrained by property are especially weighty, or how they figure in any on-balance assessment of the liberty of specific groups or whole societies. Cohen's assertion that "to think of capitalism as a realm of economic freedom is to miss half its nature"[7] is, for these reasons, only a conceptual truism – the truism that capitalism, like any set of property rules, is "a complex structure of freedom and unfreedom."[8] Once the liberal view is granted, these conclusions follow infallibly; but they tell us nothing about the comparative merits in terms of freedom of capitalism and socialism.

The aim of the second part of Cohen's argument is, perhaps, best interpreted as that of giving a definite content to these otherwise entirely formal considerations. His thesis is that, if the freedom of any worker to become a capitalist depends on his fellow workers not similarly exercising that option, then the workers as a class remain unfree under capitalism. This is a more substantive version of the thesis of the correlativity of freedom with unfreedom than the liberal view embraces; the freedom of the few workers who become capitalists presupposes the unfreedom of the many who do not. Of course, there is nothing very determinate in this relationship of freedom with unfreedom under capitalism: we do not know *how many workers* becoming capitalists would invalidate the claim, or destroy the system. (If most workers at some point in their lives had a period as capitalists, would Cohen's argument be invalidated? Or would "capitalism" have ceased to exist?). There is, however, a more general consideration which goes far towards depriving Cohen's argument of any force it might otherwise have had. I refer to the condition of simultaneous or joint access to some

[7] Cohen, *op. cit.*, p. 15.
[8] *ibid.*, p. 12.

opportunity or status which he imposes as a condition of freedom in respect to it. Cohen's argument suggests that unless all or most workers can become capitalists, workers as a class are unfree to do so. This is at least strikingly counterintuitive: we do not ordinarily suppose that, unless any subscriber to a telephone system can use it at the same time as every other or most others, then the whole class of telephone users is rendered unfree by the system. This is a suggestion radically at variance with much of our standard thought about freedom. More importantly, it would condemn as generating unfreedom many other social institutions. It would condemn in this way institutions (proposed by C.B. Macpherson[9] and others as devices for diminishing dangers to personal liberty under socialism) such as the guaranteed minimum income, whose existence depends upon their being used by only a few: for the freedom of any citizen to take up his guaranteed income, and to live on that alone, depends upon the unfreedom of most others, whose labors support the system. It is, in fact, a common feature of social institutions that their existence or viability depends upon their restricted use, and this feature alone never entitles us to condemn an institution as conferring unfreedom on its users taken as a class. Only if the distribution of chances of access to the institutions could be shown to be skewed by factors relevant to principles of freedom could such a judgment be sustained; but, though this is indeed one of the chief uses of Marxian class theory, it is nowhere developed Cohen's paper. Unless some such argument is forthcoming, however, the conclusion that the proletariat is an imprisoned class under capitalism is as banal as the claim that capitalism is a complex structure of freedom and unfreedom.

Cohen's conceptual truisms, incontestable as they are within the liberal view, are devoid of content so far as any comparison of the impact on freedom of different property systems is concerned. But could a content be given to these truisms which did have something to say about the comparison? It is not altogether clear that it could, since Cohen, noting that "Each form of society [capitalist or socialist] is by its nature congenial and hostile to various sorts of liberty, for variously placed people," goes on to remark that "Which form is better for liberty, all things considered, is a question which may have no answer in the abstract. Which form is better for liberty may depend on the historical circumstances."[10] The difficulty to which Cohen alludes here is the familiar difficulty in the liberal theory of freedom of making on-balance assessments of comparative liberty. It is, in part, this difficulty which motivates Rawls's decomposition of liberty into the basic liberties. Rawls's is a helpful move, since it would at least allow us to

---

[9] C.B. Macpherson, *Democratic Theory* (Oxford: Clarendon Press, 1973), p. 154.
[10] Cohen, *op. cit.*, p. 15.

compare capitalist and socialist societies as to the presence within them of these basic liberties. Rawls's basic liberties are, for the most part, the civil liberties to which Cohen refers when he tells us that these freedoms (of speech, assembly, worship, publication, movement, political participation, and so on) are not necessary concomitants of capitalism.[11] We *can* assess capitalist and socialist systems in respect of these liberties, since, though it is true that they do not always accompany capitalism, it is no less true that they have never been found in the absence of capitalism: there is not a single historical example of a socialist society, for example, in which these basic or civil liberties are respected.

Rawls's suggestion does not take us all the way, however, and it is not much help to Cohen, since it depends on excluding entitlement to property from the class of basic liberties. Since property rights, individual or communal, do not figure among the basic liberties as Rawls conceives them, the choice of capitalism or socialism cannot turn on how their respective property institutions create and restrict liberty. (The choice may, indeed, be informed by a conjecture about the causal role of capitalist and socialist institutions in supporting the basic liberties – but that is another question.) For Cohen, on the other hand, it seems that the institution of property is a centrally important factor in the creation and restriction of liberty. Thus, a society might curb some of the basic liberties and yet, because its property institutions extended liberty in important ways, do better from the standpoint of liberty than a society in which the basic liberties were perfectly protected. This is, after all, the view of many Leninists about the Soviet Union. What is lacking in Cohen's argument is some indication of how any such assessment is to be made, even in concrete historical circumstances: How are the losses in basic liberties to be weighed against the gains in liberty made through the adoption of a communal property system? How are even the various liberties created by different property systems to be weighed? Cohen's homespun example of an augmentation of liberty following upon two households bringing their tools into partly common ownership shows that he believes a well-founded comparison of on-balance liberty can sometimes be made between different property systems: a communal system operating by the rule that "each may take and use a tool belonging to the other without permission provided that the other is not using it and that he returns it when he no longer needs it, or when the other needs it, whichever comes first" would, he contends, "increase tool-using freedom on any reasonable view."[12] Cohen's judgment seems to me far from self-evidently sound. The partly communal system of ownership he envisages has the serious disadvantage

[11] *ibid.*, p. 15.
[12] *ibid.*, p. 17.

that, since the tools can be taken at any time without permission, neither household can effectively engage in long-term planning about when they will use the tools. If freedom is conceived, in liberal fashion, roughly in terms of the nonrestriction of options, it is clear that *both* households have suffered some loss of freedom under Cohen's communalist system. It is, for that matter, just this loss of freedom resulting from the inability to make long term plans that has in many societies led to usufructuary rules of property being replaced by ones based on individual ownership and permitting contractual arrangements for the renting of tools and assets. Even in Cohen's example, then, there is no simple enlargement of liberty but, instead, a trade-off of liberties whose bearing on on-balance liberty remains obscure.

In arguing that the impact on liberty of property rules remains obscure even in Cohen's example, I do not for a moment want to deny that well-founded comparative judgments about liberty can often be made, or that the systems of property rules under consideration may sometimes be crucial in making such on-balance assessments. It is an important argument against socialism that, in transferring the control of employment from a diversity of competing employers to a single public authority, it will unavoidably curtail the options of the employed. As Hayek has put it: "That the freedom of the employed depends upon the existence of a great number and variety of employers is clear when we consider the situation that would exist if there were only one employer – namely, the state – and if taking employment were the only permitted means of livelihood ... a consistent application of socialist principles, however much it might be disguised by the delegation of the power of employment to nominally independent public corporations and the like, would necessarily lead to the presence of a single employer. Whether this employer acted directly or indirectly he would clearly possess unlimited power to coerce the individual."[13] Or, as Leon Trotsky, one of the architects of Soviet totalitarianism put it: "In a country where the sole employer is the state, opposition means death by slow starvation. The old principle, who does not work shall not eat, has been replaced by a new one: who does not obey shall not eat."[14] This is to say that, in a socialist economy, the legal rights of workers will not be matched by corresponding effective powers. It is precisely the dependency of workers' freedom on dispersed ownership of the means of production that is neglected by Cohen when he observes that workers "face a structure generated by a history of market transactions in which, it is reasonable to say, they are *forced* to work for some or other person or group. Their natural rights are not matched by corres-

---

[13] F. A Hayek, *The Constitution of Liberty* (Chicago: Henry Regnery, 1960), p. 121.
[14] Leon Trotsky, *The Revolution Betrayed* (New York: Pathfinder Books, 1937), p. 76.

ponding effective powers."[15] Again, systems of property rights may be relevant to freedom since communal systems of ownership of productive resources may find it hard to permit minorities to advance, or novel practices to find a foothold, perhaps especially when they are operated by democratic procedures. Consider what would have been the fate of immigrants of alien cultural traditions, in England and the United States, if they had had to gain access to productive sources solely via the democratic process. Even when discriminating majorities are lacking, it remains a defect of communal systems of property from the standpoint of freedom that, as Hayek has perceived, "action by collective agreement is limited to instances where previous efforts have already created a common view, where opinion about what is desirable has become settled, and where the problem is that of choosing between possibilities already generally recognised, not that of discovering new possibilities."[16] Whereas I do not say that these considerations by themselves settle the issue between capitalism and socialism, they demonstrate that the freedoms generated by private property are not only those enjoyed or exercised by its holders. This should be a weighty consideration in any on-balance assessment which deploys Cohen's liberal conceptions of freedom.

Cohen's liberal view is to be contrasted with the views of Marx and Nozick. In Nozick's conception, freedom is a moral notion whose scope is given by a theory of justice. It is this conception which Cohen calls the moralized view of freedom and which (for reasons that are unclear to me) he thinks to be "false."[17] The falsity of Nozick's view seems to be revealed to Cohen by the fact that *justified* interferences remain interferences with freedom. In Nozick's theory, however, in which the domain of individual freedom is specified by principles of justice, justified violation of the freedoms demanded by justice remains a violation of freedom: if we violate side-constraints in order to prevent a moral catastrophe, we curtail liberty and justify doing so by reference to the broader morality within which considerations of justice are usually paramount.[18] What Nozick's view excludes as a possibility is not, then, justified restraints on liberty, but *justicizable* restraints on liberty – that is to say, restraints justifiable in terms of justice. Justice cannot compete with liberty, but morality may *in extremis* license a violation of the liberty demanded by justice. Nozick's conception does not have the feature which Cohen thinks shows its falsity, and the only reason I can see that might otherwise give this result is the deviation of Nozick's view from the intuitions embodied in our ordinary-language deliberations. But ordi-

[15] Cohen, *op. cit.*, p. 19.
[16] Hayek, *op. cit.*, p. 126.
[17] Cohen, *op. cit.*, p. 19.
[18] Robert Nozick, *Anarchy, State and Utopia* (Oxford: Basil Blackwell, 1974), p. 30, footnote.

nary language has no special authority here, if Nozick's conception is compelling for other reasons. If, for example, it suggests that the would-be rapist loses no freedom under laws forbidding sexual assault, because he is not entitled to subject another to forcible sexual intercourse, then I think that squares with our moral intuitions better than does the liberal view. For Nozick's view disqualifies, what the liberal view necessitates, weighing in the scales the rapist's liberty against that of his victim.[19] What is required to evaluate Nozick's conception of freedom as a moral notion is not servility to the supposed deliverances of ordinary language but, rather, something akin to Rawlsian reflective equilibrium, in which the claims of the larger theory of justice are matched against the whole body of our intuitions. The Nozickian conception may in the end fail, but not for any of the reasons Cohen has advanced.

The Nozickian and the Marxian conceptions of freedom are alike in that they treat freedom as a moral notion whose content is given by a larger theory. In Marx, this is not a theory of justice, but of alienation: indeed, the necessity of justice is seen by Marx as one among the marks of alienation. What, however, does Marx understand by alienation? As against those scholars who wish to divide Marx's work into two phases, metaphysical humanist and historical materialist, and who situate his use of a theory of alienation primarily in the early, metaphysical phase, I contend that Marx's conception of alienation remains substantially unchanged throughout the *corpus* of his writings. From the Paris *Manuscripts* to *Capital*, Marx's social theory is informed by a conception of alienation, owing something to Hegel but more to Feurbach, according to which man suffers an alienation of his essence whenever he comes to be ruled by something of his own making. In religious alienation, man constructs from his moral hopes and needs the image of a deity which (losing his grasp on the origin of this deity in his own creative powers) he then worships and believes himself to be governed by. In his social and economic thought, Marx generalizes Feurbach's analysis of religious alienation, so that alienation is found whenever human beings are governed in their activities by institutions and practices of their own creation. Marx's critique of classical economics, like his criticism of ethical or utopian socialism, consists in large part of an attempt to de-reify the social objects and laws, the moral notions and principles, in which human creative activity is embodied and by which it is thereby estranged from the human beings to whom it belongs. Alienation is found, then, wherever social objects and

---

[19] Cohen has argued in conversation with me that his writings do not support the view that the liberty of the rapist has value, but only that it is the rapist's liberty that is lost when rape is prohibited. I am not sure I accept Cohen's account of his writings on this point. Even if it is correct, however, the central contrast between Cohen's view and Nozick's view of freedom as a moral notion whose content is given by a theory of justice remains valid.

forces have an autonomous life of their own which constrains the activities of the human beings who are their creators and authors.

Marx's condemnation of capitalist society does not rest on any claim that capitalists enjoy a freedom denied to workers. Contrary to Cohen, Marx conceives workers and capitalists alike as enslaved by capitalism. The alienation and estrangement from self of both the capitalist and the worker issues from the domination of their lives by autonomous social forces – the so-called laws of classical economic theory. The loss of human creative power in capitalism, which afflicts capitalist as well as worker, consists in the government of human activity by the alien power of market forces. To be sure, such alienation exists in every class society but, according to Marx, it is nowhere more pronounced than in capitalism. This is because in capitalism, as the highest form of commodity production, relations between men are transformed into relations between things: "[Capitalist] production does not produce man only as a *commodity*, the *human commodity*, man in the form of a *commodity*; it also produces him as a *mentally* and physically *dehumanized* being . . . Its product is the *self-conscious* and *self-acting commodity – the human commodity*."[20] Or, as he puts it in *Capital*: exchange values "vary continually, independently of the will, foresight, and actions of the producers. To them their own social action takes the form of the action of objects, which rule the producers instead of being ruled by them."[21] Thus it is that "Capital is dead labor, that vampire-like, only lives by sucking living labour, and lives the more, the more labor it sucks."[22]

My thesis is that it is in Marx's conception of alienation that his central idea of human unfreedom is found. Further, this conception motivates his rejection of capitalism and provides the most fundamental defining feature of capitalism's negation in socialism.[23] Accordingly, the problem with capitalism for Marx is not the distribution of income it generates, nor even its dependency upon private property, but *the mode of production* which capitalism instantiates or exemplifies – the mode of commodity production. For it is in the government of their activities by commodities and by the laws whereby commodities are exchanged that the loss of men's freedom in capitalist society lies. As Marx states it programmatically in the *Grundrisse*.

> To have *circulation*, what is essential is that exchange appear as a process, a fluid whole of purchases and sales. Its first presupposition is the circulation of commodities themselves, as a natural,

---

[20] *ibid.*, p. 336.
[21] Karl Marx, *Capital*, vol. 1 (New York: International Publishers, 1967), p. 75.
[22] *ibid.*, p. 233.
[23] I am indebted here, and throughout my account, to Paul Craig Roberts and Matthew A. Stephenson, *Marx's Theory of Exchange, Alienation and Crisis* (New York: Praeger Publishers, 1973).

many-sided circulation of those commodities. The precondition of commodity circulation is that they be produced as *exchange values*, not as *immediate use values*, but as mediated through exchange value. Appropriation through and by means of divestiture [Entäusserung] and alienation [Veräusserung] is the fundamental condition. Circulation as the realization of exchange values implies: (1) that my product is a product only in so far as it is for others; hence suspended singularity, generality; (2) that it is a product for me only in so far as it has been alienated, become for others; (3) that it is for the other only in so far as he himself alienates his product; which already implies (4) that production is not an end in itself for me, but a means. Circulation is the movement in which the general alienation appears as general appropriation and general appropriation as general alienation. As much, then, as the whole of this movement appears as a social process, and as much as the individual moments of this movement arise from the conscious will and particular purposes of individuals, so much does the totality of the process appear as an objective interrelation, which arises spontaneously from nature; arising, it is true, from the mutual influence of conscious individuals on one another, but neither located in their consciousness, nor subsumed under them as a whole. Their own collisions with one another produce an *alien* social power standing above them, produce their mutual interaction as a process and power independent of them. Circulation, because a totality of the social process, is also the first form in which the social relation appears as something independent of the individuals, but not only as, say, in a coin or in exchange value, but extending to the whole of the social movement itself. The social relation of individuals to one another as a power over the individuals has become autonomous, whether conceived as a natural force, as chance or in whatever other form, as a necessary result of the fact that the point of departure is not the free social individual. Circulation as the first totality among the economic categories is well suited to bring this to light.

Alienation is overcome, and human freedom achieved, when the autonomous life of social objects and forces is destroyed. *Socialism*, for this reason, consists centrally in the abolition of that commodity production of which capitalism is the highest form. Socialism is the *conscious, purposive* ordering of production by the producers: for "what distinguishes the worst architect from the best of bees is this, that the architect raises his structure in imagination before he erects it in reality."[24] Thus, Marx tells us that "the life

[24] Karl Marx, *Grundrisse* (Harmondsworth: Penguin Books, 1973), pp. 196–7.

process of society, which is based on the process of material production, does not strip off its mystical veil until it is treated as production by freely associated men, and *is consciously regulated by them in accordance with a settled plan.*"[25]

In socialism, then, the mode of production has been transformed from production of commodities for exchange to production of goods for use. As the dialectical negation of capitalism, socialism can only be understood as the suppression or transcendence of the organizing principle of capitalism-commodity production. Whatever else it may mean in Marx's writings, overcoming alienation means at least this, and centrally this, that human productive activities be direct and no longer mediated by the institutions of commodity production. The freedom that men attain under socialism is not, then, Cohen's freedom of noninterference, nor yet a positive individual freedom of exercise or enjoyment; it is freedom from autonomous social forces and laws, a freedom which they *have* with the abolition of capitalist commodity production and which they *exercise* in the conscious planning of production. Socialism and planned production are, as I interpret Marx, aspects of one and the same mode of production, and central planning is not an incidental institution of actually existing socialist economies, but socialism's very essence. The freedom which socialism promises is not liberal freedom – the freedom of individual human beings to act without interference by their fellows – but something incommensurable with it. It is the freedom of men as associated producers, classless instances of their species, united in the common project of realizing human powers in cooperative productive activity.

This is the conception of freedom as alienation transcended which informs all of Marx's works. It is also that which inspired our century's revolutionary socialist movements, and which is an unstated postulate of much popular criticism of market economies as anarchic and chaotic. It captures, better than most subsequent statements do, the core of the moral criticism of capitalism as involving submission to blind, impersonal forces, and of socialism as the realization of human freedom in collective self-determination. In the Marxian conception, then, capitalism is morally condemned on the ground that it alienates the freedom of workers and capitalists by enslaving all to impersonal social forces. In a socialist society, by contrast, human freedom is embodied in the conscious and collective control of production without the mediation of market forces and processes. Among the presuppositions of Marx's condemnation of capitalism as an embodiment of unfreedom, however, is the thesis that socialism – the conscious regulation of production by the producers according to a definite plan – is possible.

[25] Karl Marx, *Capital*, vol. 1 (New York: International Publishers, 1967), p. 80.

("Ought" implies "can".) As against this, I wish to argue that Marxian socialism and communism encompass an impossibility which Marx failed to detect because of his lack of understanding of the epistemological or information functions of market pricing.

II. *The Impossibilities of Marxian Socialism and Communism*

The standard argument for the impossibility of Marxian socialism and communism attacks Marxian moral psychology and, most particularly, the plausibility of Marx's assumptions about the motivation of socialist man. In its most vulgar form, this standard argument invokes a conception of man's moral imperfection as being rooted in his intractable egoism, and the impossibility of Marxian socialism is located in the motivational transformation – from egoism to altruism – which it presupposes. For several reasons, this is not the argument I wish to develop here. For one thing, any such argument rests on a postulate of the fixity of human nature which, though it has been powerfully defended in recent sociobiological speculation,[26] remains in the realm of opinion rather than that of objective knowledge. Again, this standard argument trades on a traditional moral condemnation of egoism, and an association of the socialist ideal with moral perfection, which I am far from wishing to endorse. Yet again, there is nothing self-evidently compelling about the Marxian ideal of a universal, conflict-free society from which distinctive cultural traditions have disappeared. Many of man's greatest cultural achievements depend, in all likelihood, upon the existence of particular loyalties and local attachments – to specific ways of life and religious and national traditions – which Marxian communism would be bound to extinguish. It is arguable that these particular and exclusive attachments, with all the conflicts they engender, are not a contingency of human history thus far, which may one day be transcended but, instead, are an expression of the essential variety of human nature. They express the primordially human need for self-definition by identification with a definite social group. If this is so, the Marxian universalist ideal of a human world purged of conflicting traditions and cultures is a chimera, or else a project whose realization involves a massive and dehumanizing loss of distinctive cultural values. The Marxian vision of a conflict-free universal society seems, in any case, to presuppose a perfection in moral conformism which can have little appeal to those who value the diversity of human life.

For these and other reasons, my argument does not trade on any assumption of human moral imperfectibility. It rests on another sort of imperfection

---

[26] See, especially, E. O. Wilson, *On Human Nature* (New York: Bantam Books, 1978).

or limitation – that of the human intellect – and it finds an impossibility in the demands made by socialist planning on the knowledge of the central planner. In sketching this argument, I can do no more than gesture towards the important and neglected literature in which Ludvig von Mises, F.A. Hayek, Michael Polanyi, and more recent writers such as P.C. Roberts and Thoman Sowell[27] have explored in more systematic fashion the epistemological impossibilities of socialist planning. In its most essential elements, however, the argument of all these writers is fundamentally simple. It is that no central planner could possess the detailed knowledge required for rational resource allocation (and so for successful planning). Before we explore the reasons for this limitation, it is worth noting that the argument is perfectly general in its application to Marxian projects for a post-market economic order. Nothing in it turns on the supposition that the central planning agency is part of a totalitarian bureaucratic apparatus: if sound, the argument holds just as much for a planning agency whose activities are subject to some sort of democratic accountability. Equally, it does not matter whether or not the planning agency seeks to respect consumer preferences. To be sure, part of the argument is that the planners will find it impossible to identify the preferences of the consumers, but their fundamental problem – that of allocating productive resources rationally – will remain even if they decide to neglect or overrule them. Nor is the argument limited in its application to any phase of socialist development. If I am right in my claim that socialism is the dialectical negation of capitalism, where capitalism's essence lies in commodity production, then both Marxian socialism and communism will be social orders in which the coordination of economic activities by market pricing has been replaced by central planning. The differences between socialism and communism can then be only in their distributive arrangements and in the fact that communist society dispenses with the apparatus of coercive state power preserved under socialism. Important as this pair of differences may be for some purposes, it is immaterial to my argument. It is arguable, to be sure, that in the absence of a coercive state apparatus, central economic planning ceases even to be imaginable. If this is true, it still does not affect my argument, but shows instead simply that Marx specified no mechanism for economic coordination under communism. Either way, socialism and communism are both defined by the absence of market competition.

---

[27] The definitive history of the calculation debate is Don Lavoie's *Rivalry and Central Planning: The Socialist Calculation Debate Reconsidered* (Cambridge: Cambridge University Press, 1985). The important later contributions are by Michael Polanyi, *The Logic of Liberty* (Chicago: University of Chicago, 1951); Paul Craig Roberts, *Alienation and the Soviet Economy* (Albuquerque: University of New Mexico Press, 1971); and Thomas Sowell, *Knowledge and Decisions* (New York: Basic Books, 1980).

The thesis is that socialist planners are bound to lack the knowledge required for rational allocation of productive resources, so that socialist economic planning – or, at least, *successful* socialist economic planning – is an impossibility. "Rational allocation of resources" refers here to the attainment of economic goals with the least expenditure of assets (including labor), and the knowledge which is denied to the planner (in the absence of market pricing) is that of relative costs and scarcities among resources. Note that rationality in economic life is not here *identified* with calculation in market prices: rather, market pricing is seen as a *discovery procedure* for ascertaining the underlying and massively complex pattern of resource scarcity. Why is it, though, that the planner is denied this detailed knowledge of relative costs? In part, this knowledge already exists, but is dispersed across society in the knowledge of millions of individuals. The project of centralizing this knowledge comes up, in the first place, against the fact that, often enough, it is local knowledge of transitory circumstances and is soon dated. Again, this knowledge is often not articulated, and may sometimes be inarticulable: it is embodied knowledge, knowledge stored in the tacit responses and practical skills of workers, managers, and entrepreneurs. If (as seems clear) much knowledge of relative costs is of this tacit or practical kind, then its centralization in a single body, or in a single mechanical device, will pose insuperable difficulties.[28] Yet again, market pricing generates knowledge of relative costs which no one possesses, even tacitly, in the absence of market pricing of resources: for market pricing allows for the integration, imperfect as this may be, of the various plans of activity of different economic agents, by the use by each of them of prices as signals of relative cheapness and scarcity. The claim of the Austrian economists in the great "calculation debate" of the 1920s and 1930s was that, without the knowledge generated and transmitted by market pricing, rational calculation of costs was impossible and with it, successful economic planning.

It would be to attempt too much to try to summarize in any detail the vast literature on this debate, but a few conclusions stand out as nearly indisputable. First, the arguments of Enrico Barone, Oscar Lange, and Joseph Schumpeter[29] to the effect that a coordination of economic activities can be mathematically modelled *given knowledge of the relevant data* precisely neglect the nub of the Austrian critique, which is in the claim that, because we live in a non-stationary world of unpredictably changing preferences, technologies, and practices, the relevant data could be available to us only in the imaginary (and barely coherent) world of general equilibrium theory. Second, the

---

[28] I have set out this argument in greater detail in my *Hayek on Liberty* (Oxford: Basil Blackwell, 1984), pp. 34–40.

[29] See Joseph Schumpeter, *Capitalism, Socialism and Democracy* (London: Unwin, 1943), Ch. XV.

insight into the indispensable role of tacit or practical knowledge in economic life, found particularly in the refinements of the calculation debate made
by Polanyi and Roberts, suggests – what historical experience amply confirms – that socialist economic systems will in the event be compelled to rely
upon the embodiment of such practical knowledge in historic prices and
world prices and in the ubiquitous black and gray markets. Finally, we
should note that the Austrian critique incorporates (though it does not
depend upon) a view of the subjectivity of costs and expectations which was
unavailable to Marx as the last great classical economist. The argument
against central planning, and in favor of dispersed decision making via
market competition, becomes all the stronger if we accept the essentially
subjective character of some of the central phenomena of economic life.

I have alluded already to attempts made by a number of writers during the
heyday of the calculation debate to resist or refute the arguments of Mises
and Hayek. I have said little of these attempts since, despite Schumpeter's
cavalier assertions to the contrary, I think there is little doubt that the Austrian
critique won a decisive victory – only now being rescued from the intellectual
memory hole[30] – over its socialist opponents. It is by now generally agreed
that the "competitive solution" proposed by Lange to the problems of
socialist calculation, because it leaves determination of the prices of all but
consumer goods and wages to the Central Planning Board, fails to confront
adequately the problem of knowledge faced by the Central Planning Board
with respect to the price relativities of the various productive resources. It is
worth remarking here that, whatever its merits and difficulties, Lange's
competitive solution is not the market socialism advanced by many recent
writers who have acknowledged the vast costs in efficiency of the command
economy. As it is envisaged by David Miller, Jon Elster, and others,[31] market
socialism differs from the Lange model in that there is to be no price fixing
by a Central Planning Board of any commodity but rather market pricing (of
labor, raw materials and so on) right across the board. Further, and crucially,
they make clear that the institutional unit of the socialist market is to be the
worker cooperative (instead of any industry-wide corporation, for example).
The vision suggested by these writers is that of an economy from which the
capitalist relationship of worker to owner is abolished, but relations between
the worker-owned enterprises are those of market competition. As Elster has
put the case for this sort of solution:

> Autonomy in the work-place is one form of self-realization that
> would be open to everybody. Corresponding to the large-scale

---

[30] See Lavoie's superb book, cited in footnote 27 above.
[31] I am indebted to David Miller for discussion on these questions, and for letting me see his
Marx, communism and markets (unpublished draft). Jon Elster's endorsement of market
socialism can be found in *Making Sense of Marx* (Cambridge University Press, 1985), p. 527ff.

character of modern industry, it would have to be autonomy mainly at the collective level, in workers' cooperatives. This, certainly, is less than what Marx hoped for; equally certainly, far more than we have today. Central planning is out, being incompatible with autonomy and with efficiency. Instead there would have to be a conflictual political process to decide on the specific form of political intervention and regulation.[32]

Market socialism of this variety certainly does not succumb to the impossibilties attendant upon the socialist command economy, but it has serious disadvantages from a Marxist point of view. It does not abolish commodity production and so leaves the pattern of economic activity to be determined by the unintended consequences of human action rather than the collective will of the producers. It cannot, therefore, promote the overcoming of alienation as Marx conceived it. The concepts of autonomy and self-realization with which this variant of socialism is defended are, like market socialism itself, wholly un-Marxian and, in fact, embody the liquidation of Marx's distinctive contributions (and their recuperation by liberal ideology).

The un-Marxian pedigree of market socialism aside, it has costs and difficulties which greatly diminish its promise as an institutional vehicle for the promotion of autonomy and self-realization. The fusion of job holding with capital ownership which is the essence of the system produces resistance to new entrants into the worker cooperatives and is probably largely responsible for the magnitude of youth unemployment in worker-managed economies such as Yugoslavia.[33] Like other forms of inefficiency and inequity produced by market socialism, this maldistribution of employment opportunities is remediable in practice only by governmental interventions which seriously hamper the autonomy of the worker cooperatives. Market socialism has other difficulties, connected with its inherent inability to promote technological innovation, the scale on which it is to be implemented and the economies which such implementation would involve sacrificing, and a central obscurity about how new investment capital is to be acquired. Its fatal flaw, however, is that the intervention and regulation required to control the interaction of the worker enterprises so as to protect socialist (but non-Marxian) values of equity severely curb self-management, to the point of reducing it to a charade. As Barrington Moore has summed up the case against market socialism:

> In the form of self-management (autogestion) the notion (of participatory democracy) is ... inherently contradictory and

---

[32] Elster, *op. cit.*, p. 527.
[33] See James Dorn, "Markets, true and false: the case of Yugoslavia," *Journal of Libertarian Studies*, vol. 3 (Fall 1978), pp. 243–68.

impossible to realise in practice. . . . The main difficulty with self-management on any wide scale is that the procedure as such contains no way to take account of the larger requirements of the whole society. It cannot solve the general problems of social order. Each individual plant or economic unit tends to pursue its local and selfish interests, as has been repeatedly discovered in practice. Pushed to its logical conclusion, when these selfish interests balance each other without outside intervention the system would amount to no more than the classic model of competitive capitalism ruled by an impersonal market. As a practical matter under socialism, it may be a very good device to leave a considerable degree of autonomy to individual plants to carry on production within the framework of some overall plan and one in which these plants have some voice in drawing up, as they did in practice even in the most totalitarian phase of the Soviet experience. But then there is no use pretending that real self-management or workers' control exists, because fundamental decisions are made elsewhere. Likewise, there may be highly desirable features in André Gorz's proposal that the workers in regions allowed to stagnate because of profit considerations under capitalism get together and insist on a more humane use of the area's natural and human resources. In their essentials, however, such actions are no different from the tugging and hauling among competing interest groups that take place under pluralist democracy. In effect, then, self-management is a device to oppose the abuses of the powers that be, capitalist or socialist. It is not a possible substitute for a central authority.[34]

This seems to me to amount to an obituary of market socialism if it be conceived as a successor to Marx's vision of a post-market order. There is a fundamental contradiction in market socialism as an economic system in that, whereas the form of worker management is adopted in order to protect the liberal socialist values of self-realization and autonomy, central governmental intervention of a continuous and permanent kind, which reduces the scope of self-management severely, is required in order to protect the values of equity and equality. The messy pluralism which market socialism would embody represents a refinement of or variation on Western social democracy and not an alternative to it, and it is as a development of current institutions that it is to be evaluated. I have already suggested some of its costs and disadvantages, which are clear in the Yugoslav case. It remains to show that, whereas the danger to liberty might be less under market socialism than it is

[34] Barrington Moore, Jr., *Reflections on the causes of human misery* (London: Penguin Books, 1972), p. 68.

under a socialist command economy, there are reasons in theory and practice for thinking that the danger is serious and insoluble in both variants of the socialist project.

III. *Political Consequences of the Impossibility of Marxian Socialism*

If the Marxian project of supplanting market competition by central planning encompasses an impossibility, it seems likely that at least one sort of freedom will from the outset be compromised in a Marxian socialist order – that of intellectual inquiry into the causes of the failures of the socialist economic system. Ubiquitous shortages, malinvestments, and corruption will have to be accounted for in terms which do not threaten the central tenets of Marxian theory, and to this end an apparatus of ideological control will soon be needed.[35] It is this development which is often fastened upon by Western academic critics of the socialist regimes as the chief mark of their authoritarian character. I will not follow this line of thought, partly because I do not share the conventional academic conviction that intellectual freedom is always the chief among human liberties, but mainly because its eclipse is only a moment in the broader extinction of liberties which I claim to be unavoidable in a socialist order. What, then, are the principal reasons for the incompatibility of individual freedom with socialist planning?

The first of these stems from the fact that socialist economic planning, unlike the macroeconomic controls adopted in most Western countries during the postwar period, is structural planning: it involves making and implementing decisions about the detailed pattern of economic activity. This is to say that the central planning board will need to rank in order of their claims on assets, industry against agriculture, the provision of consumer goods against heavy industry, and so on. Again, in each industry, decisions about rates of investment and depreciation of capital stock, location of plant and methods of working, and so on will have to be made and enforced. All of these decisions, which are made by individual firms within the market order, have to be taken consciously and collectively in any system which seeks the suppression of market relations. It seems obvious that, whatever Marx's hopes for it may have been, central economic planning cannot be conducted by anything like a democratic process. The impossible complexity of these trade-offs among costs, preferences, and opportunities which characterizes any such structural plan itself renders delusive the hope that it could be the

---

[35] See on this the first-hand account of Eugene Lyons in *Assignment in Utopia* (New York: Twin Circle Publishing Co., Inc., 1967). Lyons's is by far the best account of life in the early years of the Soviet system.

subject of real democratic debate. Even if this obstacle could in the end somehow be overcome, the scarcity of expert knowledge among the general population and the vast costs of popular participation in economic planning would inevitably attenuate its democratic character. In addition, there are well-known problems associated with the aggregating of preferences and with doing so in a way which avoids paradoxes of collective choice,[36] problems which would soon force oligarchical decision making on the planners even if they began with a serious commitment to the democratic process.

Oligarchic decision making is still not tyranny, however, and we need to go further in our explorations if we are to recover the logic of the relationship between socialist planning and the loss of individual freedom. We may note, further, then, that the idea of a largely noncoercive form of socialist planning presupposes a degree of moral consensus or conformism which exists in no developed society. Nowhere is there to be found a real convergence on the just or desirable remuneration of different occupations, the appropriate rate of investment or saving, the claims of future generations, or the acceptability of cheap but risky technologies. Whereas the lack of such consensus is tolerable and even desirable in a system in which the functions of democratic government are limited, it is a fatal flaw in proposals to extend the scope of democratic governance into areas currently subject to control by convention, market competition, or some mixture of the two. The incommensurability of preferences and values in modern societies, which contain a diversity of traditions and ways of life, is evaded by theories of basic needs or primary goods which suppose that these can be made the objects of public provision by institutions whose mode of operation is subject to democratic control. Not only is the ranking among basic needs a matter of intractable dispute, unsettleable by reason, even where the basic needs are satiable,[37] but the content and definition of the needs itself will vary across different traditions and ways of life in a pluralist culture such as those in which we all now live. It may be possible to devise income transfer schemes which enhance the power of the poor to satisfy their own self-defined needs, but the project of organizing production directly for the satisfaction of needs comes up against the insuperable obstacle of the thorough lack of consensus about the definition and content of needs. In the absence of the required degree of

---

[36] See Mancur Olson, *The Logic of Collective Action* (Cambridge, Mass.: Harvard University Press, 1965), for a seminal account of the paradoxes of collective choice.

[37] That needs may be basic but nonsatiable is a fact often ignored by Marxian and other socialist theorists. I have explored the political implications of the nonsatiability of basic needs in my paper, "Classical liberalism, positional goods and the politicization of poverty," Adrian Ellis and Krishnan Kurtan, eds., *Dilemmas of Liberal Democracies* (London: Tavistock, 1983), pp. 174–84.

moral consensus, the planners will have no alternative but to impose their own judgments about the relative priority of needs and values. In so doing, they will be bound to distort the life plans of individuals at the same time as they hamper the activity of the distinctive traditions which the socialist society will inherit from the past. If the plan is to be formulated at all, decisions will have to be taken which involve ranking needs, wants, and values connected with rival traditions whose contents are, in fact, rationally incommensurable. If it does not come to grief on the social fact of the pluralism of values in contemporary cultures, socialist economic planning is bound to attempt to destroy it.

Once it has been formulated, implementing and enforcing an economic plan will include imposing serious costs on various sectors of the community, even if a moral consensus exists. Decisions to abandon long-established techniques of production disrupt the lives of workers and sometimes spell the death of their communities. Whether it occurs in a market or in a socialist context, economic change inflicts costs as it alters relative levels of income, employment opportunities and working methods, and promotes the mobility of capital and labor. In Western democracies, the costs of economic change are in part accepted as incidents in the market process, and in part resisted by governmental intervention and the power of trade unions. The costs of such intervention are considerable, even if they result in short-term benefits for some groups, since they initiate a political process of distributional conflict which damages production and destroys wealth.[38] Where all major allocative decisions are politicized, the costs of distributional conflict will be prohibitive rather than merely high, and some semblance of collective rationality will be restored only by recourse to coercive measures. In this phase of socialist development, the freedoms to be extinguished will be, first and foremost, those of the workers, as the direction of labor by planners restricts workers' choice of occupation, and deprives them of the opportunity for autonomous trade union organization. These developments, which have been observed in every socialist society, are in fact rational responses by socialist planners seeking to contain the threats to the implementation of the plan posed by the exercise of individual choice and the protection of group interests on the part of the workers themselves.

I have spent some time exploring the reasons for the abandonment of democratic process in socialist planning and its replacement by an oligarchy whose policies are bound to curb the liberty of workers and others. There is, however, a very fundamental objection to central planning which I have not yet discussed and whose force in no way turns on the oligarchical character

---

[38] See on this Samuel Brittan, *The Role and Limits of Government: essays in political economy* (London: Maurice Temple Smith, 1983), Ch. 3.

which central planning always exhibits in practice. I refer here to the insights generated by theorists of collective action and, above all, by the Public Choice School of James Buchanan and Gordon Tulloch,[39] into the impact of small, concentrated groups on political life. The central insight of this approach is that, insofar as political life is open to manipulation by special interests which are organized in small groups able to act collusively, such groups will tend to colonize public institutions and to control public policy to their own advantage. In part, the public choice approach consists in the extension to political life of the economic understanding which it is usual to apply primarily to market behavior. Through the use of this technique, the Public Choice School has made a major contribution to correcting the unbalanced combination of contempt for market processes with voluntarism about political life which is characteristic of much recent political thought. In its exploration of political instances of the Prisoner's Dilemma, however, the public choice approach goes beyond ordinary economic theory and helps to explain why a political order which injures all may nonetheless be supported by most. In its applications to the political economy of the socialist command system, the public choice approach would predict the colonization of planning institutions by organized and collusive interests. Further, it would expect large-scale popular participation in informal networks of graft and corruption which would be generated in the first instance, often enough, as defensive stratagems against the political struggle for resources. All of these expectations are amply borne out by the evidence we have from Soviet-type systems.

In its most general formulation, the argument for the inevitability of unfreedom under socialism invokes the vast concentration of power which is inseparable from central economic planning. The informational impossibilities of successful planning in the absence of market pricing, and various insights of collective action theory, go far to supply a compelling theoretical account of the nemesis to individual freedom in socialist systems. It remains to consider briefly an *ad hoc* stratagem of socialist thought which has often been adopted to evade these results. I refer to the thesis – so nearly universal that it has become part of the common stock of academic conventional wisdom – that the eclipse of individual freedom in the Soviet Union is to be explained by certain peculiarities of Russian tradition and culture, rather than as an unavoidable outcome of a serious attempt to realize the Marxian project. This hackneyed tale typically includes adversions to Muscovite tyranny, to the weakness of civic life in Tsarist Russia, to the pan-Slavist aspirations of Russia's rulers, and so on, and often concludes with the

[39] For the best introduction to the public choice approach, see James Buchanan, *The Limits of Liberty: between Anarchy and Leviathan* (Chicago and London: University Press, 1975).

assertion that the Soviet Union is merely the embodiment in Bolshevik form of Tsarist political traditions of tyranny and imperialism. The Soviet Union is only Russia, with all its inherited vices, and no more.

The first point to be made in criticism of this view is that it attributes a degree of autonomy to cultural tradition which sits well with conservatism, but which is hard to square with Marxian materialism. A more fundamental criticism, however, is one which attacks the very autonomy of cultural tradition which this view presupposes. The crucial point here is that the illiberal practices which are attributed to the Russian political tradition – forced labor, violations of the rule of law, mass executions, and so forth – are replicated in all socialist systems of which we have knowledge. The culturalist explanation, with its emphasis on the supposed peculiarities of Russian tradition, fails utterly to account for the structural identity of totalitarian practices in the socialist blocs. It is true that real differences of degree exist among the socialist states in their recourse to terror and forced labor, but this by no means supports the culturalist view. The already partly industrialized states of Eastern Europe did not need (as the rulers of the People's Republic of China and the USSR did) to accumulate capital by way of a vast Gulag of slave laborers, but this represents a difference of circumstances, not of cultural tradition. Again, the Eastern European states suffered the imposition of socialism from without, but it was a form of the socialist command economy that had retreated from the radicalism of the Soviet War Communism period and had made significant concessions to commodity production and market pricing. It is the abandonment by the Soviet Union in the postwar period of the most radical aspects of the Marxist project, rather than the absence of local traditions of tyranny in Eastern Europe, which explains the differences in the human cost of socialism as it is practiced in the Eastern European states and the Soviet Union.

The culturalist interpretation of the Russian experience rests in any case on a tissue of historical errors and half-truths. Whereas it was not a liberal society, Tsarist Russia during its last half-century was an open, dynamic, progressive authoritarian society with a record of economic progress and cultural achievement which few other nations could at that time match. Contrary to conventional opinion, it contained no forced labor camps, the rule of law was largely respected, censorship was inconsiderable, literacy was growing, and the apparatus of enforcement was slight.[40] Even at its worst, when the authorities did little to repress (or, in some cases, connived at) anti-Semetic outrages and pursued policies of Russification of small nationalities, oppression under the last Tsars was incomparably less severe, more spor-

---

[40] For an excellent historical account of the last decades of Tsarism, see Norman Stone, *Europe Transformed* (London: Fontana, 1983), pp. 201–2.

adic, and less efficient than that in the post-revolutionary regime. In terms of respect for individual freedom, Tsarist Russia in its last five decades compares favorably with Bismarck's Prussia and extraordinarily well with most developing nations in our own time. The Bolshevik Revolution, which broke the normal path of Russian development and impoverished the Russian nation to such a degree that it remains the poorest people within the European portion of the Soviet bloc, represents a discontinuity rather than a development in Russian history and culture. If there is any major strand of continuity, it is in the continued dependency of the Soviet Union on Western capital and technology, which has been a feature of Soviet development from the outset[41] (and but which is now compounded by a dependency on Western food supplies which was never a feature of the Tsarist system). If the culturalist view is powerless in the face of the structural identity of totalitarianism in the Soviet Union and other socialist states, it also invokes a thoroughly mistaken historical interpretation of Russian history and development, and fails to make the crucial distinction between the *traditional authoritarianism* of the Tsars and the *radical totalitarianism* of their communist successors. At the back of the culturalist view, perhaps, is a conservative inability or refusal to perceive in the Soviet system a novelty, a state like no other, whose behavior cannot be understood by means of an antique typology of civic and tyrannous regimes.[42]

IV. *Conclusion*

The Marxian idea of freedom is not any variant of liberal conceptions of noninterference or self-realization as deployed by contemporary analytical Marxists. Rather, Marx's idea of freedom embodied collective self-government through rational planning of economic and social life. Marxian freedom is the other face of the idea of alienation as the loss of self in domination by impersonal social laws and forces. The self that is lost in Marxian alienation is not, however, that which makes each of us unique but, instead, it is simply what we all have in common as instances of the human species. It is only because Marx writes out conflict and divergence from the human essence that he is able to imagine that the abolition of classes will end social division and struggle. Marx fails to address the problem of coordination in a

---

[41] Western aid to the Soviet Union is exhaustively detailed in Anthony Sutton, *Western Technology and Soviet Economic Development* (Stanford Calif.: Hoover Institution, 1968–73). Western involvement in the Soviet economy began with a trade agreement with Germany in 1921, and includes the construction by Ford Motors in the late twenties of a vast integrated plant at Gorkii and the design and construction by the McKee Corporation of Cleveland of the famous Magnitogorsk steel mill in the thirites. As Sutton has put it (p.329): "From 1930 to 1945 Soviet technology was in effect Western technology converted to the metric system".

[42] A brilliant account of the uniqueness of the Soviet system is given by KAlain Besançon in *The Soviet Syndrome* (New York: Harcourt Brace Jovanovich, 1976).

post-market order partly because he supposes a convergence on ends, goals, and needs to be the natural outcome of the overthrow of class society. He fails to specify mechanisms for the resolution of conflicts and the arbitration of disputes and, instead, relies solely on the possibilities of collaborative discussion, primarily because he treats value-conflict as substantially epiphenomenal. His neglect of provisions for the legal protection of individual freedom has another and different source: such protection could only endanger or limit the practice of freedom as he conceived it – the conscious, cooperative planning of social life. For, if it means anything, individual liberty means the right to act without consulting any collectivity, or respecting any social decision-procedure other than the rule of law which protects liberty itself.

If Marxian freedom is not liberal freedom refined or transcended, but more like its antithesis or negation, we may be tempted to see in actually existing socialist systems the authentic realization of the Marxian project, and an outcome which Marx might have welcomed. In large part, we would be right to succumb to this temptation, since much in the socialist states – contempt for law and for the interests of minorities, primitive peoples, and small nations, the incessant campaign against religion and the bourgeois cult of technological optimism – has an authentic Marxian pedigree. At the same time, the most genuinely Marxian feature of actually existing socialist systems, their attempt to do without the mechanisms of market competition and pricing, also marks the profoundest divergence of reality from the Marxian vision. Rather than the plenty predicted by Marx, abolishing the market has produced penury. I have argued that the impossibility of the Marxian project has its source in the character of our knowledge and in its inherent limitations. Marxian freedom is a chimera, because there cannot be conscious collective planning of economic activity or rational control over social life as a whole. The character of much of our social knowledge – its character as tacit local knowledge, usually untheorized and in an important part untheorizable – throws up an insuperable obstacle to comprehensive economic planning. Attempts to achieve the impossible, in actually existing socialist regimes, have resulted in a wasteful depletion of the common stock of social knowledge and, in turn, in a squandering on a vast scale of inherited natural and human resources. Insofar as the reality belies at every point the Marxian vision of socialist abundance, we are justified in regarding the twentieth-century history of Marxian socialism as its practical self-refutation. In seeking a new sort of freedom, it has indeed created something new – but only a form of servitude unknown to human society until our own century.

Behind the epistemological impossibility there is a deeper impossibility in Marxian socialism, and that is in the speculative anthropology which the

Marxian project presupposes. For Marxian anthropology requires something we have good reason to suppose false – the thesis that divergence, variety, and conflict in forms of life and thought are contingent accidents in the life of our species, rather than expressions of its very essence. It is the partial indeterminacy of human nature, its openness to self-transformation and its alterability by experiments in living, that gives us a reason for valuing human individuality as a permanent condition of the good life. It is, indeed, the extirpation of this human individuality rooted in our partial freedom to shape ourselves that Marxian socialism would achieve, if – *per impossibile*, mercifully – its conception of freedom were ever to be realized in practice. In the real world of human history and culture, we may be assured that Marxian communism will always remain the dialectical negation of the vision of its founders – a desolate utopia in which the reality of human freedom is affirmed by the brute fact of its ceaseless repression.

Politics, Oxford University

MARXISM, VIOLENCE, AND TYRANNY

GEORGE FRIEDMAN

The problem of Marxism is the problem of tyranny. The central argument against Marxism is an empirical one: the universally tyrannical nature of all hitherto existing Marxist regimes. Defenders of Marxism must continually defend themselves against the charge that Marxism, when it comes to power, increases the sum total of human misery by increasing political oppression. Marxists have answered in several ways. Some have argued that the social and economic benefits of Marxism outweigh the political misery it causes.[1] Others have argued that while tyranny might count against any particular regime, it is not intrinsic to Marxist regimes as such.[2] Some have argued that tyranny is a transitional phase, necessary but impermanent.[3] Finally, some Marxists have denied that the regimes they defend are tyrannical at all.[4]

In any event, it is obvious that the practical connection between Marxism and tyranny is the pivot on which any political debate about or within Marxism must revolve. At the very least, if tyranny is necessary, then this defines the character of Marxism in general. To begin my analysis, I must ask a simple question: How necessary is tyranny to Marxism?

[1] Palmiro Togliatti, in the course of condemning Stalinism in 1956, paused to say that, "It must not be forgotten, then, that even when this power of his [Stalin's] was established, the successes of Soviet society were not lacking. There were successes in the economic field, in the political field, in the cultural field, in the military field, and in the field of international relations. No one will be able to deny that the Soviet Union in 1953 was incomparably stronger, more developed in every sense, more solid internally, and more authoritative in its foreign relations than it was, for example, at the time of the first Five-Year plan." Palmiro Togliatti, "Questions on Stalinism," D. Jacobs, ed., *From Marx to Mao and Marchais* (New York: Longman, 1979), pp. 243–244.

[2] So, for example, Roger Garaudy, a member of the French Communist party at the time, wrote that, "The Soviet Socialist model is characterized by the identification of collective ownership of the means of production with State ownership. But it is by no means axiomatic that the revolutionary role of the proletarian state should be transformed into an administrative one." Roger Garaudy, *The Crisis in Communism* (New York: Grove Press, 1970), p. 140.

[3] This has been the standard Soviet position, and the one most faithful to Marx's own understanding of the matter. See V. I. Lenin, *The Lenin Anthology*, ed. Robert C. Tucker (New York: W.W. Norton & Co., 1975, pp. 320–325. Also see Marx's similar comments in the *1844 Manuscripts* and in his *Critique of the Gotha Program*. For the former see Karl Marx, *Marx-Engels Werke* (Berlin: Dietz Verlag, 1974), Erganzungsband, pp. 535–537. For the latter, see *ibid.*, Volume 19, pp. 20–22.

[4] Antonio Gramsci, for example, defended Stalin, saying that "Confusion of class-State and regulated society is peculiar to the middle classes and petty intellectuals, who would be glad of any regularization that would prevent sharp class struggles and upheavals." Antonio Gramsci, "State and Civil Society," *Prison Notebooks* (New York: International Publishers, 1971), p.258.

I

Tyranny is the ability of a ruler to command obedience through unmediated violence. All political rule implies violence, but it is characteristic of tyrannies that violence is monopolized by one or a few, and that the omnipresence of violence permeates the fabric of the social order.[5]

Now, if we consider the relationship between tyranny and violence, we see that there is another political phenomenon which has a similar relationship to violence: revolution. Just as tyranny is formless, just as it is the antithesis of a regime, so too, revolution defines its form as it goes along. Neither is political in the strict sense of the word. Politics, in the classical (i.e., Aristotelian) sense of the word, is something which exists over and against private life. The virtue of politics is to be found in the manner in which it causes men to transcend the narrow concerns of their households in favor of the interests of the polity. It is in this transcendence of the private and economic considerations of men that we find the emergence of what Aristotle considered the human virtues. Tyranny is not, therefore, political, because it turns the *polis* back into a household, where everything once considered part of public life becomes an instrument in service to the tyrant. So too, the citizens, reduced to the status of subjects, lose their public concerns and turn back to the narrow problems of the household and away from the now nonexistent political life. Also, revolution is not strictly speaking political, because it stands in opposition to the *polis*, destroying it and, more important, because the motives of the revolutionary flow from the private, economic concerns of the household, rather than from genuine concern for the polity.[6]

It is worth noting in this context that Marxism represents, in its extreme form, the privatization of politics. It is private motives which are understood to compel men to act in public life. Indeed, for Marx, all ideology was a sham, inasmuch as it tried to make universal claims for itself, thereby obscuring the real private motives behind all human action. According to Marx, men act always out of private concerns.[7] This privatization reaches its most extreme point in capitalism, and in the period immediately following

[5] See, for example, Xenephon, *Hiero or Tyrannicus*, ed. Leo Strauss (Ithaca: Cornell University Press, 1975), p. 12, sections 12–14.

[6] For example, see Aristotle, *The Politics*, trans. Ernest Barker (New York: Oxford University Press, 1958), p. 226, Book V, Chap. vii: "Men tend to become revolutionaries from circumstances connected with their private lives."

[7] In *The German Ideology*, Marx and Engels write that, "For each new class which puts itself in the place of one ruling before it, is forced, merely in order to carry through its aim, to represent its interest to be identical to the interest of all members of society . . ." in *Marx-Engels Werke*, Volume 3, p. 47. Marx understood part of his task to be that of showing these universalistic claims to be false. What motivated men were needs, and these needs were, to Marx, radically material and hence radically private in nature.

the revolution. But this private concern might also be seen in communist society. Marx's famous dictum, "From each according to his ability, to each according to his need," is not a principle of political life. Rather, it is the governing doctrine of any healthy family. Marx sees the deformed private interests of bourgeois society as being replaced by a healthy, and yet still private, familial principle. Nevertheless, immediately following the revolution, the level of deformed privatization might only then reach its fullest expression. It follows naturally that the regime that is founded by Marxists should have, at least in its first instance, the result of institutionalizing these private motives of men.[8]

Thus, private motives unify tyranny and revolution. However, another quality linking them is even simpler and more obvious: violence. A tyrant governs by direct violence. So too, a revolution, for whatever end, is carried out with direct violence. Other political forms mediate violence through some institution. Only tyranny and revolution use violence without mediation. Thus, the starting point for any enquiry concerning the tyrannical nature of revolutionary socialism ought to be an examination of violence, or at least what Marx thought about violence.

This is in no way meant to suggest that it is revolution which assures the tyrannical nature of a regime. There have been revolutions which have not yielded tyranny or, at least, not much tyranny. At the same time, it is obvious that there is a connection between revolution and tyranny, and that that connection must, in some way, be bound up with the formless violence of both political phenomena.

The question which we must address here is not the general relationship between revolution and tyranny (a mixed and complex relationship at best) but, rather, the peculiar consistency with which Marxist regimes fall into tyranny. Now, one reason might be, as I pointed out, that Marxist regimes, like tyrannies, privatize politics. Marx certainly understood this to be the case, and predicted a transitional, tyrannical phase as inevitable and necessary. But we, unlike Marx, must be struck by the singular permanence of that tyranny; from the historical examples to date, it is clear that it never willingly departs. One explanation might be the inability of a public life to regenerate

---

[8] Thus, in both is *Critique of the Gotha Program* and in the section entitled "Private Property and Communism" in the *Economic and Philosophic Manuscripts of 1844*, Marx speaks of the universalization of privatization in the political organization of the first stage of socialism. In the *1844 Manuscripts*, Marx writes that, "In negating the personality of man in every sphere, this type of communism is really nothing but the logical expression of private property, which is this negation. General envy constituting itself as a power . . ." *Marx-Engels Werke*, Erganzungs-band, pp. 535–536. (It should be added that some have seen this as a critique of a particular idea *about* communism. Given the exact textual context, and his much later references in *The Critique of the Gotha Program*, others have argued more persuasively that this is a description of stages.)

itself once it has been made private. Capitalism's continual shift between public and private life, however, makes this an insufficient explanation. If one link between revolution and tyranny is privatization, another is violence. The practice of all revolutions is violence, but there is an understanding of violence and revolution peculiar to Marx which causes Marxist regimes to remain tyrannical long after the transitional phase appears to have been completed. I speak here not of his tactical understanding of violence, but rather of a deeper and more psychological understanding. In spite of his dispute with Mikhail Bakunin, Marx saw redemptive elements in revolutionary violence, elements far from merely utilitarian and instrumental.

The Marxist understanding of revolution and tyranny clearly leaves some room for violence as a tactical measure. Thus, someone like Lenin or Mao would, at the very least, see violence as an instrumentality, whether in a revolutionary context or in the context of ruling a Marxist state. If this is all that violence is to a Marxist, however, then violence, as pure instrument, cannot be said to color the regime beyond a certain necessary point. If violence is purely instrumental, its presence is purely utilitarian. As such, it is dispensable. If the occasions which necessitated violence were to disappear, so too would the need for violence. Thus, the need for violent revolution would become a practical matter, and the need for tyrannical dictatorship would also become purely practical. Its only function would be its use.[9]

If this is true, then Marxism does not ineluctably give rise to tyranny, nor must it arise directly from revolution. Granted, for Marx the circumstances were less than malleable, and therefore the revolution and the regime might have to follow a given, violent course, by the nature of the circumstances. However, even if this were true, Marxism understands itself as breaking free of the condition of need and, therefore, as breaking free from violence. Circumstances would hold no Godlike grip on society, nor would violence. Therefore, whether the circumstance demanded violence or not, violence as mere instrument would be dispensable to the Marxist polity or movement. Marxism would not be inevitably bound to violence nor, therefore, to tyranny.

It is this argument which is the ground for Marxist defenders of Marxism. Their argument is that, at worst, violence is an instrument of rule and the attainment of rule, and not intrinsic to socialist development. However, this

---

[9] This tactical side to Marx's understanding of the role of violence can be seen in a speech he made in 1872: "But we have not asserted that the ways to achieve that goal are everywhere the same. You know that the institutions, mores and traditions of various countries must be taken into consideration, and we do not deny that there are countries – such as America, England, and if I were more familiar to your institutions, I would perhaps also add Holland – where workers can attain their goal by peaceful means. This being the case, we must also recognize the fact that in most countries on the Continent the lever of our revolution must be force . . . " *The Marx-Engels Reader*, ed. Robert C. Tucker (New York: W.W. Norton, 1978), p. 523.

argument seems insufficiently radical. It seems too comfortable with distinguishing the practice of socialist rule from socialism itself. In viewing violence as pure instrument, this defense of Marxism seems undialectical. It sees only one side of violence, its utility, and not the other side, a side that Marx took at least as seriously, that of man remaking himself. It is in this sphere of man's self-creation that violence plays, for Marx, an indispensable role. For example, in *The German Ideology*, Marx writes that:

> This appropriation [of the instruments of production] is further determined by the manner in which it must be effected. It can only be fulfilled by a union, which by the character of the proletariat itself can again only be a universal one, and through a revolution, in which, on the one hand, the power of the prior mode of production and intercourse and social organization is overthrown, and, on the other hand, there develops the universal character and the energy of the proletariat, without which the revolution cannot be accomplished: and in which, further, the proletariat rids itself of everything that still clings to it from its previous position in society.[10]

It is in this further dimension of revolution, in which the proletariat remakes itself for its new role in society, that we must seek the connection between Marxism and violence that is more than purely utilitarian. It is this which will, I hope, persuade us that the connection between Marxism and tyranny is more than either contingent or transitory. Violence and tyranny must be understood as intrinsically part of Marxism. In order to understand the Marxist polity, we must begin with the genesis of that polity, revolution, and consider the connection between Marxism, revolution, and violence in that light.

II

What precisely is a revolution? How can we distinguish between an authentic revolution and the illusion of one? The term revolution conjures up different images for different people and cultures. For some, a revolution evokes images of *Mitteleuropeans*, shabbily dressed, huddled around sputtering candles, furtively mumbling to one another about hidden and mysterious plots. For others, revolution is a vision of massed action, the storming of the Bastille eternally returning. For others, revolution is armed combat, the revolutionary army arrayed against the army of the rulers. (And the ambiguous character of revolution is replicated when one tries to define reform.)

[10] *Marx-Engels Werke*, Volume 3, p. 68.

The purpose of these metaphors, stark and limited as they are, is to point out the problem which Marx faced when he tried to speak of revolution and its practice. Marx's apparent theoretical clarity concerning revolution, which he saw as the transendence of a decadent society, deteriorates into practical ambiguity as soon as one tries to apply the metaphors to concrete situations. In theory, revolution can be but one thing; in practice, it can show itself in many, deceptively different ways. This problem is by no means new. Aristotle, in his discussion of Hippodamus in *The Politics*, commented on the dangerous ambiguity involved in distinguishing between reform and revolution.[11] Marxist tradition leaves us, in a sense, with the same ambiguity. But it is not an ambiguity present in Marx himself. Marx clearly desires revolution; what he means by revolution in practice is, I think, equally clear.

Revolution might be distinguished from other political acts in several ways. For some Marxists, for example, the distinction between revolution and reform is that revolution is necessarily illegal. Much of the debate between those wishing to participate in bourgeois democratic politics and those opposed to it revolved around whether or not one could be genuinely revolutionary without being illegal. Both sides in the debate could claim Marx and Engels for themselves, because both saw, at various times, virtue in legalism *and* illegalism.[12] Thus, by some Marxists making illegality the essence of revolution, a debate was opened concerning whether or not Marx and Engels were themselves absolutely committed to revolution. It is evident that Marx was unclear on the propriety of legalism for a revolution. In fact, he regarded legalism as a purely tactical question, and he did not regard it as in any way an essential question for revolutionaries.

What ultimately distinguishes revolution from reform, for Marx, is the presence or expectation of real, sensual violence. Marx says the following in *The Poverty of Philosophy:*

> . . . the opposition between the proletariat and the bourgeoisie is a struggle of class against class, a struggle which is carried to its highest expression in a total revolution. Indeed, is it at all suprising

[11] Aristotle, *The Politics*, trans. E. Borker (New York: Oxford University Press, 1962), p. 72.

[12] The most famous debate along these lines was that between Lenin and Karl Kautsky. Lenin charged Kautsky with turning Marx into "an ordinary liberal"; V. I. Lenin, *The Proletarian Revolution and the Renegade Kautsky* (Peking: Foreign Language Press, 1965), p. 5. Kautsky, the head of the now legal Social-Democratic Party in Germany, made the claim that, "The proletariat has, therefore, no reason to distrust parliamentary actions . . . Besides freedom of the press and the right to organize, the universal ballot is to be regarded as one of the conditions prerequisite to the sound development of the proletariat"; Karl Kautsky *The Class Struggle*, trans. W. E. Bohn (New York: W. W. Norton, 1971), p. 188. This debate, which served as the frame for the debate between Social-Democracy and Communism throughout the century, was repeated in the struggle between Maoists and official Communist parties in Europe in the late 60s and early 70s.

that a society founded on the opposition of classes should culminate in brutal contradiction, the collision of body against body as its final resolution?[13]

It is in the clash of bodies, in unabstracted violence, that revolution achieves its concrete essence.

It is here that Marx gives us a model in terms of which we can understand violent revolution. The expectation of violence would seem to have two aspects. The first, surface expectation is phenomenal, the use of violence against that which exists. But this side would appear to be a reflection of something deeper, more profound in human beings. We see in revolutionary violence the ritual assertion of the self against the world, and the realization of its authentic being through the experience of violence. In *The German Ideology*, Marx writes the following:

> Both for the production on a mass scale of this Communist consciousness, and for the success of the cause itself, the alteration of men on a mass scale is necessary, an alteration which can only take place in a practical movement, a revolution; this revolution is necessary, therefore, not only because the ruling class cannot be overthrown in any other way, but also because the class overthrowing it can only in a revolution succeed in ridding itself of all the muck of the ages [ganzen alten Dreck] and become fitted to found society anew.[14]

The revolution is necessary not only for external, tactical considerations, but also for the transfiguration of the very being of the human. In a passage redolent of Marx's later opening to the *Eighteenth Brumaire*,[15] with its call for the exorcism of the past through the ritual acting out of revolution, the experience of revolution becomes significant in the reshaping of man's internal side, which dialectically becomes the basis for the reshaping of society.

Thus, revolution becomes the midwife of the new age not merely in the brutish sense of the seizure of power, but much more profoundly, in the subliminal sense that the experience of revolution eases men's beings into the configuration of the new age. For Marx, revolution teaches men how to be men, i.e., truly human.

How does revolution transfigure men? One answer might be that the

---

[13] *Marx-Engel Werke*, Volume 4, p. 184.
[14] *Marx-Engels Werke*, Volume 3, p. 70.
[15] "The traditions of all of the dead generations weigh like a nightmare on the brain of the living"; *Marx-Engels Werke*, Volume 8, p. 116.

revolutionary experience teaches men to act communally. However, this explanation appears to be insufficient. There are, on the one hand, much better teachers of commmunalism that revolution. For Marx, the experience of the factory was much more significant in teaching the proletariat about the social nature of life than was revolution. Indeed, the understanding of human sociability was the prerequisite for the proletarian revolution, and not its consequence.[16] On the other hand, revolution's core is not social. The violence and danger of revolution casts man alone at the critical juncture. In danger, the calculus of material interest separates each man from the interest of the mass. One's death is distinct from the whole.[17] Thus, there must be something other than communality that is taught to the proletariat in a revolution.

As Marx said of commodities, so I say of violence: it appears to be a simple thing, but it is really quite mysterious. Violence and force are clearly the bedrocks of revolution to Marx. But what exactly is violence? Subliminal violence, after all, permeates the very texture of all society. Even the theoretical argument behind liberal democracy is not that force and violence have been abolished, but that they have been sublimated, that there are to be ballots instead of bullets. The clear implication is that one must see this as a symbolic substitution, and not confuse it with the utter elimination of violence from society. For Marx, this form of the sublimation of violence by bourgeois society is fraudulent and corrupting. It is fraudulent in the obvious sense that it does not abolish violence but merely refines and legitimizes it, and in the further sense that it serves the interests of an anti-historical ideology. Its pretensions to nonviolence are pretensions of universality and permanence. Its claims are the claims of those denying change.

For the proletariat to adopt this stance other than tactically is to be led into docility. It is thus corrupting. But it is corrupting also in the deeper sense of leading one further away from real, sensual life. The corruption of the bourgeois rests not only in his historical role, but also in his distance from history's material essence. The bourgeois pretense of nonviolence is the political counterpart of the late bourgeois's unwillingness to dirty his hands in labor. His distance from the factory, a relationship now mediated through the abstract symbolism of finance capitalism, affirms the passing into reaction of the bourgeoisie. The time at which the bourgeois got his hands

---

[16] The distinction between the sense of proletarian unity engendered by the factory and by the experience of the revolution can be seen in *Capital, Marx-Engels Werke*, Volume 23, p. v. The same distinction is maintained in *The German Ideology, Marx-Engels Werke*, Volume 3, pp. 75–77, although the revolution is seen as expanding and deepening the sense of unit. Also see the *Introduction to the Critique of Hegel's Philosophy of Right, Marx-Engels Werke*, Volume 1, p. 390, and *The Poverty of Philosophy, Marx-Engels Werke*, Volume 4, pp. 182–183.

[17] Marx *The Economic and Philosophic Manuscripts of 1844, Marx-Engels Werke*, Erganzungsband, p. 539.

dirty coincided with his progressivism. His corruption manifested itself in his unwillingness to labor any longer. So too, his political corruption and downfall are proclaimed by the abstract symbolism of bourgeois democracy. He is no longer in contact with the stuff of history. The proletarian, on the other hand, is in contact with it, first in the factory and then in the street. Just as the economic act must be more than the exchange of symbols, of money, so the political act must be more than symbolic. The concretion of the political act is war and violence.

Clearly, the violent act must be more than symbolic. At the same time, Marx would obviously recognize the violence of brute terrorism as being insufficient.[18] Brute violence is unreflective; hence, it teaches nothing. The task of revolution, of violence, is the task of the educator. Merely shooting someone would not constitute an authentic and sufficient revolutionary act.[19] The violence must rest somewhere between the symbolic and the brutish. But its location is, at first glance, utterly mysterious, for between brute and symbolic violence there appears to be little room.

Violence must have an object, and it must be an object outside the realm of the brutishly political. Political power is attainable through various means, if one thinks of political power in its ordinary sense. But merely seizing power is not enough, for the mere seizure of power, as an experienced act, tends to leave the lives of those who act out the seizure, in its abstract bourgeois democratic form, untouched. Seizing power by itself is, from Marx's point of view, superficial. How one seizes power is critical. It is, however, not critical because of tactical considerations, but for deeper, personal reasons. How one seizes power transforms one's being.

Revolution is the introduction of the hitherto powerless to power. It introduces them to power by being, in and of itself, the experience of power.

---

[18] Avineri in *The Social and Political Thought of Karl Marx* Cambridge: Cambridge University Press, 1968), pp. 188–194, is correct in arguing that Marx rejected terrorism. But all violence is not terrorism. For Marx, terrorism was merely individuated violence, without a mass base. Thus, Avineri's use of Marx's critique of terrorism as a base from which to attack the notion that Marx endorsed the necessity of mass violence (pp. 202–214) is erroneous. This can be seen most clearly on p. 217, the only mention by Avineri of praxis in relation to violence. Here, Avineri argues that violence is contingent, inasmuch as the nature of praxis precludes *a priori* knowledge of its concrete form. When (p. 194) Avineri argues that Blanquism is merely political, and hence alienated, he belies this position by being able to demonstrate through Marx what revolution is not. But what praxis must be is also knowable, since one can know its ends and know that its ends must be reflected in the means of attaining those ends. Thus, a radical transformation of being requires a radical, suprapolitical means. To argue that Blanquism is merely political presupposes the other side of the argument, that what is even more obviously merely political (reform politics) is equally unacceptable because it too, like Blanquism, represents only a limited and, hence, insufficiently radical side of revolutionary praxis.

[19] See Engels's letter to Cuno, January 24, 1872, in *Marx-Engels Werke*, Volume 33, pp. 387–393, esp. p. 389.

The essence of power, its first moment, rests in the annihilation of what stands before it. Power is the active intervention into the texture of space and time, annihilating both the object and its temporality. For a Marxist such as Walter Benjamin, it constitutes the "blasting (of) a specific life out of the era or a specific work out of lifework."[20] For Marx too, revolution is, at least at first, a cleansing. But it cannot be only a symbolic cleansing. Rather, it must be concrete, sensual, and practical: a material act, performed against the real texture of history.

Power must be sensualized. Sensualized power, in its first moment, is violence, the real, material, cleansing of space and time of the unwanted. Thus, the revolutionary act, without violence, and mass violence at that, leaves our being untouched. Hence, it is impractical. We may have cooperated, we may have determined the shape of our lives to some extent, but in some profound sense, our lives, from Marx's point of view, have been untouched in a peaceful revolution. Without violence, one remains alienated from both texture of history and, more importantly, from the essence of one's self.

The intention of revolution in general, albeit a possibly unconscious intention, is the realization of one's species-being and the annihilation of the past. Thus, the violence of revolution must be related to these tasks. This is something which Marx hints at in the opening of his *Eighteenth Brumaire*. Here Marx claims that history repeats itself, each time in dramatic forms, once as tragedy and then as farce. What these two forms share is the denouement, the moment of catharsis, in which the burdens of the past are thrown off in an empathetic and, hence, species-wide moment. Both tragedy and comedy concretize a universal moment into a particular form, forcing the universalization of the viewers' sensibilities through empathy with a particular moment of the universal. In that moment of empathy, pathos and laughter cleanse the soul, causing it, in a sense, to be reborn. The soul throws off the muck of the past, and gains a sense of the universality of the particular condition it faces, i.e., a sense of its species-being. From the point of view of revolution, then, it does not matter which genre the revolution manifests, and, indeed, the implication of this passage is that each recapitulates, in different moments, the other. The point of revolution is catharsis, albeit not mimetic catharsis, for in revolution the pathos of distance must be abolished, as viewer and viewed, actor and audience, subject and object are merged in the dialectics of the revolutionary act. But while mimesis must be abolished, catharsis remains central and necessary.

Thus, violence is useful as a cleansing of the past from the soul. Marx says this explicitly in *The German Ideology*,[21] and the dramatic reformulation of this

---

[20] Walter Benjamin *Illuminations* (New York: Schoken, 1969), p. 162.
[21] *Marx-Engels Werke*, Volume 3, pp. 67–69.

in the *Eighteenth Brumaire*,[22] merely confirms and deepens the point. Violence cleanses the soul, one might speculate, by slaying "the dead which weigh like a nightmare on the brain of the living." Through force, the past is abolished, not only as a binding social norm, but also as a subliminal hold on the brains of the living. Violence, since it is rooted in the dark recesses of being, as well as in need, makes itself real and stark. It reflexively abolishes those subliminal things which held hegemony over the violent possibilities of men, those same things which were the manifestations of alienation, the distortion of the human self through the powers of false and illusory consciousness. Violence springs from the very substance of alienation within the human being.[23]

Only violence can abolish violence. But it can do this only by becoming utterly real, thereby crushing the bonds which held it in check. It must become so real as to brook no sublimation, and thus abolish the distance between the subject and itself, imposed by alienation. Violence is catharsis, a cleansing self-realization of the self acting out its fate tragicomically. It is tragic in that it needs to be done, comic in its endless but fated repetitiveness. Violence first cleanses the human of his own self-mystery. This prepares the ground for creation.

Species-being presents itself as the other side of the catharsis of violence, as its future. In *On the Jewish Question*, Marx writes the following:

> Human emancipation will only be complete when the real individual man has absorbed into himself the abstract citizen; when as individual man, in his empirical life, in his individual work, and in his individual relationships, he has become a species-being; and when he has recognized and organized his own powers as social power so that he no longer separates this social power from himself as political power.[24]

The individual must end his radical individuation with a recognition of his concrete and sensual universality. This is what revolution is the preface and midwife to. In its cathartic moment, as a dramatic form, it concretizes the theoretical understanding of universality. It does this through radically

---

[22] "The tradition of all the dead generations weighs on the brain of the living like a nightmare. And just when they seem engaged in revolutionizing themselves and things, in creating something entirely new, precisely in such epochs of revolutionary crisis, they anxiously conjure up the spirits of the past to their service . . . " However, Marx says, "Earlier revolutions required world-historical recollections in order to drug themselves concerning their own content. In order to arrive at its content, the revolution of the nineteenth century must let the dead bury their dead"; *Marx-Engels Werke*, Volume 8, pp. 115–117.

[23] Marx, *Marx-Engels Werke*, Erganzungsban, pp. 518–521. The origin of violence is in the radical estrangement of the worker from the things, the people, and even the society which surrounds him.

[24] *Marx-Engels Werke*, Volume 1, p. 370.

personalizing the act, and in the next moment universalizing the now sensually known personal fact and act of personhood.

It is the violence of the revolutionary act which confirms the transcendence of theoretical knowledge. Until this point, the revolution has existed purely as theory. Once violence has taken place, once the radical, personal, danger of revolution is driven home, then there can no longer be any doubt that the purely theoretical nature of revolution has been abolished. In addition, it is the violence of the act which introduces to the individual his own powers. Marx and Engels wrote in 1850 that:

> Far from opposing so called excesses, these examples of popular revenge against hated individuals or public buildings that are associated only with hateful recollections, such instances must not only be tolerated, but the leadership of them taken in hand.[25]

What is known only abstractly at the start, that is, the abstract knowledge of being human, becomes clear to the proletarian at the moment when he experiences practically the phenomenal form of being human through experiencing its *power*. But he knows and appropriates this power insufficiently in the moment when he only thinks about it. It is the sensual experience of the destruction of the muck of the ages which finally introduces the proletarian to his power, in an utterly practical fashion, via the unmimetic catharsis of the revolutionary act. The personal violence must be universalized through the external side of revolution, the revolutionary party, and in its struggle for concrete goals in a social context. The distinction between violence and revolutionary violence is to be found in this externalization and universalization of the violent act. Simple violence is undialectical. Revolutionary violence is the particularization of the universal, and the universalization of the particular. Once, as Marx and Engels imply, proper leadership and guidance is provided by a communist party, violence becomes transcendental in nature and promise.

The other side of violence, its danger, serves to further expand its species character, and its service to species-being. In *The Economic and Philosophic Manuscripts of 1844*, Marx wrote that:

> Death seems to be a harsh victory of the species over the definite individual and to contradict their unity. But the determinate individual is only a determinate species-being, and as such, mortal.[26]

Violence has, as one of its determinate possibilities, death. It is on the surface peculiar that Marx, in one sense (an expanded Hobbesian one) a

[25] Marx and Engels, "Address to the Communist League," *Marx-Engels Werke*, Volume 7, p. 378.
[26] *Marx-Engels Werke*, Erganzungsband, p. 539.

hedonist, could reasonably argue for revolutionary sacrifice and risk on the part of the individual revolutionary. After all, the primary call to revolution arises from self-interest. In any calculus of interest, the act of revolutionary martyrdom, a certain fate for some, must be outweighed by the individual's interest in surviving. Hence, at a certain point, the point at which prudence and chance intersect, the revolutionary subject should seem irrational if he does not retreat.[27]

But on a deeper level, Marx seems to argue, death reinforces the consciousness of one's species-being. In exhibiting the mere determinacy of the individual, and hence his inevitable contingency, death reinforces the universal side of man. As a practical matter, man's death is always contingent. The revolutionary risk, on the contrary, liberates death from its contingent moment by uniting it with species (that is, with universal) requirements. Thus, violence not only introduces the individual to his species-being through introducing him to his own power, it also gives meaning to death's perpetual threat by placing it on the continuum of history. Hence, violence liberates man both from a false universality (the past) and from a false personalism (contingent life) by dialectically wedding him, through the experience of violence and risk, to an authentic dimension of both.

The function of violence is, therefore, not merely tactical and utilitarian, but psychological and even ontological. It has been commented frequently that Marx lacks a true psychology to go along with the rest of this theoretical framework.[28] While this is certainly true, he does possess what we might call the preface to psychology, which is a theory of the agencies of psychological affect. Marx postulates certain forces which would tend to change the human being's internal life, and certain directions in which that change will and ought to move. Violence, as I have tried to show, is one of these pivotal agents of change, and is therefore necessary not only to attain political ends, but for deeper reasons as well.

In all theories of revolutionary socialism, Leninist, Maoist, Debreist, or whatever, violence is present. On the surface, the discussion of violence is tactical. Mao argues that a revolutionary army ought to be massive and based among the peasants. Debre argues that it ought to be small and separate

---

[27] What motivates all men is need. Even man's relationship to a class arises not from choice but from necessity. It is this necessity that leads men both to class solidarity, and to species-being as well. See, in *The Economic and Philosophic Manuscripts of 1844*, the section called "Estranged Labor" for a sketch of this process; *Marx-Engels Werke*, Erganzungsband, pp. 510–522.

[28] Marx himself said this in *The Economic and Philosophic Manuscripts of 1844*; see *Marx-Engels Werke*, Erganzungsband, p. 543. It was this self-described and self-justified lack which caused a good portion of what is today called Western Marxism to try to create a Marxist psychology by way of Freud. The most powerful of these attempts was Herbert Marcuse's in his *Eros and Civilization* (New York: Vintage, 1962); see in particular pp. 144–156.

from the masses. So the debate goes on. Beneath the surface of this debate, we see hints of Marx's deeper teaching. We can see hints not only among quasi-Marxists, such as Sartre and Merleau-Ponty,[29] but also among more orthodox and consequential Marxists like Lenin.

Lenin, in *The State and Revolution*, quotes Engels approvingly.

> [Engels] And this in spite of the immense moral and spiritual impetus which has been given by every victorious revolution! And this in Germany, where a violent collision – which may after all, be forced on the people – would at least have the advantage of wiping out the servility which has penetrated the nation's mentality following the humiliation of the Thirty Years' War.

> [Lenin] . . . The necessity of systematically imbuing the masses with this and precisely this view of violent revolution lies at the root of the entire theory of Marx and Engels.[30]

Taking Lenin at his word, that is precisely this theory of revolution that is at the root of Marx's work, we see that one of the critical functions of revolution is to abolish the servility of men. It is the violence of revolution which makes men into men, rather than servile and craven creatures.

Lenin also understood the difficulty of this position for Marx's overall view of man. In the same section of *The State and Revolution*, he writes:

> How can this panegyric on violent revolution, which Engels insistently brought to the attention of the German Social Democrats between 1878 and 1894, i.e., right up to the time of his death, be combined with the theory of the "withering away" of the state to form a single theory?[31]

Lenin answered this question in a way that is consistent with Marx's understanding of post-revolutionary transitional phase, in which the proletariat creates a state for the coercive, violent suppression of its class enemies. With the withering of the proletariat's class enemies, there will come a withering away of the state.

Lenin, like Marx, understood that the transition would be difficult.

---

[29] See Sartre's famous introduction to Franz Fanon's *Wretched of the Earth*. See also Merleau-Ponty's defense of violence in *Humanism and Terror*, (Boston: Beacon, 1969), particularly p. 34.

[30] Lenin, *The Lenin Anthology*, "The State and Revolution," ed. Robert C. Tucker (New York: W.W. Norton, 1975), pp. 324–325.

[31] *ibid.*, p. 324.

Believing, as they did, in the class nature of the state, they had confidence
that tyranny would be transitory. Lenin, perhaps more than Marx, belies a
sense that the transition needs explaining, that there is something problematic about it.

There has been no withering of the Leninist state, nor of any other
revolutionary socialist state. They may fall, they may grow corrupt, but they
do not wither. And on the whole, they simply remain what they were at the
outset: tyrannies with unmediated violence.

There are, perhaps, a number of reasons for the inability of revolutionary
Marxist regimes to transcend their tyrannical nature. Some analysts have
suggested an iron law of oligarchy, others international circumstances. I
would suggest a more radical and profound reason – Marxism's deep
theoretical attachment to violence. Marx understood violence to be necessary not only to seize power, but also to create a species of man capable of
holding power, of being powerful. Violence, the autonomous seizure of
power, the striking out against the symbols which cause men to recollect
their submission, represents a means of recovering one's humanity as well as
a means of overthrowing the old regime.

Other revolutions, liberal revolutions, viewed violence as nothing more
than a means toward a political end. Marxist revolutions understand violence
as having a more private, radically unpolitical end. Thus, in this sense and on
this level, violence becomes a private and personal act. In making a political
act private and personal, Marxism turns revolution into a nonpolitical end.

Marx understood socialism to be the abolition of politics. With the
abolition of classes and scarcity, there would come the abolition of the
distinction between public and private. The principle, "From each according
to his ability, to each according to his need," represents the principle of
private life, of the family, and not of public life, or of a world divided between
public and private. For Marx, the ability of men to live not only socially, with
their species-being fully attained, required the creation of a truly human,
private realm. It was in the creation of this realm that Marx saw violence as
indispensable. Species-being and violent assertion of the self against oppression became intimately bound up.

III

It is here that Marx leaves us without guidance and here that the problem
of tyranny emerges. We understand the social uselessness of violence once
class antagonisms have been abolished. But what about the individual's need
for violence? If the discovery of being human comes, in some way, through
violence, can men who have never experienced it be fully human? Mao faced
this problem when he tried to institutionalize his revolution so that the young

might know what it was to struggle. But Lenin, perhaps more honestly, also faced it when he wrote in a slightly different context, "when you live among wolves you must howl like a wolf, while as for exterminating all the wolves . . . we shall act as to the wise Russian proverb: 'Boast not before but after the battle.'"[32]

In revolution, men learn to become wolves. It is not clear that they can forget the pleasure of being wolves. Nor is it clear that Marx's argument about the uses of violence can be confined only to periods of class distinction. Given that Marx predicted a period of tyranny, of dictatorship, after the revolution, the attachment of Marxism to violence raises the question of whether or not within the context of a Marxist regime, violence can ever be contained.

I began by pointing out that there are two connections between revolution and tyranny. One is that they are both directed against politics. The other is that they are both violent in an unmediated fashion. What Marx says concerning revolution celebrates precisely these unpolitical dimensions of revolution. This is reasonable, inasmuch as his ultimate end is the abolition of politics as such. However, in so doing, he opens the door to revolution's coordinate element, tyranny. He does this intentionally when he discusses the transition from capitalism to socialism. He does it unintentionally when he creates an explicitly tyrannical regime without showing the limits of violence.

Marxist regimes are tyrannical because they neither know how to, nor wish to stop being violent. For Marxists, violence is too important to be left behind in history. Marx concluded his *Address to the Communist League* with the words, "Their battle cry must be: The Revolution in Permanence."[33] Years before, he concluded his *The Poverty of Philosophy*, with a passage from George Sand:

> Combat or death: bloody struggle or extinction. It is thus that the question is inexorably put.[34]

These two understandings of revolution, as something permanent and as something bloody, must inform our own understanding of Marx. And they do much to explain the condition of regimes which today consider themselves Marxist.

Political Science, Dickinson College

---

[32] Lenin, *The Lenin Anthology*, "The Importance of Gold Now and After the Complete Victory of Socialism," ed. Robert C. Tucker (New York: W.W. Norton, 1975), p. 515.
[33] Marx & Engels, "Address to the Communist League," in *The Marx-Engels Reader*, p. 511.
[34] *ibid.*, p. 219.

MARXISM AND DIRTY HANDS

STEVEN LUKES

Lenin asked the question: what is to be done? A second question, which Lenin did not ask is: what is not to be done? A third question arises when answering the first and second yields incompatible directives. How are we to understand and respond to such situations, in which, as Machiavelli put it, the Prince must learn, "among so many who are not good," how "to enter evil when necessity commands" for the good of the Republic? This is the classical problem of dirty hands. What, if anything, does Marxism have to say about it?

I

As it happens, some of the twentieth century's most compelling represen-tations of this problem – or, rather, of the conflict between Marxist and non-Marxist approaches to it – come from two Marxist playwrights: Brecht and Sartre. Brecht addressed it in his remarkable play *Die Massnahme (The Measures Taken)*, written in 1929–30, which has been accurately described as "an exact and horrifying anticipation of the great confession trials of the Stalinist era."[1] In this play, 'Four Agitators' decide to shoot a soft-hearted 'Young Comrade' who has flouted Party discipline, in order to relieve suffering because, as he puts it, "misery cannot wait". The 'Young Com-rade's' action had placed the 'Four Agitators' and the revolution in danger. The 'Four Agitators' explain:

> And so we decided: we now
> Had to cut off a member of our own body.
> *It is a terrible thing to kill.*
> We would not only kill others, but ourselves as well,
> if the need arose.
> For violence is the only means whereby this deadly
> World may be changed, as
> Every living being knows.
> And yet, we said
> We are not permitted to kill. At one with the

[1] Martin Esslin, *Brecht: A Choice of Evils*, 3rd revised edition (London: Eyre Methuen, 1980), p. 144.

Inflexible will to change the world, we formulated
The measures taken.

To which the 'Control Chorus' responds:

It was not easy to do what was right.
It was not you who sentenced him, but
Reality.

For "what is needed to change the world" are

Anger and tenacity, knowledge and indignation
Swift action, utmost deliberation
Cold endurance, unending perseverance
Comprehension of the individual and comprehension of the whole:
Taught only by reality can
Reality be changed.[2]

Elsewhere in the play, the Control Chorus expresses its view even more clearly:

With whom would the just man not sit
To help justice?
What medicine is too bitter
For the man who's dying?
What violence should you not suffer to
Annihilate violence?
If at last you could change the world, what
Could make you too good to do so?
Who are you?
Sink in filth
Embrace the butcher but
Change the world: it needs it![3]

Eight years later, Brecht was to write in a less ruthless vein, seeking some understanding for the present perpetrators of necessary evils from their future beneficiaries:

You who will emerge from the flood
In which we have gone under
Remember
When you speak of our failings

---

[2] B. Brecht, *The Measures Taken and Other Lehrstucke*, trans. Stefan Brecht (London: Eyre Methuen, 1977), pp. 32–34.,
[3] *ibid.*, p. 25.

The dark time too
Which you have escaped.

For we went, changing countries oftener than our shoes
Through the wars of the classes, despairing
When there was injustice only, and no rebellion.

And yet we know:
Hatred, even of meanness
Contorts the features.
Anger, even against injustice
Makes the voice hoarse. Oh, we
Who wanted to prepare the ground for friendliness
Could not ourselves be friendly.

But you, when the time comes at last
And man is a helper to man
Think of us
With forbearance.[4]

Sartre confronted the problem most directly in his plays *Les Mains sales* (1948) and *Le Diable et le bon Dieu* (1951). In the latter play, Sartre has the violent revolutionary peasant leader say to the pacifist Tolstoyan, Goetz: "In a single day of virtue you have created more deaths than in thirty-five years of malice" and Goetz reflects: "On the Earth at present Good and Evil are inseparable."[5] And in *Les Mains sales*, Sartre's 'Young Comrade', Hugo, argues thus with the Party secretary, Hoederer:

> HUGO: I've never lied to our comrades. I . . . What use would it be to fight for the liberation of mankind if you despised them enough to stuff their heads with lies?
> HOEDERER: I lie when I must and I despise no one. I didn't invent the idea of lying; it was born of a society divided into classes and each of us inherited it at our birth. We shan't abolish lies by refusing to lie ourselves; we must use every weapon that comes to hand to suppress class differences.
> HUGO: Not all methods are good.
> HOEDERER: All methods are good when they are effective.
> HUGO: Then what right have you to condemn the Regent's policy? He declared war on the U.S.S.R. because it was the best way of safeguarding our national independence.
> HOEDERER: Do you imagine I *condemn* him? I've no time to

[4] B. Brecht, "To Those Born Later" in *Bertholt Brecht Poems 1913–1956* ed. and trans. J. Willett *et. al.*, (London: Methuen, 1976), pp. 319–320.
[5] J.-P. Sartre, *De Diable et le Bon Dieu* (Paris: Livre de Poche, 1961), p. 224.

waste. He did what any poor fool of his caste would have done in his place. We're not fighting men or a policy, but against the class which produced that policy and those men.

HUGO: And the best method you can find to carry on this fight is to offer to share the power with them?

HOEDERER: Exactly. Today, it is the best method. (*Pause*) How attached to your purity you are my boy! How frightened you are of soiling your hands! All right, stay pure! Who does it help, and why did you come to us? Purity is an ideal for a fakir or a monk.

You intellectuals, you bourgeois anarchists, you use it as an excuse for doing nothing. Do nothing, stay put, keep your elbows to your sides, wear kid gloves. My hands are filthy. I've dipped them up to the elbows in blood and slime. So what? Do you think you can govern and keep your spirit white?[6]

This, most dramatically put, is the problem of dirty hands. It has an interesting structure that is worth analyzing. Sometimes, the problem is unhelpfully posed in the form of the question: 'Does the end justify the means?' There are several things seriously wrong with this question. To begin with it is doubly ambiguous. In the first place, 'the end' could mean the 'end-in-view' at the time of action, or the end likely to be achieved by it, or the end in fact achieved. And, second, the formula of the end justifying the means could mean either that given certain ends (which?), in whichever of these three senses, any means could be justified; or it could mean that, when it comes to justifying means, the nature of the end, in whichever of the three senses indicated, makes a difference (but what difference?). But the question is misleading for a deeper reason, too. It assumes that, in justifying 'means', there is an overall metric, a unified scheme of evaluation within which the values of means and ends alike are commensurable: that they can be impartially assessed or *weighed* (and, on the most ruthless interpretation of the formula, the costs of means will always be *outweighed* by the positive value of certain ends).

Yet this assumption of commensurability is precisely what the problem of dirty hands puts in question. For the problem arises when what is, from one point of view, the overall good is attainable only by the committing of what, from another point of view, are wrongful acts. On the one hand, we endorse and pursue the attainable good; on the other, we condemn and regret the uncancelled wrongs committed in its pursuit. Machiavelli captured this dual structure perfectly when he said that in such cases, "while the act accuses, the result excuses." The point is that both the accusation and the excuse

---

[6] J.-P. Sartre, *Les Mains Sales* translated by Kitty Black as *Crime Passionel* (London: Methuen, 1961), pp. 94–95.

stand. As Michael Walzer has observed, commenting on Machiavelli's argument:

> His political judgments are indeed consequentialist in character, but not his moral judgments. We know whether cruelty is used well or badly by its effects over time. But that it is bad to use cruelty we know in some other way. The deceitful and cruel politician is excused (if he succeeds) only in the sense that the rest of us come to agree that the results were 'worth it' or, more likely, that we simply forget his crimes when we praise his success.[7]

The problem of dirty hands is, of course, a completely general and familiar one, arising in all spheres of life. It arises whenever, while doing the best thing in the circumstances, we know that we have done wrong. It tends, however, to be peculiarly stark in political cases where the good attained tends to be general and the wrongs committed specific. The Defence of the Realm, the Cause of the Revolution, the Glory of the Republic may have been furthered, but particular people have been betrayed, lied to, or done in.

The issue is how to put together the points of view from which the former is endorsed and the latter condemned. Is there after all an overall, unified consequentialist theory within which each can be fitted, yielding a determinate solution, all things considered, to the question of what is to be done? Or is a Kantian, deontological, agent-relative position the only defensible one, in which moral principles set firm constraints by which all action – including political action – is to be finally judged. Or are we rather caught 'between utility and rights', committed on the one hand to the maximizing consequentialist picture and, on the other, to a narrow view of morality to which the notion of rights, justice, and the protection of basic liberties and interests of individuals is central? If so, the problem of dirty hands is the *locus classicus* of such a conflict. Indeed, we shall see that only if some such conflict is presupposed, is the problem of dirty hands a problem.

II

There are, I believe, four main ways of responding to this problem that are worth indicating briefly. The first three, in different ways, seek to dissolve or defuse the problem; only the fourth faces it directly.

First, there is what I shall call the *ideological response*. I here use 'ideological' in a quasi-Marxist sense to indicate a view that makes claims to objectivity, comprehensiveness, and universality of application, while being

---

[7] Michael Walzer, "Political Action: The Problem of Dirty Hands," *Philosophy and Public Affairs*, vol. 2 (Winter 1973), p. 175.

one-sided, abstract, and distortive of the reality it purports to represent, and all to the advantage of some social interests against others. On this view, there is essentially no problem of dirty hands, since, provided that overall good is attained, *dirty hands are really clean*. The problem is dissolved or thought away by theoretical fiat. This response can take a *consequentialist* form, of which the most familiar version is utilitarianism, or it can take what I shall call an *Orwellian* form, for reasons that will appear shortly.

The consequentialist form simply asserts that actions and policies are to be judged solely by whether they contribute to the best available outcome overall, all things considered. In any given case, there is only one correct answer to the question: what is it right to do? If the appropriate calculations show what is the right thing to do in the circumstances, then that is the right thing to do. Of course, a utilitarian, for example, may well go on to give a utilitarian explanation of and justification for ordinary moral rules (by which 'the right thing to do' might be judged wrong): he may account for the principles of justice and the rights and obligations by which we ordinarily live and, further, for the sense of obligation that we attach to these and the guilt we feel when we violate them. But if, in any given case, the right answer to the question, what is it right to do? requires us to override the constraints of ordinary morality, then in that case, to do so could not be wrong.

The consequentialist or utilitarian merely says that dirty hands, in this case, are clean. The Orwellian goes further: he redescribes the means in the light of the end pursued. Here, the means are purified or sanctified; the dirty hands are washed clean by the nobility or the correctness of the cause. Actions that might appear to be (in Machiavelli's phrase) contrary to "those things by which men are considered good" are ideologically redefined. You do not kill heretics; you maintain and protect the faith. You do not torture or wrongfully arrest or imprison people; you maintain law and order or eliminate the class enemy. You do not repress freedom of speech; you eliminate harmful opinions, and prevent obscenity and the spread of corruption. You do not intervene in other countries' affairs; you liberate freedom-loving peoples. You do not invade a country; you offer friendly assistance against counterrevolutionary subversion.

Second, there is what I shall call the *moralistic response*. This is a high-minded view of politics, according to which *politicians should always have clean hands*. It advances a view of political life as, in principle, no less subject to ethical principles than other spheres of social life, either as things actually are or as they could be. This response thus takes two forms: the *liberal* and the *utopian*.

The liberal form of the moralistic response relies on a deontological theory that is in turn justified by reference to the will of God or the Moral Law or some notion of personal integrity or respect for persons. It applies to politics, as to the rest of life, a moral theory that is, at least in its moralistic form, consequence-insensitive. As with the utilitarian, there are determinate answers to problems of practical judgment which, in this case, stem from a Theory of the Right (or rights); if the theory is rigorously followed, it will enable its practitioners to keep their spirits white.

The utopian form looks forward to a coming transformation of political life that will overcome the ethical irrationalities of the present world. Thenceforward, political life will be purified, and the problem of dirty hands will disappear – not through the imposition or the manipulation or the engineering of consensus, but through enlightenment and insight. This utopian vision can often take a chiliastic form well described by Max Weber:

> In the world of realities, as a rule, we encounter the ever-renewed experience that the adherent of an ethic of ultimate ends suddenly turns into a chiliastic prophet. Those, for example, who have just preached 'love against violence' now call for the use of force for the *last* violent deed, which would then lead to a state of affairs in which all violence is annihilated.[8]

There is (to anticipate) a strong strain of this in Marxism and no better exemplar of it than Trotsky, who held that "a society without social contradictions will naturally be a society without lies and violence. However, there is no way of building a bridge to that society save by revolutionary, that is violent means."[9] As he wrote in 1920,

> the road to socialism lies through a period of the highest possible intensification of the principle of the state. . . . Just as a lamp, before going out, shoots up a brilliant flame, so the state, before disappearing, assumes the form of the dictatorship of the proletariat, i.e. . . . the most ruthless form of state, which embraces the lives of the citizens authoritatively in every direction.[10]

Third, there is what we may call the *cynical response*. This is low rather than high-minded, and it usually relies upon a sharp dichotomy between public (or political) and everyday (or private) life. On this view, *everyone in politics has dirty hands*: politics is a sink of curruption, self-interest, and ambition. This response tends to exist at the level of popular attitude rather than developed theory, and it can often represent a rational, if politically

---

[8] Max Weber, "Politics as a Vocation," in *From Max Weber: Essays in Sociology* ed. and trans. H. H. Gerth and C. Wright Mills (London: Routledge and Kegan Paul, 1948), p. 122.

[9] L. Trotsky, *Their Morals and Ours*, 4th edition (New York: Pathfinder Press, 1969), p. 27.

[10] L. Trotsky, *Terrorism and Communism* (Ann Arbor: University of Michigan Press, 1961), p. 177.

dangerous, response to prevalent political practice. It is a view traditionally, but wholly falsely, attributed to Machiavelli and labelled "Machiavellian." Machiavelli, on the contrary, firmly advocated the fourth response.

This is what I shall (tendentiously) call the *political response*, which alone recognizes the problem of dirty hands as a problem with which politicians, citizens, and, under modern conditions, the institutions of a democratic system must come to terms. It involves seeing what, in their quite different ways, both Machiavelli and Max Weber saw: that there is in political life no impartial arbiter, no neutral standpoint from which "correct" practical conclusions can be derived. It involves recognizing the consequences for the character of politicians and the virtues they typically develop of the fact that, by virtue of their role, they must regularly confront this problem on behalf of the rest of us, in routine and small forms as well as heroic and tragic ones.[11] It involves establishing and maintaining institutions and social conditions which sustain the necessary tension within the dualistic structure to which I have referred. It is vital to keep alive the sense, among politicians and citizens alike, that deception, betrayal, and worse, when they are committed for the public good, violate morally important principles and commit uncancelled wrongs. And it is important to call those who violate such principles to explain and excuse. In short, there must be public watchfulness, journalistic scrutiny, a tradition of and effective mechanisms for public accountability. For all this a free press, an independent judiciary, and a competitive party system appear to be minimum preconditions.

III

How, then, does Marxism respond to the problem? To begin with, I need hardly allude to the complex and rich variety of strands within the Marxist tradition. That tradition is, of course, a contested terrain, in which the solemn orthodoxies of the Second and Third Internationals have faced many and various forms of heterodoxy and revisionism, from Bernstein and the Austro-Marxists to the Frankfurt and the Budapest Schools. I see orthodox, Russified Marxism as only one line of (arrested) development within the Marxist tradition, one which happens to have had momentous world-historical effects in practice, while others have undoubtedly been far truer to the letter and the spirit of Marx's thought. Nevertheless, I strongly disagree with my friend Bertell Ollman who, responding to Professor Walicki's fine piece on Marx and Freedom in the *New York Review of Books*, proclaimed that:

[11] See Bernard Williams. "Politics and Moral Character" in his *Moral Luck* (Cambridge: Cambridge University Press, 1981).

Most Western Marxists have come to understand that there is little to learn about socialism (understood as a form of society that can be built in our countries) from the experience of the 'socialist' world. Unfortunately, and with a few outstanding exceptions, these same distorting experiences have meant that there is little to learn about Marxist theory (especially as it applies to the unfolding potential of capitalism, its/our possible future) in the works which have come out of these countries, whether communist or anti-communist.[12]

On the contrary, the "distorting experience" of "actually existing socialism" exhibits repeated failures of Marxist theory and ideology, both within and outside the "socialist" world, to provide a basis for resisting measures taken in its name, despite some critical counter-currents in the last few decades. Are there features of the original theory that have disabled its inheritors from offering such resistance? I myself think that there are. I believe that Marxism has from its beginning exhibited a certain approach to moral questions that has disabled it from offering moral resistance to measures taken in its name; in particular, despite its rich view of freedom and compelling vision of human liberation, it has been unable to offer an adequate account of justice, rights, and the means-ends problem and, thus, an adequate response to injustice, the violation of rights, and the resort to impermissible means in the present. I believe that this disability was transmitted from the original theory to its main descendants. I also believe that it has characterized Marxist ideology far and wide. The experience of the Eastern bloc and the rich literature that has come out of it, and that of other socialist countries as well, is centrally important in the exploration of these issues, which should be of even greater concern to socialists than to their opponents.

My principal claim is that there is a central core or structure of moral thinking fashioned by Marx and Engels that is partly constitutive of the bibliocentric tradition that is Marxism, by which even the heterodox have been deeply imprinted. I shall briefly seek to analyze that structure, in order to delineate Marxism's response to the problem of dirty hands.

That structure can be best understood if we draw a distinction between what I shall call the morality of *Recht* and the morality of *emancipation*. The first comprises what Herbert Hart has called "an area of morality (the morality of law) which has special characteristics . . . occupied by the concepts of justice, fairness, rights and obligation."[13] The second denotes a setting free from the pre-history of human bondage, which culminated in wage-slavery and exploitation, and thus it refers to that ideal of transparent

---

[12] Bertell Ollman, letter to *New York Review of Books*, vol. xxxi, 4 (March 15, 1981), p. 48.
[13] H. L. A. Hart, "Are there any natural rights?" *Philosophical Review*, vol. 64 (1955), pp. 177–178.

social unity and individual self-realization in which "the contradiction between the interest of the separate individual or the individual family and the common interest of all individuals who have intercourse with one another has been abolished."[14] It is the morality of *Recht* that Marxism condemns as ideological and anachronistic, and the morality of emancipation that it adopts as its own. Indeed, human emancipation in part consists precisely in emancipation from *Recht* and the conditions that call it into being.

How did Marx and Engels and their followers conceive of *Recht*? Marx wrote of relations governed by *Recht (Rechtverhältnisse)* that, "like forms of state, [they] are to be grasped neither from themselves nor from the so-called general development of the human mind, but rather have their roots in the material conditions of life, the sum total of which Hegel . . . combines under the name 'civil society' whose anatomy is to be sought in political economy."[15] For Hegel, 'civil society' meant "the war of each against all" to be found in the capitalist marketplace: it denoted the competitive, egoistic relations of emergent bourgeois society in which individuals pursued their respective particular interests, treating one another as means to their respective ends and exercising what Hegel called 'subjective freedom'. Hegel saw certain rights and principles as governing such relations (e.g., private property rights and the principles of contractual justice), and he saw the State as the sphere of citizenship, of 'objective freedom', institutionalizing internally-accepted norms of ethical life and providing the framework within which the mutually destructive forces of civil society could be contained. In this way, a rational synthesis of subjective and objective freedom is attained in the modern bourgeois state.

For Marx, on the contrary, both the rights and the principles governing the relations of civil society, and the state itself, were rooted in and a means of stabilizing the production relations and thus the class relations of a given social order. The principles of *Recht* were to be understood only in this perspective. As Engels wrote, "social justice or injustice is decided by the science which deals with the actual facts of production and exchange, the science of political economy."[16] In short, the principles of *Recht* are to be understood neither (through themselves) as a set of objective norms, a set of independent rational standards by which to assess social relations nor, following Hegel, as a rational way of ordering such relations which finally

---

[14] K. Marx and F. Engels, *Collected Works* (London: Lawrence and Wishart, 1975 onwards; hereafter referred to as MECW), vol. 5, p. 46.

[15] K. Marx, Preface to *A Contribution to Political Economy*, in Marx and Engels, *Selected Works* (Moscow: Foreign Languages Publishing House, 1962), vol. 1, p. 362.

[16] Cited in Allen Wood, "The Marxian Critique of Justice," *Philosophy and Public Affairs*, vol. 1, no. 3 (Spring 1972), p. 15.

unites subjective with objective freedom. Rather, the principles of *Recht* must always be explained as arising, like the social relations they govern and stabilize, out of given material conditions.

This suggests the first Marxist reason for opposing *Recht*, namely, that it is inherently ideological. It claims to offer 'objective' principles specifying what is 'just' and 'fair' and defining 'rights' and 'obligations'; it claims that these are universally valid and serve the interests of all the members of society (and perhaps all members of any society); and it claims to be independent of particular partisan or sectional interests. But from a Marxist point of view, all these claims are spurious and illusory. They serve to conceal the real function of principles of *Recht*, which is to protect the social relations of the existing order, a function that is better fulfilled to the extent that the claims are widely accepted as 'objectively' valid. Marxism, in short, purports to unmask the self-understanding of *Recht* by revealing its real functions and the bourgeois interests that lurk in ambush behind it.

It does not, of course, follow from this that all communists should become immoralists, violating every bourgeois right and obligation in sight. That would, in any case, be poor tactics. What does follow is that the principles of *Recht* should have, for the communist, no rationally compelling force. And it follows from this that it makes no sense to criticize capitalism for failing to live up to such principles – for being unjust, violating the rights of workers, etc. (except as a tactical move).

But there is a further and deeper reason for communism's opposition to *Recht*, which can be unearthed if we ask the question, To what problem are the principles of *Recht* a response? To this question jurists and philosophers give different answers, but these answers have in common a view of human life as inherently conflictual, and potentially catastrophically so, thus requiring a framework of authoritative rules, sometimes needing coercive enforcement, that can be rationally justified as serving the interests of all. *Recht* is a response to what one might call the 'conditions of *Recht*', inherent in the human condition, and these may be more or less acute, just as the response will take different forms in different societies.

Consider David Hume's summary account of the conditions of *Recht*; for Hume, "'tis only from the selfishness and confin'd generosity of men, along with the scanty provision nature has made for his wants, that justice derives its origin."[17] In his recent book on ethics, John Mackie, citing this statement of Hume's alongside Protagoras and Hobbes, sought to identify what he calls a 'narrow sense of morality' (which looks very much like *Recht*) as a "system of a particular sort of constraints on conduct – ones whose central task is to

---

[17] D. Hume, *A Treatise of Human Nature*, ed. L. A. Selby-Bigge (Oxford: Clarendon Press, 1951), p. 495.

protect the interests of persons other than the agent and which present themselves to an agent as checks on his natural inclinations or spontaneous tendencies to act." Mackie argues, following Hume, that morality – in the narrow sense thus defined – is needed to solve a basic problem in the human predicament, that "limited resources and limited sympathies together generate both competition leading to conflict, and an absence of what would be mutually beneficial co-operation."[18] Or consider Kant's celebrated discussion of man's 'unsocial sociality' and of the problem to which the *Rechtstaat* is the solution:

> Given a multitidue of rational beings who, in a body, require general laws for their own preservation, but each of whom, as an individual, is secretly inclined to exempt himself from this restraint: how are we to order their affairs and establish for them a constitution such that, although their private dispositions may be really antagonistic, they may yet so act as a check upon one another, that, in their public relations, the effect is the same as if they had no such evil sentiments.[19]

Or consider, finally John Rawls's account of what I have called the conditions of *Recht* and what he calls the "circumstances of justice": these are "the normal conditions under which human co-operation is both possible and necessary," and they "obtain wherever mutually disinterested persons put forward conflicting claims to the division of social advantages under conditions of moderate scarcity."[20] These are "elementary facts about persons and their place in nature" and, for justice to obtain, "human freedom is to be regulated by principles chosen in the light of these natural restrictions."[21]

These various suggestions combine to identify three jointly sufficient conditions for the existence of justice and rights. (Whether in their imagined absence there would be a need for principles of justice and the recognition of rights is a question largely unaddressed within Marxism.) Clearly scarcity, or limits to desired goods, and egoism, or at least the absence of total and unconditional altruism, generate conflicting claims, and thus the need to adjudicate which claims are valid and, of these, which have priority. More deeply (and this is what Rawls's account implicitly adds to Hume's and Kant's), it is the conflict of interests, resulting from different individuals'

---

[18] J. L. Mackie, *Ethics: Inventing Right and Wrong* (Harmondsworth: Penguin, 1977), pp. 106, 111.

[19] I. Kant, *Perpetual Peace. A Philosophical Essay* ed. and trans. M. Campbell Smith (New York: Garland, 1972), p. 154.

[20] J. Rawls, *A Theory of Justice* (Oxford: Clarendon, 1972), pp. 126, 128.

[21] *ibid.*, p. 257.

(and groups') different and conflicting conceptions of the good that define those interests, which renders such adjudication, and the protections rights afford, necessary. Hume mistakenly thought that if you increase "to a sufficient degree the benevolence of men, or the bounty of nature . . . you render justice useless, by supplying its place with much nobler virtues, and more favourable blessings."[22] But even under conditions of co-operative abundance and altruism, there will – if conceptions of the good conflict – be a need for the fair allocation of benefits and burdens, for the assigning of duties and the protection of rights: but we should then need them in the face of the benevolence rather than the selfishness of others. Altruists, sincerely and conscientiously pursuing their respective conceptions of the good, could certainly cause injustice and violate rights. For every conception of the good favors certain social relationships and forms of life, and certain ways of defining individuals' interests – or, more precisely, certain ways of conceiving and ranking the various interests, deriving from their roles and functions, that individuals have. It also disfavors other conceptions. In a world in which no such conception is fully realized and universally accepted, even the non-egoistic adherents of one threaten the adherents of others: hence the need for justice and rights.

But what if divergent conceptions of the good, and of interests, were to converge within a single moral and political consensus? Here, a fourth condition comes into view: the lack of perfect information and understanding. For even under co-operative abundance, total altruism, and the unification of interests within a common conception of the good, people may get it wrong. They may fail to act as they should towards others, because they do not know how to or because they make mistakes, with resulting misallocations of burdens and benefits, and damage to individuals' interests. We may, therefore, say that if these four conditions obtain, a necessity exists for finding principles of justice for distributing social advantages and disadvantages, and principles specifying rights and duties to protect us from one another's depredations and abuses, whether these be selfish or benevolent, intended or unintended.

Now, it is a peculiar and distinctive feature of Marxism that it denies that these conditions of *Recht* are inherent in human life. *Recht*, Marx and Engels wrote, "arises from the material relations of people and the resulting antagonism of people against one another."[23] Both could, and would, be overcome. Marxism specifically denies that scarcity, egoism, and social and moral antagonisms are invariant features inherent in the human condition, and it looks forward to a 'transparent' form of social unity, in which social life

---

[22] Hume, *op. cit.*, pp. 494–495.
[23] MECW, vol.5, p. 318.

will be under the rational control of all. In short, it envisages the removal of the basic causes of significant conflicts of interest in society. As Marx and Engels wrote in *The Holy Family*:

> If enlightened self-interest is the principle of all morality, man's private interests must be made to coincide with the interest of humanity . . . If man is shaped by environment, his environment must be made human.[24]

Marxism maintains that the conditions of *Recht* are historically determined, specific to class-societies, and imminently removable. Neither limits to desired goods, nor limited sympathies, nor antagonistic social relations, and corresponding moral ideologies, nor the opaqueness or reified character of social relations are essential to the human predicament. To assume that they are is itself an ideological illusion (propagated by *Recht*) – ideological in serving to perpetuate the existing class-bound social order. Marxism supposes that a transparent and unified society of abundance – a society in which the very distinctions between egoism and altruism, the public sphere of politics and the private sphere of civil society, and "the division of the human being into a *public man* and a *private man*"[25] have been overcome – is not merely capable of being brought about, but is on the historical agenda and, indeed, that the working class is in principle motivated to bring it about and is capable of doing so.

Thus, *Recht* is not merely inherently ideological, stabilizing class societies and concealing class interests, and falsely purporting to adjudicate competing claims, limit freedoms, and distribute costs and benefits in a universally fair, objective, and mutually advantageous manner. It also presupposes an account of the conditions that call it forth, an account that Marxism denies. For Marxists hold that, broadly, all significant conflicts are to be traced back to class divisions. So, for example, Marx and Engels could speak of communism as "the *genuine* resolution of the conflict between man and nature and between man and man,"[26] speculate about the abolition of crime under communism, and suggest that 'social peace' might succeed 'social war'; and Trotsky, as we have seen, could proclaim that the future "society without social contradictions will naturally be a society without lies and violence."[27] Certainly, the Marxist canon has virtually nothing to say about any bases of conflict, whether social or psychological, other than class. It is virtually innocent (and totally so at the level of theory) of any serious consideration of all the interpersonal and intrapersonal sources of conflict and frustration that

[24] MECW, vol.4, p. 131 (amended translation, S. L.).
[25] MECW, vol.3, p. 155.
[26] *ibid.*, p. 296.
[27] Trotsky, *Their Morals and Ours*, p. 27.

cannot, or can no longer, plausibly be traced, even remotely, to class divisions.

By furnishing principles for the regulation of conflicting claims and interests, *Recht* serves to promote class compromise and thereby delay the revolutionary change that will make possible a form of social life that has no need of *Recht* because the conditions of *Recht* or the circumstances of justice will no longer obtain. In this respect, I think that Marx's view of morality as *Recht* is exactly parallel to his view of religion, concerning which he wrote: "To abolish religion as the *illusory* happiness of the people is to demand their *real* happiness. The demand to give up illusion about the existing state of affairs is the *demand to give up a state of affairs which needs illusions.*"[28] Analogously, the demand to give up illusions about the 'rights of man' and 'justice' is the demand to give up the conditions of *Recht* and the circumstances of justice. Once emancipation from such conditions or circumstances arrives on the historical agenda, the morality of emancipation dictates the bringing into being of a world in which the morality of *Recht* is unnecessary. In that world, the conditions that made such a morality necessary will, as Engels put it, have been not only overcome but forgotten in practical life. This is the meaning of Lukács's accurate statement that the "ultimate objective of communism is the construction of a society in which freedom of morality will take the place of the constraints of *Recht* in the regulation of all behaviour."[29]

In such a society, principles of justice, and more generally of *Recht*, are asumed to have withered away: they have, as Engels said, been forgotten in practical life. By what principles or standards, then, is this society to be judged superior? What kind of morality is the "really human morality" that it embodies? How are its claims to be validated? By an appeal to intuition? Much of Marx's and Marxist writings could be seen in that light: frequent appeal is made to the reader's sense of indignation and sympathy, and also his sense of what is "worthy of human nature." Yet it is an elementary Marxist thought that moral intuitions will be prime candidates for class-related bias. There seems to be no good Marxist reason to suppose such intuitions to be universally shared, even by fully reflective agents, let alone to appeal to them in practical reasoning. Is the indicated morality deontological, then, perhaps Kantian? There is, as the neo-Kantians saw, much to support this view in the canonical texts – as, for example, in Marx's condemnation of capitalist exchange relations as social relations in which each becomes a means of the other and, more generally, in his frequent talk of the slavery,

---

[28] MECW, vol. 3, p. 176.
[29] G. Lukács, *Political Writings: 1919–29*, ed. Rodney Livingstone (London: New Left Books, 1972), p. 48.

perhaps why Marx and Engels rejected Max Stirner's view that "in communist society there can be a question of 'duties' and interests," holding these
to be "two complementary aspects of an antithesis which exists only in
bourgeois society."[35] This, I believe, is why they thought that:

> Communism differs from all previous movements in that it over-
> turns the basis of all earlier relations of production and intercourse,
> and for the first time treats all naturally evolved premises as the
> creations of hitherto existing men, strips them of their natural
> character and subjugates them to the power of the united indi-
> viduals. . . . The reality which communism creates is precisely the
> true basis for rendering it impossible that anything should exist
> independently of individuals, insofar as reality is nevertheless only a
> product of the preceding intercourse of individuals.[36]

But if this is a correct interpretation, then a host of questions crowds in
upon us. What makes a purpose count as extraneous? Not (unless Marx is
saddled with a purely subjective, phenomenological notion of alienation)
whatever the agent counts as such. But what, then, are individuals' authentic,
non-extraneous purposes? Marx imagines a world in which the question
does not even arise, because its answer is both not in doubt and correctly
understood, both obvious and true (a world, therefore, free of moral skepticism). And are there not natural necessities which human activity (including
labor) must fulfill as a prerequisite of social co-operation in general and (as
both Weber and Durkheim thought) of a complex modern social order in
particular? And as for social *duties* (this takes us back to the withering away of
Recht), is their disappearance conceivable, even in a world inconceivably
more abundant and co-operative than our own – either in the sense that the
required tasks now conceived as duties would disappear or that they would
no longer be seen as duties? And many further and wider questions arise,
which we cannot explore here.

I hope, however, to have said enough to display what I have called the core
moral structure of Marxism. This is, in brief, a form of consequentialism
that is long-range and perfectionist. It therefore comes as no surprise that
Marxism has throughout its history been deeply and unremittingly anti-
deontological: hence the systematic hostilities among the orthodox to Kant
and Kantianism. Mainline Marxism has always required an exclusive commitment to the attainment of emancipation. "He who fights for Communism," wrote Brecht, "has of all virtues only one: that he fights for

[35] MECW, vol. 5, p. 213.
[36] *ibid.*, p. 81.

Communism."[37] The purportedly 'eternal', 'universal', and 'abstract' principles adduced by deontological theories are, from a Marxist viewpoint, both
without foundation and, if applied, irrelevant to and obstructive of the
consequences Marxism requires action to promote.

IV

My conclusion is that, in its response to the problem of dirty hands in
politics, Marxism combines, in a distinctive way, ideology and utopia. It is
ideological, first, in the purely consequentialist form. It one-sidedly rules out
or ignores, in the assessment of human action and character, all that it holds
to be irrelevant to the project of human emancipation. In particular, Marxism ignores the interests of persons in the here and now and immediate
future, both victims (intended and unintended) and agents, in so far as these
have no bearing on that project. It is like utilitarianism in offering an
explanation for the constraints of ordinary morality (though it offers a
different explanation), but unlike it in offering little scope for justifying
them: on the contrary, it holds that such constraints are likely to be class
deceptions lying in ambush to trap the unwary. Moreover, the justification
for such constraints that a utilitarian can offer will incorporate in its calculations benefits to agents in the here and now and the foreseeable future. For
the Marxist, such benefits are, in themselves, irrelevant. The long-term
character of Marxist consequentialism, its focus on future benefits to future
persons, makes it markedly less sensitive than even utilitarianism to the
moral requirement of respecting the basic interests and liberties of persons
in the present and immediate future.

All this explains why Marxism has throughout its history been at best
ambivalent about the domain and the language of *Recht*. Moral vocabulary of
this kind gets in the way of a clear-headed pursuit of the emancipatory
project. Marx was wont to call it "obsolete verbal rubbish" and "ideological
nonsense": the conceptions of *Recht* are, Marx and Engels thought, conceptions which people "ought to get out of their heads."[38] Removing those
conceptions, and the vocabulary within which they are couched, would
enable one to see present injustices and violations of rights not as such but,
rather, as either obstacles or means to future emancipation. In this way, the
ground for the Orwellian response is prepared: the language of morals is to
be revised to purge it of *Recht*-like features.

But Marxism is also utopian, as we have seen, though in a very special

---

[37] Brecht, *The Measures Taken*, p. 13.
[38] Marx, *Critique of the Gotha Programme*, in Marx and Engels, *Selected Works* (Moscow: Foreign
Languages Publishing House, 1962), p. 25.; and MECW, vol. 5, p. 362.

way. It is a kind of anti-utopian utopianism, with a built-in inhibition against specifying the nature of the utopia to whose realization it is committed. Its anti-utopianism, for which there are several reasons, has consistently inhibited Marxists from spelling out what the morality of emancipation implies for the future constitution and organization of society. It has repeatedly presumed to foresee the future, in which that emancipation is somehow guaranteed, while foreswearing the clarification of the long-term consequences by which alternative courses of action can be judged. In short, it has offered the unsubstantiated promise of a world "without lies and violence," thereby rendering their acceptance in this world easier than it might have been.

I believe that the structure of thinking that I have sought to sketch here is to be found throughout the Marxist tradition. It is to be found among the Bolsheviks and among their major Marxist critics, Luxemburg and Kautsky. It is, above all, to be found, in splendidly lucid and forthright expression, in the writings of Trotsky, who would doubtless have regarded this paper as yet another instance of "Kantian-priestly and vegetarian-Quaker prattle."[39]

Politics, Oxford University

---

[39] Trotsky, *Terrorism and Communism*, p. 82.